'An illuminating glimpse of the chain reactions of human and physical geography.' – *Financial Times*

'This is a chance to see the world anew through the eyes of a wonderfully curious new writer.' – *Guardian*

'*Invisible Lines* is a fascinating, detailed exploration of the hidden boundaries that carve up the world ... it is a pleasure to accompany Samson to the Malaria Belt, inside eruvim (markers of a single domestic space within which fewer Sabbath regulations apply), or along the border of Portugal to discover why vultures prefer not to cross it.' – *Telegraph*

'[An] intricately detailed explanation of how each invisible line came to be, as well as what it can tell us about the world and our place within it ... a fascinating read.' – *Geographical*, Book of the Month

'Old worlds enhanced, new worlds exposed and challenged ... a wise and thought-provoking series of raids across borders we thought we knew and others made visible to us, by Maxim Samson's forensic eye, for the first time.' – Iain Sinclair, author of *The Gold Machine* and *The Last London*

'Utterly engrossing! Samson's literary atlas of the world's unseen boundaries and how they've shaped our lives demands to be read.' – Lewis Dartnell, author of *Origins: How Earth's History Shaped Human History*

'A fascinating book ... a truly original adventure into new ways of exploring what we mean by a sense of place.' – Simon Jenkins, author of *The Celts* and *A Short History of England*

'The world is a mesh of lines. We don't normally see them, and so we blunder on, unaware of where we really are and missing out on so much. Samson's iconoclastic new geography will make the scales fall from your eyes. A tremendous and important read.' – Charles Foster, author of *Cry of the Wild*

'A journey to the unmarked and unseen borders that shape our world … a fascinating, extraordinary and insightful exploration of the many boundaries that define us.' – Alastair Bonnett, author of *The Age of Islands* and *Off the Map*

'This absorbing book is an accessible and wide-ranging read, built upon erudition, curiosity and careful compilation. It reveals and reflects upon many types of divisions between places – stretching from the Antarctic to the Urals, and from the turfs of passionate soccer fans in Buenos Aires to linguisitic divisions in Brittany, to name but a few.' – Cliff Hague OBE, Emeritus Professor of Planning and Spatial Development at Heriot-Watt University

INVISIBLE LINES

Boundaries and Belts That Define the World

MAXIM SAMSON

ANANSI
INTERNATIONAL

Copyright © 2024 Maxim Samson

Published in Canada in 2024 and the USA in 2024 by House of Anansi Press Inc.
houseofanansi.com

All rights reserved. No part of this publication may be reproduced or transmitted in any form or by any means, electronic or mechanical, including photocopying, recording, or any information storage and retrieval system, without permission in writing from the publisher.

House of Anansi Press is committed to protecting our natural environment. This book is made of material from well-managed FSC®-certified forests, recycled materials, and other controlled sources.

House of Anansi Press is a Global Certified Accessible™ (GCA by Benetech) publisher. The ebook version of this book meets stringent accessibility standards and is available to readers with print disabilities.

28 27 26 25 24   1 2 3 4 5

Library and Archives Canada Cataloguing in Publication
Title: Invisible lines : boundaries and belts that define the world / Maxim Samson.
Names: Samson, Maxim, author.
Description: Includes bibliographical references.
Identifiers: Canadiana (print) 20230547605 | Canadiana (ebook) 20230547613 | ISBN 9781487012847 (softcover) | ISBN 9781487012854 (EPUB)
Subjects: LCSH: Human geography. | LCSH: Geography—Social aspects. | LCSH: Difference (Philosophy)—Social aspects. | LCSH: Distinction (Philosophy)—Social aspects.
Classification: LCC GF50 .S26 2024 | DDC 304.2—dc23

Cover design: Greg Tabor
Typeset in Sabon by MacGuru Ltd
Maps produced by Dominic Beddow

Kind permission to reproduce the quote on p. 333 has been granted by ASTERIX®- OBELIX®- IDEFIX® / © 2023 LES EDITIONS ALBERT RENE / GOSCINNY – UDERZO.

While every effort has been made to contact copyright holders of copyright material, the author and publishers would be grateful for information where they have been unable to trace them, and would be glad to make amendments in further editions.

House of Anansi Press is grateful for the privilege to work on and create from the Traditional Territory of many Nations, including the Anishinabeg, the Wendat, and the Haudenosaunee, as well as the Treaty Lands of the Mississaugas of the Credit.

 Canada Council   Conseil des Arts
for the Arts   du Canada

 ONTARIO ARTS COUNCIL
CONSEIL DES ARTS DE L'ONTARIO
an Ontario government agency
un organisme du gouvernement de l'Ontario

With the participation of the Government of Canada
Avec la participation du gouvernement du Canada | Canadä

We acknowledge for their financial support of our publishing program the Canada Council for the Arts, the Ontario Arts Council, and the Government of Canada.

Printed and bound in Canada

FSC
www.fsc.org
MIX
Paper from
responsible sources
FSC® C103567

To Eleanor and our continued adventures

No matter how thin you slice it, there
will always be two sides.

Baruch Spinoza

The most dangerous worldview is the worldview
of those who have not viewed the world.

Alexander von Humboldt

Contents

Introduction

Walking around Chicago, the city I currently call home, I am regularly struck by a feeling of having crossed some kind of invisible line. Travelling south from the downtown 'Loop', beyond the rattling and clattering of the city's overhead 'L' trains, the bustle of commuters quickly gives way to a more passive energy of apartments and parks. The contrasts of the city centre, with its clash of architectural styles and functions, are replaced by an element of consistency, if not harmony. Suddenly, my composure is disturbed as a sharp gust between two high-rises nearly knocks me off my feet. Making a mental note to circumvent this canyonesque intersection on blustery days in the future, this being far from my first experience of contending with Chicago's distinct microclimates, I proceed, now to the south-west. The city changes again: Cantonese emerges among English, sandwich shops are replaced by noodle houses, the colour red becomes more prevalent. And yet a little further west, I have crossed another invisible line: the main language is now Spanish, the walls are adorned with murals, the churches are prevailingly Catholic. Moreover, in people's home and car windows I notice that the stickers and flags that so many Chicagoans use to show their loyalty to one of the city's baseball teams have changed, the red 'C' and blue bear of the Cubs superseded by the snaking black 'S' of their South Side adversaries, the White Sox.

Every day, each of us encounters and crosses invisible lines which shape how we act, how we feel and how we live. Somewhere around our bedrooms we probably imagine a line defining our willingness to wear (or at least be seen in) our boxers. Putting on shoes that we possibly choose to leave on the far side of another invisible line, this time distinguishing the parts of our abode we want to keep unsullied by dirt from the outside, we step outside, at some point crossing the boundary of our home. Throughout the world, children and teenagers in school playgrounds recognise invisible lines defining where a particular game is to be played, to the exclusion of other forms of fun. Athletes must negotiate various invisible lines (some of which are made visible simply for the purposes of refereeing and spectating), like the offside line in football and the strike zone in baseball. And this is by no means a phenomenon limited to humans: animals also acknowledge the existence of invisible lines, marking their territories using scents and sounds as well as visual markings.

This book is concerned with such lines, which operate as *boundaries* distinguishing one side from another. I define a boundary simply as a *dividing line*, which is necessarily spatial and as such can be mapped. However, rather than more formal *borders*, I am interested in the types of lines that rarely appear on our physical and political maps and, when they do, have impacts that go far beyond what is generally shown. Some are so subtle as to be perceptible only to a small population, to whom they nevertheless have great significance. Others are more subjective, and so different people position them in different places on a map. Certain boundaries move over time, whether on a regular basis throughout the year or more intermittently, often linked with broader changes in society. Most of the boundaries represent lines that quite effectively divide one side from another. However, a few mark broader *belts* where the transition is more gradual, and so in a sense one can identify dividing lines on either side of a distinct, broadly linear-shaped zone. All the examples used here are important somewhere in the world, in some cases to millions of people across thousands of kilometres, while others are more localised.

Why do we tend to engage with our surroundings through such lines? In a nutshell, *because they are the easiest thing one can draw*. We may like to think of ourselves as complicated beings, but when it comes to the world and its own complexity, we struggle to resist searching for a shortcut. And so, consciously or not, we draw lines to simplify and adapt our complex planet to our needs and desires. Drawing lines helps us distinguish one place from another and thereby assume some level of control over our surroundings. By simplifying our world in this way, it doesn't seem quite so complex any more. In this sense, boundaries encapsulate humans' engagement with the world in general: wanting to understand it, but also to shape it.

Why do I describe these lines as 'invisible'? Streets, rivers and mountain ranges are all types of boundaries that can be discerned by the eyes. However, often it is not the physical entity that holds the power, but rather the intangible meaning and possible consequences associated with it. Consider a 'no trespassing' sign: even without the presence of a material barrier, we know not to step any further. Similarly, where a physical barrier is removed, we often retain a sense that the other side is, somehow, different. Instead of simply concentrating on the material that gives *substance* to a boundary, we need to foreground the boundary itself. After all, there are numerous types of boundaries we scarcely notice or cannot see at all, but which undoubtedly affect people's lives in manifold ways. For this reason, when I teach university students my subject, geography, I like to signpost boundaries that many – maybe most – have never considered. These range from inconspicuous evidence of a religious community's presence (eruvim, which I use as an example in this book, provide a perfect example) to the ways in which planning policies in different wards affect the services we receive and, by extension, our life chances.

Geographers are well placed to understand these dynamics, being fundamentally concerned with the distribution and interactions of diverse phenomena on our planet. We have long attended to the ways in which humans assign meaning to specific locations, converting abstract, loosely defined 'space' into distinguishable, consequential 'place'. Given that we cannot fully understand a place without knowing where it begins and where it ends, the boundaries separating it from its surroundings are crucial. Even our use of language reflects the interdependence of places and boundaries. For instance, we may speak of events occurring within a *region* or *territory* in the same way as we would of events occurring within the same area's *boundaries* or *borders*. When we discuss conflict *zones*, our attention is drawn to the boundaries, notably the front *lines* and the shifting *frontiers* of the warring parties. The slippage between places and their boundaries is additionally reflected in the fact that the English word for a certain kind of place, 'town', is derived from the Old English *tun*, meaning 'enclosure', which in turn is related to the Dutch word for 'garden', *tuin*, but also the German word for 'fence', *Zaun*. In short, to comprehend any place on the planet, we need to consider its boundaries.

Often boundaries are created intentionally, for reasons of protection, whether we understand this physically, economically, culturally or otherwise. Some are formalised through law: the criminalisation of sleeping rough and begging within a set distance of specific public amenities, geographical variations in laws concerning matters as diverse as alcohol and abortion, disputes over fishing rights, and the gerrymandering of electoral and school districts are just a few examples. Others emerge more informally (such as the colloquial distinction centred on England's River Medway between Kentish Men and Maids on the one hand, and Men and Maids of Kent on the other), exist as legends (the Bermuda Triangle), or continue to be perceived by residents even where they are no longer recognised by governments (another English example is the historical county of Middlesex, which was officially absorbed by Greater London in 1965, but lives on in the form of a first-class cricket club and in some residents' addresses).

Others are natural features that are often perceived to be visual manifestations of some kind of boundary, even where this is scientifically spurious or an oversimplification – the Grand Canyon, for instance. It is also important to remember that even those boundaries that demarcate natural differences and hence appear to be involuntary, are defined and specified by humans – and not always consistently. For this reason, they too can prove both consequential and contentious.

Furthermore, given that boundaries and their positioning are often subjective, questions of power – in the form of competition, domination, influence – are rarely far away. Russia's war with Ukraine is a case in point: a conflict rooted in competing narratives of national and cultural identity and geopolitical spheres of influence, notably between broad and often simplistic categories of 'West' and 'East'. However, even those of us far from conflict engage with power-laden boundaries all the time. For example, when we erect a fence, what are we indicating to those on either side, as well as ourselves? When we draw a map – of anything at all – what are we emphasising, and what are we ignoring? When we refer to ideas such as 'north–south divide', 'city' and 'suburb', 'neighbourhood' and 'ghetto', all of which involve the drawing of boundaries, what are we suggesting about identity and belonging? We rarely think about these questions, and yet somewhere deep in the subconscious, we maintain a sense of where we 'fit', where we can go, where our surroundings 'feel' different. We learn these boundaries. Our acknowledgement and reinforcement of these invisible lines can have significant implications for other people's interactions with the world, too. In *Invisible Lines*, we will see how boundaries can exist in the mind, sometimes far from the place in question, as well as locally 'on the ground'.

It is also necessary to recognise that numerous boundaries that are conceived for a specific purpose can have profound, unforeseen consequences. We can see many boundaries as exemplifications of the butterfly effect, the idea that seemingly minor actions in one place can have enormous ramifications elsewhere. The writing of graffiti, the signing of a contract, the construction of a new road can all have long-term implications for how we and others engage with people and places both locally and beyond. I regard geography as the butterfly effect discipline, because it pays attention to assorted issues and events and their complex interrelationships across space, affecting people, wildlife and places in many different ways. Whether we are speaking of the long-standing habit of many people in northern China to wear facemasks as an outcome of the government's heating policy, the tendency of detritus to accumulate in specific parts of the ocean, or the continued refusal of red deer to cross the former Iron Curtain in Central Europe, boundaries have real, enduring, practical impacts on life on this planet.

Clearly, then, there is no one type of boundary, even if certain parallels can be identified. In this book, I demonstrate the five key ways in which invisible lines operate, with wide-ranging impacts on our lives and our relationships with the world around us. First, some lines are drawn to help us improve our understanding of the planet, through revealing the distinguishing characteristics on either side and from there pinpointing the processes at play. Second, certain lines are marked not to comprehend the planet, but to transform it in some way, so that it can better accommodate us and our needs. Third, innumerable lines are drawn or perceived by groups determined to take a portion of the planet for themselves, provoking competition and even conflict where others have territorial claims of their own. Fourth, combining elements of all three of the above, some lines constitute imaginary boundaries between places, allowing people to divide 'us' on one side from 'them' on the other. And fifth, assorted lines across the world are marked or recognised as means of allowing specific groups, keen to preserve some kind of cultural distinctiveness, to maintain a degree of separation from the larger society. Within these five themes, comprising six examples each, we will see the varied ways in which the world is divided, from meteorology and ecology to race and religion. Some of my examples have both a 'natural' and a 'human' component. In several, the existence – or perceived existence – of one boundary has spawned additional boundaries. Whatever the story may be, in each case, a simple map – ever the geographer's friend – is provided to make what are in many cases incredibly complex boundaries and belts that little bit more visually distinct.

I like to think that my students come away from class with a new perspective on the world around them, noticing aspects they had never noticed before but which reflect and reinforce our efforts to categorise, distinguish and divide. *Invisible Lines* introduces the reader to a range of boundaries that inform our understanding of the world and affect our engagement with it. Readers will be able to apply some of the dynamics here to places familiar to them, and hopefully come to see, experience and think about their surroundings as well as the planet more generally in a deeper way. Considering how many boundaries exist at all sorts of scales, this book does not claim to be an exhaustive account of the globe's invisible lines. Rather, it introduces a variety of fascinating examples that I find particularly helpful in understanding our planet and our relationship with it, both consistent and messy all at once.

How Invisible Lines Help Us Understand Planet Earth

As humans, we are imbued with a desire for knowledge, and accordingly derive great pleasure from learning something new. Unsurprisingly, given its obvious relevance to our lives, planet Earth has for millennia been studied by philosophers, mathematicians, astronomers and, of course, geographers, seeking to understand its multitudinous processes. Nevertheless, an interest in learning about the planet is by no means limited to scholars. Perhaps such natural feelings – a phenomenon often called 'epistemic curiosity' – are what stimulated you to pick up this book! Whether consciously or not, we all seek to familiarise ourselves with the world around us.

Boundaries and belts are fundamental to how we understand and experience the planet, because they compel us to question what distinguishes any place – however widely or narrowly described – from another. Answering this question of course raises other questions. Do we feel different there – more or less comfortable, perhaps – compared to how we feel elsewhere? Is the place changing in a way that causes it to stand out? Fundamentally, what is it about the place that is somehow unique?

By drawing or imagining invisible lines, we can streamline our thinking. As the boundary between the Earth's two hemispheres, the Equator – perhaps the most famous invisible line of all – provides us with copious information about our seasons, the shape, circumference and orbit of our planet, and the movement of ocean currents and winds. It also acts as an invisible line of latitude, zero degrees, along with the tropics of Cancer and Capricorn and the Arctic and Antarctic circles, which, although drawn strictly according to their distance to the north or south, are sometimes seen as unofficial boundaries between climate zones. And not only do many maps include lines of latitude or longitude like these, allowing us to pinpoint any location, but they may also display contour lines connecting spots at the same height above or below sea level, rendering these markings invisible gradient boundaries. Think too of continental divides, which, despite being far more intricate than any of the above, are indisputably invisible lines, partitioning the watersheds of a major portion of land. Even if it is not necessarily obvious while we are travelling, it is astonishing that the water flowing from one mountain headwater may well end up in an ocean on the opposite side of the continent to another headwater nearby. More pertinently, with growing populations needing more and more water – while also contributing increasing amounts of pollutants that can contaminate water supplies downstream – identifying the location of continental divides is critical to our use, management and conservation of our most essential resource.

Sometimes, though, the precise location of an invisible line is less clear-cut. In such cases, it can be more useful or convenient to draw lines that mark, even just roughly, the edges of a broader belt, which we can reconsider and gradually refine as our understanding increases. Consider the Sahel, an immense, shifting transition zone of semi-arid land that runs for the best part of 6,000 kilometres across the African continent, from the Atlantic Ocean in the west to the Red Sea in the east. From north to south it can stretch up to a thousand kilometres, dividing the arid Sahara in the north, with its towering sand dunes, stony plains and barren plateaus, from a belt of humid savannahs in the south, typified by long grasses, scattered trees and many of the animals in Simba's kingdom. Representing a kind of middle ground· with umbrella-shaped acacia trees not dissimilar to what can be found to the south, but also clump tussock grasses suggestive of a desert, the Sahel is often perceived as a place at the edge, a boundary land between two very different biomes.* And with climate change allowing the Sahara to stretch further and further south, the Sahel's invisible frontiers are necessarily sought in order to monitor the availability of fertile lands able to support a rapidly growing population.

In this first part we will see six examples of how people have drawn lines which, although invisible 'on the ground', encapsulate how dissimilar or distinctive the places on either side can be, and thereby provide essential insights into the workings of our planet. The Wallace Line demonstrates how different species can only be found in certain places, enabling us to view idiosyncratic evolutionary trends over time. The loosely defined Tornado Alley is crucial to our understanding of the disproportionately common occurrence of frequent and severe tornadoes across a specific swathe of the United States. The doldrums and the Sargasso Sea collectively show not only the dangers involved in ocean exploration, but also humans' often harmful impacts on fragile ecosystems. The Antarctic Circumpolar Current and the Antarctic Convergence mark the boundaries between the enigmatic White Continent and the rest of the world in terms of physical geography, climate and wildlife, with important implications for life on either side. The Arctic tree line demarcates another delicate part of the world, and by acting as an indicator of dynamic climatic and soil conditions, it provides a helpful marker of global warming. And finally, malaria, plausibly the greatest killer of all time, relies on some specific geographical factors, making the identification and monitoring of the Malaria Belt's changing and changeable boundaries essential to saving lives and fighting poverty in the future.

---

*This notion is even reflected in its Arabic name, sāḥil, which means 'coast' or 'shore'. By contrast, the Sahara's Arabic name, ṣaḥra, is far more prosaic, translating simply to 'desert'.

13

The Wallace Line

In this archipelago there are two distinct faunas rigidly circumscribed, which differ as much as those of S. Am. [South America] & Africa, & more than those of Europe & N. Am. [North America] yet there is nothing on the map or on the face of the islands to mark their limits.

Alfred Russel Wallace

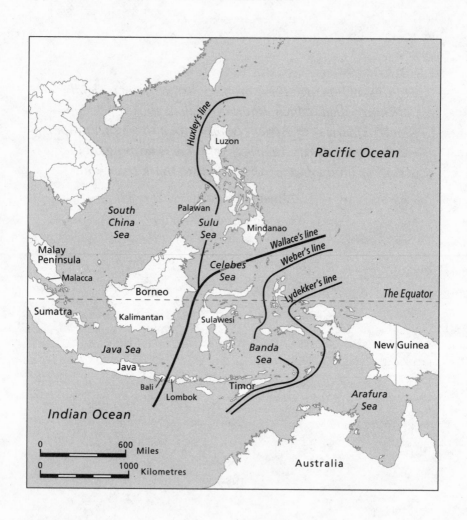

At their closest points, there are fewer than 40 kilometres between the Indonesian islands of Bali and Lombok. However, making the short journey from west to east can feel like travelling to a different continent. Whereas much of Bali is inundated with tourists visiting its beautiful beaches, rice paddies and volcanoes, Lombok is calmer, slower, less developed. Hinduism gives way to Islam, temples to mosques, suckling pig to beef satay. Particularly perceptive visitors may notice differences between the Balinese and Sasak languages. Honeymooners often descend on Bali, whereas adventure travellers may be more inclined towards Lombok. The waters may seem the same, but much else gives the impression of a stark juxtaposition.

It is when the islands' wildlife is considered that the contrast becomes particularly obvious. In Bali, the fauna is 'Asian', including civets and woodpeckers, and historically tigers, as well. In Lombok, the fauna is 'Australian', comprising porcupines, white cockatoos and helmeted friarbirds. How can just a hop, skip and a jump across the Lombok Strait reveal such a clear-cut difference? And what can we learn about the wider world from this dissimilarity? We have one of history's most unfairly overlooked scientists to thank for the answers to these questions.

Ask a stranger on the street to name the man who discovered evolution and they will almost invariably say Charles Darwin. They may then be surprised to learn that while Darwin was developing his ideas based largely on his experiences in the Galapagos

Islands, a younger, less renowned naturalist was drawing analogous conclusions over 16,000 kilometres away. Fittingly for two men with a keen eye for variance, Alfred Russel Wallace was in several ways the antithesis of his more illustrious contemporary. Whereas Darwin was born into a wealthy family and studied at both Edinburgh and Cambridge universities, Wallace dropped out of school aged fourteen because his father had gone bankrupt and could no longer afford his education. Darwin was somewhat reluctant to express his political beliefs throughout his lifetime, although he was the grandson of the prominent abolitionists Josiah Wedgwood and Erasmus Darwin.* By contrast, Wallace wrote articles in support of land nationalisation and women's suffrage, openly regarded himself a socialist and was critical of the United Kingdom's free trade policies and militarism. He also claimed to be a direct descendant of the thirteenth-century Scottish independence leader William Wallace. He was accustomed to being largely self-sufficient and in most of his endeavours was self-taught, though his future discoveries would be built in part on his experience of surveying, which he learnt from apprenticing under his eldest brother, also named William.

Wallace garnered important experience in the Amazon rainforest, which he explored from 1848 to 1852 while still in his twenties. Here he produced a remarkably detailed and accurate map of the Rio Negro, made copious notes on the people and places he visited, and collected thousands of animal specimens, although he lost almost everything when his ship caught fire and sank on the voyage home. But it is his pioneering work in the Malay archipelago for which he is today best known. From 1854 to 1862, he travelled extensively across this region, collecting more

---

*Following in his grandfathers' footsteps, Charles's most explicit political stance was his opposition to enslavement, although he did also sympathise with various common liberal causes of the time, including individualism, self-help, the free market and humanitarianism.

than 125,000 specimens, primarily insects and birds, including the Rajah Brooke's birdwing and Malayan leafwing butterflies,* the yellow-sided flowerpecker, the racquet-tailed kingfisher and the Moluccan scrubfowl. His description of the flying frog, a 'new' species that he anticipated would interest Darwinians owing to 'the variability of the toes . . . modified for purposes of swimming and adhesive climbing', also proved especially noteworthy in Western science circles. Through meticulously examining the archipelago's fauna, he started to spot patterns that would help change our understanding of biology and geography for ever.

Scientists were already aware that species vary geographically,[†] but what particularly caught Wallace's attention in South-East Asia was how even across short distances like the Lombok Strait, there could be abrupt changes in species. Usually, sharp differences in plant and animal communities across space can be attributed to significant boundaries in the natural environment, such as mountain ranges and deserts, but between islands such as Borneo and Sulawesi there is just a short stretch of sea. Recognising this quirk, Wallace contended that there is an invisible line running north to south through the archipelago, dividing animal species on the west side, which are more like those in Asia, from those on the east side, which are more akin to those in Australia.

We know far more about geology and glaciation today, and the theory of plate tectonics would not enjoy widespread

---

* Wallace named the former *Ornithoptera brookeana* after his friend Sir James Brooke, the Rajah of Sarawak. He described the latter's resemblance to 'a dead leaf attached to a twig' as a form of adaptation that is 'perhaps the most perfect case of protective imitation known' and thus clear evidence of natural selection.

† For instance, Georges-Louis Leclerc, Comte de Buffon, had a century earlier described in detail how different regions across the world are home to distinctive species, even where they share a similar climate. This idea, 'Buffon's Law', would later become a key principle of the field of biogeography.

scientific acceptance for another hundred years; yet Wallace correctly identified that the water between the islands on either side of his line was much deeper than elsewhere in the region. He knew that, during past ice ages, many seas would have been locked up as ice and thus the general sea level was far lower, at times well over 100 metres. Most of the seas in the region would simply not have existed, allowing land-based species to migrate; but the contemporary bodies of water marking his line would still have been sufficiently deep to prevent any animal species that could not swim or fly long distances from migrating. As a result, the species on either side would have evolved separately. This invisible division between 'Asia' and 'Australia' would come to be called the 'Wallace Line', after another influential scientist, Thomas Henry Huxley, in 1868 amended it slightly to extend northwards to divide the Palawan archipelago from the rest of the Philippines to better account for the distribution of different types of gallinaceous birds.*

We now know that a complex series of tectonic plate boundaries runs along Wallace's line, helping to account for the surprising variations in species Wallace observed (this also helps explain why the animals of North and South America are so different, as the two present-day continents were separate until *just* a few million

---

* Specifically, Huxley noted how *Peristeropodes* (like megapodes, also known as mound-builders) can be found on the 'Australian' side of the line, whereas *Alectoropodes* (including those birds within the Phasianidæ family, for instance partridges and pheasants) can be found on the 'Asian' side. Interestingly, another of Huxley's most influential legacies was his coining of the word 'agnostic' at a meeting of the Metaphysical Society in London in 1869, as a challenge to those who believed they had 'solved the problem of existence', a question Huxley deemed 'insoluble'. As he remarked, 'I took thought, and invented what I conceived to be the appropriate title of "agnostic." It came into my head as suggestively antithetic to the "gnostic" of Church history, who professed to know so much about the very things of which I was ignorant.'

years ago). Geologically, the western part sits on the Sunda extension of the South-East Asian continental shelf, whereas the eastern side forms part of Australia's Sahul shelf, with a deep-water trench separating them for over 50 million years, easily enough time for evolution to proceed very differently on either side. Consequently, most large terrestrial mammals as well as flightless and weak-flying birds can only be found on one side of the line. Around two-thirds of the world's marsupial species (such as kangaroos, wallabies, koalas, wombats, Tasmanian devils and bandicoots) and all extant monotremes (for instance, platypuses and echidnas) are endemic to the eastern side. By contrast, very few placentals (including cats, lutungs and squirrels) are native species here. Flora do not adhere to the division so clearly, and were less interesting to Wallace during his fieldwork, although we can note that most species of eucalyptus are only found to the east.

More broadly, Wallace's fieldwork enabled him to make remarkably similar inferences to Darwin, independently originating a theory of evolution through natural selection. He sent a paper outlining his ideas to Darwin to review. Impressed but uncertain of how to proceed, Darwin asked his friends and fellow scientists Charles Lyell and Joseph Hooker for advice. It was decided that both men's essays should be presented together at the influential Linnean Society of London, to resolve any priority dispute. The following year, while Wallace was still in South-East Asia, Darwin published his *On the Origin of Species*, gaining him public as well as professional acclaim; Darwin had been working on this text for over twenty years and ultimately condensed it so that it would be read before Wallace's work.* Wallace's subsequent use

---

* As Darwin admits in the Introduction to *On the Origin of Species*: 'My work is now nearly finished; but as it will take me two or three more years to complete it, and as my health is far from strong, I have been urged to publish this Abstract. I have more especially been induced to do this, as Mr Wallace,

of Darwin's term 'natural selection' as well as 'Darwinism' only reinforced the relationship between his counterpart and evolution in the public's mind, while underplaying his own contributions. Even so, the two men enjoyed a cordial and mutually respectful relationship: Wallace continued to defend Darwin's still controversial theory and dedicated his greatest work, *The Malay Archipelago*, to him 'not only as a token of personal esteem and friendship but also to express my deep admiration for his genius and his works', while Darwin helped Wallace, who continued to struggle financially, to receive a government pension for his contributions to science in 1879. Wallace did not seem to be bitter about his lesser reputation, and instead appeared to recognise that through his association with Darwin and their joint defence of the theory of evolution, his ideas would enjoy greater currency. During the rest of his life, Wallace published research not only on biogeography and evolutionary theory, but also on topics as widespread as politics, anthropology, astrobiology and spiritualism, the latter greatly at odds with established scientific thinking. He was also an early environmentalist, recognising the dangers of deforestation, soil erosion and the introduction of invasive species.

Since 1908, fifty years after the joint presentation of their ground-breaking papers, the Linnean Society of London has awarded a 'Darwin–Wallace Medal', for which Wallace was the first 'gold' winner, testament to his contributions to evolutionary research. However, it is the region of Wallacea and the line that bears his name with which he is most readily associated today. Although the scientists Richard Lydekker and Max Carl Wilhelm Weber would subsequently propose that the dividing line exists slightly further east, based on their analyses of different species,

---

who is now studying the natural history of the Malay archipelago, has arrived at almost exactly the same general conclusions that I have on the origin of species.'

Wallace's identification of a sharp divide in this part of the world has remained central to the discipline of biogeography and the concept of zoogeographic regions since the nineteenth century. More recently, the line has additionally been used to explain other differences, including with regard to human genetics, anthropology and linguistics. Papuan nationalists have long maintained that they are racially different from Indonesians and have used the notion of an invisible dividing line to this end; a similar boundary was invoked by the former Dutch and Portuguese colonial powers to defend their respective claims to the region. Wallace, an outspoken critic of eugenics, would most likely have been uncomfortable about such an appropriation of his biogeographical concept, a natural boundary commandeered as a political tool of division. This exemplifies part of lines' power: given their simplicity, they can easily be seized by those who deem themselves distinctive and seek justification for this claim, even though the original boundary is rooted in a separate form of difference that enjoys actual empirical support. Later we will see various other instances of invisible lines being used to spatially divide groups and places that are perceived to be different, giving rise to boundaries that are at least as much imaginary as scientifically factual.

Still, there are also plenty of lines that, like the Wallace Line, are primarily used to increase our understanding of the Earth's processes. This is perhaps especially true in the planet's most unusual places, although here, too, biases can interfere. Indeed, as we shall see next, the challenge is often to disentangle what we think we already know about a place from what the science is telling us.

Tornado Alley

I had never been to Oklahoma City before. I had no clue. Just heard there were a lot of tornadoes.

Chris Paul

---

* The basketball player was remarking on his first two seasons in the National Basketball Association, during which he played most of his home games not in New Orleans, where he was drafted, but in Oklahoma City, following the former city's devastation in the wake of Hurricane Katrina in 2005.

A coast-to-coast road trip is one of the most iconic experiences of the United States. Perusing a map of the country, it is hard not to feel a rush of excitement at the sites that await. Bustling cities and big skies. Lush forests and sweeping coastlines. Volcanoes and lakes. Art during the day and a show at night. So much food. In fact, there are almost *too* many things to take in. Where to begin? Where to end? Where to visit on the way? Is it better to stick to the major highways, or take the road less travelled? Are there any bathrooms on the way?

Naturally, certain places on any route will arouse greater enthusiasm than others. Whereas some may seek to feel the rush of the city, others prefer to find the enigmatic 'small-town atmosphere' of a place hitherto unknown to them. Kooky roadside attractions like model dinosaurs and upside-down houses – as well as what may be the world's worst idea, gas stations with a shooting range and liquor store attached – can help break the potential monotony of staring at thousands of kilometres of asphalt. However, in the middle of the country is a broad belt of land that typically garners little attention from travellers and daydreamers, despite its museums, trails and various styles of regional barbecue. Casual critics online, many of whom have probably never spent much time in this Great Plains region, love to rebuke central states like Nebraska, Kansas and Oklahoma for being boring; in 2018, the Nebraska Tourism Commission even chose to steer into the skid by snidely marketing the state as 'famous for our flat, boring landscape' and as offering 'nothing to do'. Still, befitting the tourism slogan 'Honestly, it's not for everyone', others see the potential for an energising experience.

Tornadoes occur on every continent apart from Antarctica, so technically a person does not need to visit the Great Plains just to see one. However, the central states provide among the best conditions in the world for a tornado to form, allowing them to become intimately associated with these mesmerising and unpredictable meteorological phenomena. Some people chase these enigmatic hazards as part of their profession, while others living in the region or just passing through do so for fun.

The genesis of a tornado remains nearly as cryptic as the wizard whom the appropriately named Kansan Dorothy Gale sought, but research is enabling meteorologists to gradually proceed on their own journey of understanding. In simple terms, a tornado can develop when contrasting air masses – one warm and humid, the other cool and dry, and travelling at different altitudes and speeds – collide. This is a common occurrence in much of the central United States, the former air mass arriving from the Gulf of Mexico, the latter from Canada and the Rocky Mountains, and meeting somewhere in the middle. In a minority of cases, an anvil-shaped supercell thunderstorm forms when the lighter warm air rapidly rises and the denser cold air sinks, while an invisible tube of air, fuelled by the differences in wind speed and direction at different heights, rotates horizontally. If the updraught is sufficiently strong, this tube can shift to a vertical position and create a spinning column of air in the sky, called a funnel cloud. If the column reaches the ground, a tornado is born. Most survive here for just five to ten minutes, although some can last for over an hour.

Only around one-fifth of all supercells produce tornadoes, and yet the United States consistently boasts more than a thousand tornadoes each year, around four times more than the rest of the world combined. Canada, in second place, sees just a tenth of its southern neighbour's total, while the United Kingdom, perhaps surprisingly, also appears near the top of the list of tornado events, with an average of thirty per year and the most relative to its land area of any country. However, whereas the UK's tornadoes are typically deemed 'weak' according to the Enhanced Fujita Scale of tornado intensity, as many as twenty of the United States' tornadoes each year are considered 'violent' – a tiny proportion, but a total that can cause great trepidation.

The yearly frequency and consistency of tornadoes in much of the central United States has earned the region the nickname 'Tornado Alley'. The phrase is believed to have been coined by two US Air Force meteorologists, Major Ernest J. Fawbush and Captain Robert C. Miller, who used it as the title of a 1952 research investigation concerning severe weather activity. Having already made the first successful tornado forecast and issued the first official tornado warning in March 1948 in Oklahoma City, prior to the use of Doppler radar and weather satellites, the two officers were regarded as leading experts on such hazards, and described Tornado Alley as an area stretching from Lubbock, Texas, through Enid, Oklahoma, to Kansas's state borders with Colorado and Nebraska. Appended by a northward extension into Nebraska and South Dakota and the westernmost section of Iowa, this wide swathe of land in the continental interior still represents what is commonly regarded as Tornado Alley. It is no coincidence that for nearly sixty years, the National Severe Storms Laboratory (NSSL), which plays a key role in researching a range of extreme events, has been based in Norman, Oklahoma, in an area very familiar with tornadoes and the destruction they can cause. A second belt, whose name 'Dixie Alley' has become more controversial in recent years due to the word's association with white supremacy (and for this reason was abandoned by the Weather Channel in March 2021), was identified in 1971 by the National Severe Storms Forecast Center director Allen Pearson, comprising parts of the southern states of the Carolinas, Georgia, Florida, Alabama, Mississippi, Tennessee, Kentucky, Arkansas,

Missouri, Louisiana and Texas. Today, some argue that the two alleys are in reality a single, continuous belt, albeit one marked by specific differences in the manifestation of tornadoes: those in the humid south-east tend to be accompanied by greater precipitation and may be spawned by hurricanes, for instance. The Ozark Mountains at the state borders of Arkansas, Missouri and Oklahoma also provide a patch of territory that is less prone to tornadoes than its surroundings.

Regardless of whether the two tornado belts are considered distinct or conjoined, the existence of a southern tornado region complicates the validity of the traditional Tornado Alley in the continental interior. Indeed, it is interesting to note that whereas the gargantuan Texas typically reports the most tornadoes each year (155 on average, far more than any country not named the United States), the state that experiences the most relative to its area tends to be Florida, while the most tornado-prone place in the country is Smith County, Mississippi. The south-eastern states Florida, Georgia, Alabama, Mississippi and Louisiana collectively experience one-fifth of all US tornadoes; furthermore, if just Alabama and Mississippi are considered together, they boast nearly as many tornadoes across only a slightly larger land area than Kansas, which is arguably the quintessential site of tornado events.

The damage caused by tornadoes in the south-eastern states also tends to be more significant than in the Great Plains, even though fewer of them are deemed 'strong' or 'violent'. There are a number of reasons: the population in the south-east is on average older and less able to reach a safe space quickly; more people live in mobile homes, often poorly anchored and far from adequate shelter; the population density is generally higher and so there are more people at risk in general; these areas have a great number of trees, which are prone to falling. Additionally, weather conditions in the south-east render tornadoes more likely to occur at night, when people may be less prepared to respond, whereas those in the country's interior conventionally occur in the mid-afternoon or early evening; and the tornadoes here typically travel faster, some over 100 kilometres per hour, and over longer distances, thereby covering more ground. The 362 tornadoes that swarmed across a crescent-shaped corridor from central Texas to upstate New York over a period of four days in April 2011, causing a record-breaking $10.2 billion of damage and killing 348 people either directly or indirectly (the majority in Alabama), provide compelling evidence of the dangers posed by these hazards far beyond what has historically been known as Tornado Alley. It is also worth noting that the deadliest tornado event in US history – that of 18 March 1925, with 695 fatalities – took place not in Texas, Oklahoma or Kansas, but in Missouri, Illinois and Indiana. Evidently, the former states may bear the Tornado Alley name, but they are by no means unique in their vulnerability. In fact, given the higher levels of awareness and preparedness typical within these places, schools and offices periodically conducting tornado drills, tornado sirens being used for a longer time and houses being more likely to have basements, they can actually prove far safer.

So why is Tornado Alley generally associated only with the Great Plains states in the south-central interior of the country? In addition to the fact that this was the first region to be described as such by Fawbush and Miller, and statistically speaking Texas, Kansas, Oklahoma and Nebraska make up four of the top five states with the most tornadoes in an average year (Florida is the other, in third), popular culture and the media have long played an important role. The films *Twister*, *Into the Storm* (both Oklahoma) and *The Wizard of Oz* (Kansas) brought this hazard to the forefront of many people's consciousness and reinforced the association between tornadoes and what tend to be relatively poorly known states. The tornadoes that characterise this region can be highly photogenic, materialising sharply above a flat or gently undulating landscape of vast fields of wheat or corn, which helps to generate media coverage, whereas those in the south-east are often partly concealed by heavy rain and trees and can therefore prove difficult to spot. However, even if they are less known for their tornadoes, the latter states have a reasonable claim to be included within Tornado Alley.

Certainly, considering how many places are vulnerable to tornadoes, the traditional boundaries of Tornado Alley are increasingly criticised for being based not on objective, empirical data across a range of locations, but on personal perceptions and assumptions. This creates the risk of the dangers faced by people across much of the country being underplayed, especially in the south-east. Some argue that the belt should be more precisely defined by frequency of tornadoes; others contend that only the most severe tornadoes ought to be taken into account. The invisible boundaries of any Tornado Alley will shift over time, thanks to climatic changes and growing numbers of people living in potentially susceptible areas. In recent years, noteworthy tornadoes have become more common to the east of the belt's traditional area, including in Missouri, Arkansas, Illinois, Indiana, Ohio, Kentucky, Tennessee and North Carolina, as well as in the south-east. Consequently, there are reasonable arguments to be made that the Tornado Alley moniker should additionally subsume substantial parts of states that have long been overlooked as sites vulnerable to these hazards and yet which periodically face substantial physical and economic damage. At the same time, there are indications that tornadoes, while still commonplace, are becoming less frequent in many parts of Texas and Oklahoma. Regardless of whether these are short-term anomalies or evidence of long-term shifts, it is apparent that the word 'alley' – implying a narrow passageway – underplays the extent to which tornadoes occur on a fairly regular basis across perhaps 40 per cent of the contiguous United States, stretching a good 2,000 kilometres from west to east.

Road trippers must therefore be cautious when travelling through a remarkably broad belt, and not just the established boundaries of Tornado Alley. In the core area of the Great Plains, the peak season of transitional weather which can generate tornadoes runs from March to June; in the warm Southern states, tornadoes can also present a hazard from October to December and even through the winter, necessitating year-round preparedness. Tornado watches may be issued where weather conditions are conducive to the formation of these hazards – especially important considering that tornadoes can form very suddenly out of seemingly tranquil skies – and warnings, which on average provide just thirteen minutes to reach a basement or storm shelter, follow if a tornado is sighted. To the possible surprise of some, lying in a ditch – and ideally grasping a tree trunk or stump – is deemed more advisable than sheltering in a mobile home, which can easily topple over. Drivers are recommended to leave the road and, if there is no shelter available, find a ditch, too, for even weak tornadoes can roll vehicles, let alone pick them up and carry them. Along with attempting to outrun a tornado – for their movement is erratic and they can throw people through car windows – one of the worst actions is to park on a bridge or in an underpass, as these can channel the wind, thereby increasing its velocity and attracting flying debris. Education about the risks has long been used in the traditional Tornado Alley but remains less common in much of the south-east, yet it is crucial to building awareness and overcoming any false sense of security that can come with living beyond the Alley's presumed boundaries.

Whether tornadoes are becoming more frequent over time remains a difficult question to answer. It is plausible that reporting is simply better today than at any point in the past, thanks not only to improved forecasting, but also to increased communication, including by individuals such as volunteer tornado 'spotters' on social media. Growing populations in many parts of the United States are enabling more people, albeit not always willingly, to view these hazards first hand. The number of tornado events can also fluctuate considerably from year to year, although in a number of risky areas fatalities are, fortunately, showing a general downward trend, thanks to improved building codes and severe weather warning systems. Nonetheless, ascertaining the precise location of where a tornado is about to emerge remains a significant challenge.

So, who says that a trip through the central United States can't be exciting? Even if the name 'Tornado Alley' struggles to reflect the breadth of tornado-prone places, it has helped bring renown to a part of the United States that is often unfairly maligned. More importantly, defining and monitoring its boundaries in the future will be crucial to determining the impacts of climate change and the associated vulnerability of millions of people, including beyond Tornado Alley's traditional centre. Indeed, although it is unknown whether a new appellation for this vast region would help increase public awareness, acknowledging the actual boundaries of severe tornado risk is necessary to enhance public safety and preparedness. Clearly, we must reconsider how we perceive a significant portion of the United States, reflecting inwardly on our biases while also contemplating the potential tornado hazards that may await across a far larger area of the country than is generally presumed. Scientific facts undoubtedly matter, but so too does perspective.

The Doldrums and the Sargasso Sea

This second arm – it is rather a collar than an arm – surrounds with its circles of warm water that portion of the cold, quiet, immovable ocean called the Sargasso Sea, a perfect lake in the open Atlantic: it takes no less than three years for the great current to pass round it. Such was the region the Nautilus was now visiting, a perfect meadow, a close carpet of seaweed, fucus, and tropical berries, so thick and so compact that the stem of a vessel could hardly tear its way through it. And Captain Nemo, not wishing to entangle his crew in this herbaceous mass, kept some yards beneath the surface of the waves.

Jules Verne, *Twenty Thousand Leagues Under the Sea*

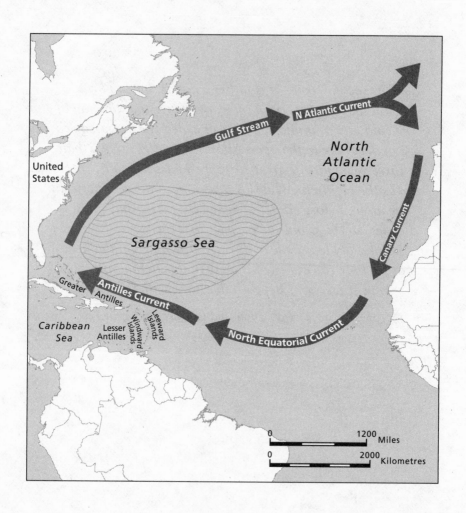

Viewing the Earth from above can be a profoundly liberating experience. Before the reader gets the impression that I've had the opportunity to 'do a Bezos' and travel to space, let me clarify that I am simply an avid user of Google Earth and can happily spend hours zooming in and out of the world's varied mountain ranges, archipelagos and street patterns. This interest stems, I believe, from my several years of avoiding otherwise mandatory morning assemblies by helping run my school's meteorological society, interpreting satellite images and synoptic charts to produce a concise daily forecast, which doubtless few read. But regardless of its (in my opinion, undeservedly) limited audience, this activity helped familiarise me with the use of lines to depict atmospheric pressure and weather fronts, both of which are invisible at ground level, yet are certainly felt and experienced. I still consider satellites truly remarkable in allowing us to observe all sorts of global features and processes, without having to come into contact with those we might want to avoid. Although many do this as part of their profession, from volcanologists monitoring the spread of volcanic ash to glaciologists tracking the melting of glaciers and ice shelves, amateurs like me can absent-mindedly scan satellite images to temporarily escape from the walls around us. Such engagement with the world is merely abstract: we see or draw lines that we do not necessarily experience personally. By contrast, those at sea and lacking the requisite technology to propel themselves can quickly feel detained if they cross certain invisible lines. In fact, one part of the ocean is so famous for its listless winds, and an associated feeling of entrapment, that it has come to be used more generally to describe feelings of depression: of 'being in the doldrums'.

How sailors, for so much of human history, would have loved to have the luxury of satellite technology before embarking on their travels (not to mention some kind of motor). Rather than relying on observations and instruments at the everyday human level, meteorologists, for instance, can today monitor and forecast the weather from space and identify patterns such as the typical routes of tropical storms. One meteorological feature worth noting in satellite images of the Earth is the crisp white band of clouds that is discernible near one of the world's best-known invisible lines, the Equator, especially above the dark seas. This belt indicates the position of the Intertropical Convergence Zone (ITCZ), which oscillates approximately five degrees north and south of the Equator over time, largely according to the position of the sun in the sky. In this way, it roughly marks the course of the (similarly invisible) *thermal* equator, connecting places at each longitude (west to east) with the highest mean annual temperature. Rather than remaining stable, the line is thus constantly on the move, primarily thanks to the Earth's tilt and consequent changing of the seasons.* For instance, during the Northern Hemisphere summer, this half of the Earth is tilted towards the Sun and hence receives more solar radiation at this time, especially at the ITCZ. Furthermore, given that warm air rises through convection before cooling at high altitudes, clouds readily develop as the water vapour within the moist air condenses. For this reason, the ITCZ is associated not only with high temperatures, but also with thick cloud cover and regular thunderstorms. During the Southern Hemisphere summer, the same process occurs: this half of the

---

* The ITCZ also veers more over landmasses than water due to them heating more quickly.

Earth is now tilted towards the Sun and the ITCZ, again distinguishable as a white band of clouds, appears at this time to the south of the Equator. The outcome is a winding and constantly shifting line which can also widen and shrink over time.

More difficult to identify but of at least as much importance are the trade winds. These blow towards the Equator from approximately thirty degrees north and south, albeit at an angle due to the Earth's rotation, via a process called the Coriolis effect.* Despite lacking the contemporary advantages of satellite technology, Portuguese sailors in the fifteenth century identified these winds and their value in propelling their ships. However, the trade winds are only helpful to seafarers up to another invisible line: where the trade winds of either hemisphere meet. This location is, again, the ITCZ. Rather than continuing to flow horizontally as surface winds, the air instead rises rapidly through convection. No longer are the winds robust; one can be considered lucky to encounter any wind at all. Although European seafarers predominantly described this phenomenon in the Atlantic Ocean for obvious geographical reasons, the same can be found in the Pacific and Indian oceans, which are also crossed by the ITCZ. In the late seventeenth century, the English astronomer and mathematician Edmond Halley described this belt of calm-to-non-existent sea winds, interspersed with fierce thunderstorms, as the 'Calms and Tornadoes', encapsulating the extremities of its winds. Eventually, however, 'doldrums' became the term of choice, likely deriving either from the Old English *dol* (dull, foolish) or the Portuguese *dolorio* (tormenting), which taken together provide much the same sentiment as Halley had intended.

Today we can monitor the position of the ITCZ and the doldrums at any time and thereby forecast the probable weather

---

*The Earth is widest at the Equator, so it rotates fastest here. Consequently, the route of any object travelling directly north or south will appear to bend, rather than remaining straight.

conditions that one will encounter in low-latitude areas, between zero and thirty degrees north or south of the Equator. But for centuries, sailors were compelled to confront whatever weather conditions the tropics presented them at a specific time of year. Ships that had advanced assuredly for hundreds of kilometres, on reaching an invisible boundary in the sea, would promptly become lethargic, proceeding with the velocity of a lunchtime post office queue in the lead-up to Christmas. The waves so typical elsewhere would disappear, leaving a shiny mirror of water beneath banks of clouds. The Age of Exploration's protagonists dreamt of seeing new places, inhabited by people unknown in Europe and replete with resources that would be of considerable value at home, but here they found themselves viewing little but a seemingly endless expanse of calm, blue sea under a beating equatorial sun. The powerful convective storms that periodically pummel this portion of the ocean provided a respite from this enforced lethargy, but brought their own discomforts. In general, however, progress would be exceptionally slow, and monotony would be the rule. Sailors would feel frustrated, drenched in sweat, progressing ever so gradually through a region characterised by heat and humidity. Most seriously, being stranded in the doldrums could be fatal, as food supplies ran low, diseases such as scurvy took hold and a range of mental illnesses set in. William Smith, a keen commentator on the Caribbean Sea's Leeward Islands and the rector of St John's parish on Nevis in the 1730s, wrote the following of a sailing master suffering from a calenture, a feverish delirium associated with heatstroke:

> He was continually laughing, and if I may be indulged in the term, merrily mad: One day in the height of his frenzy, he jumped over-board in *Charles-Town* Bay, but was luckily saved from drowning, by one of his Sailors, or from being devoured by some ravenous Shark: and then confined in our Prison, till the Ship, which he was Master of, was ready to

fail, when he went on board, and did perfectly recover his senses, before they reached *Liverpool* . . . It is now customary, when we pass the Tropick of *Cancer*, both to let blood and to purge (and, as I have heard, to vomit too, if they think their Bodies require so much cleansing).

The Anglo-Irish poet Jonathan Swift similarly conveyed how sailors, stranded and longing for the verdant fields they had long left behind, would seek escape from their suffering by jumping into the sea:

So, by a calenture misled,
The Mariner with Rapture sees,
On the smooth Ocean's azure bed,
Enamel'd fields and verdant Trees.

With eager Haste he longs to rove
In that fantastick scene, and thinks,
It must be some enchanted Grove;
And *in* he leaps, and *down* he sinks.

No wonder the doldrums were (and continue to be) regarded as the most challenging and feared belt to cross during a voyage.*
In the mid-nineteenth century, Matthew Fontaine Maury's

---

*Even so, the doldrums are not alone in pushing sailors to their limits. Most notably, the horse latitudes – high-pressure bands at roughly thirty degrees north and south of the Equator, which like the doldrums exist at the boundary between the Earth's atmospheric cells, albeit where air sinks rather than rises – are according to folklore so named because Spanish sailors would throw their horses overboard in order to conserve fresh water, knowing that weak winds could leave them stranded in this part of the ocean. This latitude can be detected on land in the form of a significant proportion of the world's deserts, the high-pressure conditions here being far from conducive to cloud formation and rain.

remarkably accurate *Wind and Current Charts of the North Atlantic* proved invaluable in advising sailors how to maximise rather than wrestle with the ocean's currents and winds. Indeed, reflecting how significantly the doldrums can impede travel, today ocean racers tend to follow the 'Doldrums Corridor Rule', which allows crews to use their engine for six degrees of latitude to prevent them from floundering here for days, or even weeks. For air travellers, too, flying through the broader ITCZ – which operates over land as well as sea – can be quite perceptible in the severity of the turbulence associated with its towering cumulonimbus clouds. Our understanding of the complexities of this belt, including its contributions to the growth of the tropical cyclones that annually batter various coastlines, continues to increase, with implications for millions around the world. And no less intriguingly, one specific portion of the doldrums called the Sargasso Sea has long piqued the interest not only of scientists but also creatives, whose fictional work has reinforced and popularised this area's reputation for entanglement, danger and inscrutability, ensuring that it be somewhat distinguished in readers' minds from the wider ocean.*

Writers are not wrong to recognise that the Sargasso Sea is an unusual place, but how so? First, whereas the rest of the world's seas are discernibly bounded by a shoreline on at least one side, the Sargasso is unique in being a sea within a sea, an oval of over 3.5 million square kilometres (which happens to be larger than India) surrounded by the Atlantic Ocean. Yet despite its lack of land boundaries, it is regarded as a distinct sea in its own right.

---

* Among other depictions, the Sargasso Sea has been represented in fiction as a place of tentacular weeds grasping doggedly for anyone unfortunate enough to pass through (*The Boats of the 'Glen Carrig'*, William Hope Hodgson), as the home of pirates who seek to hijack ships and detain their passengers (*The Sargasso Ogre*, Kenneth Robeson), and as a metaphor for being caught between two lifeworlds (*Wide Sargasso Sea*, Jean Rhys).

How can this be possible? Key to the Sargasso's existence are the ocean currents that encircle it, comprising the Gulf Stream (roughly flowing clockwise from the west to the north point of a compass), the North Atlantic Current (north to east), the Canary Current (east to south) and the North Equatorial Current and Antilles Current (south to west). Ocean currents are fuelled by various factors, including surface winds and the Earth's rotation. Together, they constitute the North Atlantic Gyre, a system of ocean currents orbiting a wide area of near-motionless water, which is the Sargasso. As a consequence, these ocean currents act as the Sargasso's unofficial, albeit shifting, boundaries. However, five such ocean gyres exist across the world: currents alone do not render the Sargasso a singular case.

Instead we must look, second, to the free-floating golden-brown *Sargassum* seaweed that lends the sea its name and which provides an ecosystem unlike any other on the planet. This seaweed accumulates as wide mats and due to its elongated appearance it is sometimes – erroneously – believed to have the capacity to ensnare ships, a common trope of fiction based in this region. Christopher Columbus, who crossed the Sargasso during his famed first voyage of 1492, described how his ship the *Santa María* was severely slowed by the *Sargassum* in combination with the gentleness of the winds here, and expected to run aground because seaweed typically indicates shallow waters:

> Most of the day it was calm, and later there was a little wind. During the day and night they did not make good more than 13 leagues. At dawn they saw so much weed that the sea appeared to be covered with it, and it came from the west. A booby was seen. The sea was very smooth, like a river, and the air the best in the world. They saw a whale, which is a sign that they were near land, because they always keep near the shore.

In fact, Columbus did not make landfall for another three weeks. His experiences of drifting sluggishly for hundreds of kilometres through thick masses of seaweed have inspired writers ever since.

The Sargasso Sea's sobriquet, the 'golden floating rainforest', epitomises both the *Sargassum*'s visual appearance and its ecological importance, being central to the life cycle of multitudinous species of fish, invertebrates, cephalopods, mammals and birds. The sea's two species of *Sargassum* – *S. natans* and *S. fluitans* – are uniquely holopelagic, meaning that they float at the surface of the open ocean using air bladders, rather than growing via a connection to the shoreline or sea floor. These bladders look rather like grapes, and it is possible that 'Sargassum' derives from a Portuguese word for this fruit, *sargaço*. By hanging at the surface in this way, the seaweed can limit the amount of sunlight that penetrates the water's surface, despite its remarkable clarity. It also offers refuge for small species of fish and young sea turtles seeking to avoid predators and, for some, represents a significant food source. Bermuda petrels and humpback and sperm whales also feed in the Sargasso as they migrate through the area each year. At least ten species are endemic to the sea, including a crab, shrimp, pipefish, snail, slug and anemone all bearing the *Sargassum* name. Within a modest mass of *Sargassum* one may come across fish, crustaceans and molluscs.* Most notably, this is the only place in the world where endangered European and American eels (*Anguilla rostrata* and *Anguilla anguilla*, respectively), among the world's most mysterious species, spawn. Their larvae subsequently travel thousands of kilometres to live in fresh water, before returning to the Sargasso Sea as adults to breed and die.

---

*By contrast, a species that is common in most of the ocean but that actually struggles to survive in the Sargasso's characteristically warm, dark, salty and still waters is plankton, meaning that any other species that depend on it as a food source are also rarely seen here.

At present, little more is known about how eels in the wild reproduce – the first direct evidence that mature American eels migrate to the Sargasso Sea was found as recently as 2015, following over a century of fruitless attempts to catch even a single adult in the open ocean – further underscoring the need to protect this habitat.*

But the Sargasso also contains danger. Its combination of thick seaweed in calm water surrounded by ocean currents means that it is especially prone to accumulating plastic and other refuse. Such materials can be transported thousands of kilometres across the Atlantic Ocean, before becoming trapped in the *Sargassum*, where they may be consumed by or injure marine animals. Chemicals such as arsenic and mercury can also accumulate in waters laden with *Sargassum* and, like plastic particles, eventually pass through the food cycle all the way to humans. The North Atlantic garbage patch was first identified here in 1972 and has been growing ever since, today stretching across several hundred kilometres. And with the ocean currents that form the gyre operating as shifting walls that prevent the detritus from escaping, they represent a boundary in an additional sense. Further anthropogenic threats include the overfishing of various species of tuna and marlin on either side of the Atlantic, and shipping-related hazards such as the discharge of sewage, oil and tar. Demarcating the Sargasso's boundaries, even just roughly, has become essential to multilateral conservation efforts over the past two decades. Unfortunately, this is a major challenge.

The starting point of attempts to map the Sargasso tends to be the clockwise-circulating North Atlantic Gyre, which bounds the sea. Towards the western edge of the gyre is the island of Bermuda,

---

* The Danish biologist Johannes Schmidt is credited with first observing eel larvae in the Atlantic Ocean in 1904, but adult eels remained elusive until a Canada-based team managed to track American eels from Nova Scotia using pop-up satellite archival tags (PSATs) in 2015.

which represents the northernmost point of the Bermuda Triangle, another loosely defined region notorious for the peculiar disappearance of aircraft and ships and which in effect borders the Sargasso Sea. The problem is that ocean currents fluctuate in strength throughout the year, so they do not represent stable boundaries and hence cannot be drawn straightforwardly as a line; at best, any line would have to follow the *average* locations of these shifting currents. The eastern boundary of the Sargasso Sea is particularly troublesome to determine because the Canary Current is relatively dispersed and weak; a solution of sorts has sometimes been found by using the Mid-Atlantic Ridge, where the North American tectonic plate moves away from its Eurasian and African counterparts, instead. Eddies, small circular currents of water, provide an additional complication, as they help mix what would otherwise be an even starker divide between the calm water within the gyre and the strong currents that constitute it.

Another aspect to consider when trying to map the Sargasso Sea is the existence of its namesake *Sargassum*, but common techniques such as satellite imagery are generally only able to detect it in high densities near the sea surface, whereas clumps of it can travel well beyond the gyre. Indeed, even though *Sargassum* is most prevalent in the Sargasso Sea, on occasions it washes up on beaches on either side of the Atlantic, disrupting local tourist economies as it reeks of rotten eggs when it decomposes. It also fluctuates in its spatial extent throughout the year and possibly over longer periods of time. Consequently, the seaweed does not in itself provide an effective visible boundary of the amorphous Sargasso. The distribution of eel spawning locations, warm water masses and areas of particularly saline, warm water are among the other criteria occasionally addressed in efforts to distinguish the Sargasso Sea from the wider Atlantic.

The oval shape generally used to depict the sea on maps represents a reasonable compromise, providing visual simplicity as well as the possibility of recognising fluidity and dynamism over time. A fixed, predictable boundary is simply not the sea's reality. Far from being inconsequential, distinguishing the Sargasso enables scientists to attain a greater understanding of a place that is still characterised by numerous uncertainties and yet which may provide clues to many of our planet's greatest ecological and environmental puzzles. It is little surprise that the Sargasso has become a vital research site, concerning the movement of ocean currents and changes over time in acidity, nutrient cycling, oxygen and carbon dioxide levels and water temperature, and by extension species numbers and climate. Nevertheless, it is not alone in being a vital place – and a delicate place at that – where studies of the Earth's key processes are conducted. It's time to head south. If only we could catch a breeze . . .

The Antarctic Circumpolar Current and the Antarctic Convergence

Great God! this is an awful place and terrible enough for us to have laboured to it without the reward of priority. Well, it is something to have got here.

Robert Falcon Scott

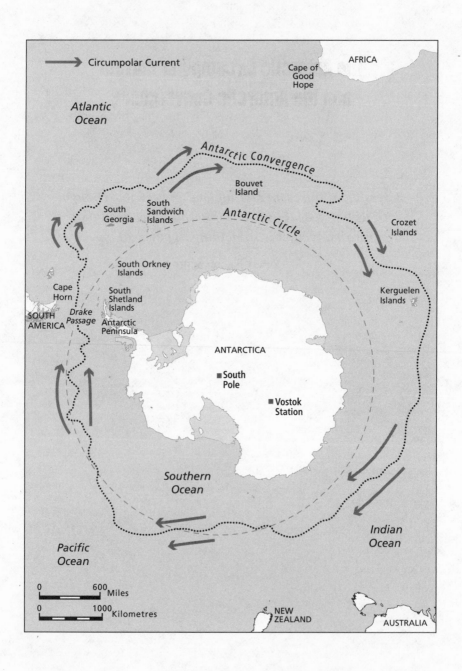

Poor Captain Scott. It wasn't bad enough that he and his four companions perished from Antarctica's acute cold, exacerbated by insufficient sustenance; he wouldn't even be immortalised as the first person to successfully lead an expedition to the South Pole, being beaten by his rival Roald Amundsen by just a month, in December 1911–January 1912. The account of Robert Falcon Scott's doomed mission has come to acquire legendary status, with Scott being memorialised across the United Kingdom in the forms of monuments and even a research institute connected to the University of Cambridge, testament to his bravery, determination and contributions to science. Scott's team was found in its icy tomb with 16 kilograms of rocks (whose fossils proved that the continent had once been warm enough to be forested), invaluable meteorological data that are still used today, and photographs of Antarctica's wildlife, seas and glaciers, accelerating our understanding of this elusive region. Along with Scott's personal diary, a rich documentation of the British team's triumphs and travails – including his companion Lawrence 'Titus' Oates's famous last words, 'I am just going outside and may be some time' – the team's methodical yet misfortunate engagement with the White Continent may explain why they and Scott specifically have garnered such affection ever since. Indeed, despite his detractors, who criticise him as a bungler lacking in foresight, Scott remains a captivating figure, representing the challenges of being human in the planet's most hostile place. By contrast, the man who made

it not only to the South Pole first but to the North Pole as well –
Amundsen – is often regarded, appropriately enough, more coolly,
perhaps due to his restrained demeanour and laconic accounts of
his travels. Yet Amundsen also saw a tragic end, his plane believed
to have crashed during a rescue mission for the *Italia* airship in
1928. Unlike Scott, his body has never been found.

Comparisons of Scott and Amundsen have certain value in
demonstrating the challenges of traversing the Antarctic continent. The two figures and their teams made vital contributions to
understanding not only the limits of human possibility but also
the intricacies of a continent that even today remains the world's
most obscure place. From its harsh climate to its lack of food
resources, and from its deep crevasses to soaring mountains, Antarctica is full of barriers to exploration. But even before these
explorers reached the South Pole, they had crossed two noteworthy, interconnected frontiers of a different sort.

The Antarctic Circumpolar Current (ACC) is one of these
boundaries, flowing continuously through the Southern Ocean
in a clockwise direction around Antarctica. This makes both the
ACC (as an ocean current) and the Southern Ocean (as a body of
water) unique in ringing a continent. However, this is not the only
way in which the ACC is distinctive: it is the world's most powerful
current, transporting well over 100 times more water than all the
planet's rivers combined. It helps make the waters around Antarctica notoriously rough, discouraging transportation from north
to south and all but preventing it from east to west through the
Southern Ocean, but speeding up travel when following its course
from west to east. The 'roaring forties', robust winds that blow
in this direction largely unhindered by landmasses, were typically
used by European sailors after rounding the Cape of Good Hope
to expedite their travel east,* and their even stronger southern

---

*The Dutch explorer and future Governor-General of the Dutch East Indies
Hendrik Brouwer is credited with discovering the 'roaring forties freeway' in

neighbours the 'furious fifties' help drive the ACC. Together these winds and the ocean current represent a formidable barrier between Antarctica and the rest of the world.

The Antarctic Convergence, also known as the Antarctic Polar Front, acts as an associated boundary. It marks a rough circle around Antarctica where the Southern Ocean meets the southern parts of the Pacific, Atlantic and Indian oceans, and hence where cold Antarctic waters encounter warmer (but still chilly) subantarctic waters. Whereas the former are dense and low in salt content due to greatly reduced evaporation in cold conditions, the latter are lighter and saltier, influenced by other ocean currents from milder climates. The result is that the denser Antarctic waters descend beneath the lighter subantarctic waters, which are forced to rise to the surface via a process known as upwelling. Nutrients become concentrated near the surface, enabling phytoplankton to photosynthesise. These phytoplankton nourish the region's bountiful Antarctic krill population, which in turn feeds the region's other animals, including fish, squid, seals, whales and birds.

The ACC and the Antarctic Convergence therefore form two interlinked boundaries, demarcating one's arrival in the Antarctic region when travelling here by sea. Whereas the general location of the ACC can be discerned in its fierce waves, the Antarctic Convergence may seem more subtle, although it has its own distinguishing features. The continent of Antarctica is of course known for its exceptionally cold temperatures, ranging from an average of $-10°C$ at the coast to an almost inconceivable -50 to $-60°C$ inland, depending on the location. On 21 July 1983, the Vostok Station recorded a ground-level temperature of $-89.2°C$! Off the coast, temperatures are also impressively frigid, although not nearly to the same level given that water is not subject to

---

the 1610s while sailing for the Dutch East India Company towards Java, in present-day Indonesia.

the same temperature swings as land. Still, there is a perceptible temperature boundary at the Antarctic Convergence: during the summer, the surface waters on the south side can be at least 3°C colder than those to the north, even if the winter temperature gradient tends to be less extreme. Although this line is in itself invisible, the presence of fog, which can appear quite suddenly, provides a visual indication that it has been crossed, while adding to the intrigue of approaching the world's least visited continent.

But ecological changes provide the clearest indication that an invisible line has been crossed. Due to the temperature boundary of the Antarctic Convergence and the physical barrier of the ACC, neither of which has changed significantly over millions of years, species exchange has remained minimal and so those to the south have been able to evolve very differently from their counterparts to the north. This is most apparent in the case of animals that rely at least in part on the presence of land: whereas even at high latitudes in the Northern Hemisphere, animals have been able to migrate in response to changes in the climate because of the widespread coverage of landmasses here, those in Antarctica have been forced to adapt to extreme environmental conditions, or otherwise die. For this reason, coping with the elements has proved a more immediate concern than developing strategies to outcompete or fend off rivals, even if some species from the north are able to cross the divide as part of their migration routes.

Why would a species that can feed and breed elsewhere choose to travel to Antarctica? The waters to the south of the Antarctic Convergence are over seven times more productive than those to the north: as long as a species can negotiate the challenges of living in this environment, food can be relatively abundant. The fact that only a small number of species possess the prerequisite resilience is reflected in Antarctica's animals' typically simple food webs, comprising just a few species rather than the smorgasbord available to consumers elsewhere on the planet. Big mammals such as whales, porpoises and dolphins tend to swim long distances, and some travel as far south as the Convergence, whereas pygmy right whales, which were believed to be extinct until 2012, appear to be limited to the Antarctic region. Crabeater (which despite their name actually eat krill), Weddell, leopard and Ross seals are largely found along the Antarctic coast, while Antarctic fur seals and southern elephant seals generally live further north, nearer the Convergence. Hardy birds tend to flourish because of the absence of terrestrial predators and the abundance of crustaceans, fish, squid and other food sources in the ocean, but only emperor penguins, Antarctic petrels and South Polar skuas breed solely south of the Antarctic Convergence.

The vast majority of the 100 or so species of fish south of the Antarctic Convergence – a tiny number considering that around 20,000 types of ocean fish have been identified – inhabit the deep sea, including Antarctic toothfish and various types of Antarctic icefish. Some nototheniod fish species here are distinctive in possessing antifreeze proteins in their blood that prevent them from freezing to death, and a few are exceptional among vertebrates in having translucent rather than red blood, lacking in haemoglobin. By contrast, pelagic fish, which live in the water column as opposed to at the sea bottom, are relatively rare south of the Convergence, given that the ice at the surface would freeze them, unless they were to develop the same antifreeze properties. Decapods like crabs are also rare to the south, largely owing to the exceptionally low temperatures here, whereas starfish and giant sea spiders are remarkably common.

With regard to plants, species must not only be able to withstand temperatures well below freezing but also contend with complete or at least considerable darkness during the winter, fierce winds and a lack of rainwater. It can be easy to overlook how Antarctica, with its negligible annual precipitation, is the world's largest desert. Plants typically grow close to the ground to avoid the continent's gales and to find any available moisture. Photosynthesis is limited to the summer, and sometimes for just a matter of days each year. Almost half of Antarctica's plants are lichens, along with mosses, liverworts, algae and fungi, which tend to be concentrated along the coast. By contrast, in territories that are consistently north of the shifting Antarctic Convergence, for example on France's Crozet Islands in the southern Indian Ocean, vascular plants like *Poa kerguelensis* (a species of tussock grass) and heather can survive as well. Thus the Antarctic Convergence is not impenetrable, even if it broadly represents a manifest species boundary, enabling Antarctica and its surrounding waters to boast one of the world's most distinctive ecosystems. It may also be the longest ecological boundary on the planet. The ACC, with its rapid waters and associated winds, only reinforces Antarctica's and its various endemic species' separateness.

These boundaries are not, however, easy to mark. Although the Antarctic Convergence tends to be found at approximately fifty-five degrees south (remarkably, the same sort of latitude south of the Equator as the UK is north), it can veer north to about forty-eight degrees and south to around sixty-one degrees over time. The Convergence is also inconsistent in its width, ranging from about 25 to 50 kilometres at points. In some places it can be broken, most notably by swirling ocean eddies, which are particularly likely to form where the Convergence moves over significant protrusions, like ridges, on the ocean bed. Meanwhile, the ACC meanders between undersea mountains and obstacles such as the Drake Passage, a gap a modest 800 kilometres wide between Cape Horn and the southern tip of South America to the north and the South Shetland Islands off the coast of the limb-like Antarctic Peninsula to the south. Differences in methodologies when measuring water temperature and salinity further complicate efforts to ascertain the precise location of the Convergence and the ACC. The Southern Ocean was officially designated as an ocean in its own right by the International Hydrographic Organization in 2000 (even though it was described as such as early as the 1770s by the British explorer James Cook) due to it being sufficiently distinctive from the southern parts of the Pacific, Atlantic and Indian oceans, largely thanks to the Convergence, but its boundaries are by extension also variable. Even the Antarctic Circle, which provides another means of defining the Antarctic region, is not stable, as it marks the northernmost point where the centre of the sun is visible above the horizon at midnight on at least one occasion per year (and by extension does not appear at noon on another day in the year), and thus changes with the Earth's gradually shifting axial tilt. It is not fixed to a line of latitude.

Nor are these boundaries solely of relevance to the general Antarctic region. The cold Antarctic waters that sink beneath the warmer subantarctic waters can travel far north of the Equator as a key driver of the 'global conveyor belt', which transports nutrients and carbon dioxide and regulates temperatures across the world's oceans. Life on the planet is dependent on the stability that Antarctica's ocean currents provide, which is why major changes to Antarctica's ice coverage cause such concern across the globe. Ozone depletion, pollution and human-induced climate change are a few of the major threats this fragile region faces today. With growing amounts of fresh water entering the increasingly warm Southern Ocean from Antarctica's melting ice, there are justified concerns that the entire system of global ocean circulation will be disrupted, with unclear consequences for the climate and by extension vital issues such as food stocks. It is plausible that the Antarctic Convergence is already moving further south, forcing many of the migratory species that rely on it, such as wandering albatrosses and baleen whales, to travel longer distances or to seek new feeding areas altogether. A combination of warming temperatures and vessel movements also poses a threat through attracting or carrying invasive species such as flea-like springtails, the midge *Eretmoptera murphyi* and potentially animals as large as shore and king crabs, which may upset the ecosystem's delicate balance. The environment that Scott and Amundsen encountered over 100 years ago has changed considerably, even if their expeditions provided the groundwork for our contemporary understanding.

Consequently, monitoring Antarctica's invisible boundaries is crucial to ascertaining the prospects for countless species' survival. Similar issues exist in the Arctic, too, even if it lacks an ocean to form a boundary in the manner of the Antarctic Convergence and the ACC. Instead, it has its own *land*-based natural division from the rest of the Northern Hemisphere.

The Arctic Tree Line

Yesterday was wood; tomorrow will be ashes.
Only today does the fire shine bright.

Inuit proverb

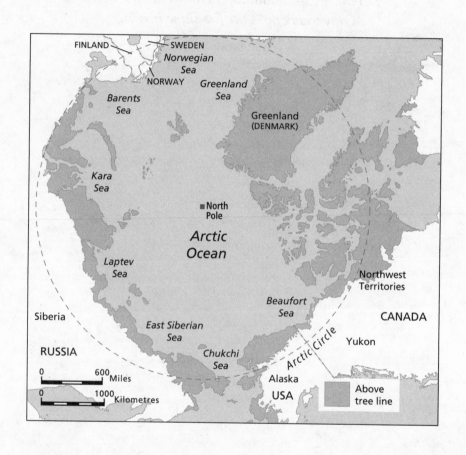

Walking north through the dense forests of Canada, you are struck by a combination of cool air and the sharp, clean aroma of pines that invigorates your mind and bolsters your spirit. Interspersed with various shades of dark green, swathes of yellow appear, larches standing tall before jagged grey mountains with a dusting of perfectly white snow. It is easy to feel nostalgic: it may be early autumn, but it feels like Christmas. The temperature cools. Signs of human activity disappear: there is no one else for miles. The tallest trees mostly block out the sky, but glimmers, sharply cutting through the canopy, offer a reminder that the sun is yet to set. The occasional rustle of a marten or hare breaks the silence. Suddenly, the tightly packed trees give way to an expanse of small shrubs and sedge meadows, boulders and bare ground. In some places, tiny lichens and mosses are the vegetative peaks. You have crossed the Arctic tree line.

There are many types of tree lines across the world, boundaries distinguishing places where trees can grow from places where they cannot. Some appear like monks' heads on tall mountains, a thick ring surrounding a bald peak. Others can be noticed along the coast, beaches spreading gently into the water, with a line of shrubs or trees some distance back. Swamps, deserts and hot springs often have their own tree lines, too. Antarctica's tree line is more subtle, being connected to the Antarctic Convergence, whereby places to the south lack the indigenous trees of places at slightly less extreme latitudes like Tierra del Fuego at the tip of South America. However, no tree line is as significant to understanding our planet as that in the Arctic, marking the northernmost points where trees can survive. Any further and the temperatures are too cold: trees' sap freezes, while permafrost prevents their roots from digging deep into the soil in search of water and nutrients as well as providing the stability they need. Cell division, essential to tissue growth, may also be inhibited.

Latitude unsurprisingly plays a key role in defining this boundary: places nearer to the North Pole are more likely to be too cold for trees to survive during the winter. Additionally, the summer growing season is short, the only time of the year when there is sufficient sunlight for photosynthesis given the Earth's tilt. Even so, latitude is not the sole factor at the local scale. Latitude's anagram, altitude, is also worth noting, as the temperature generally cools with height, affecting the types of species that can live at a particular elevation. Aspect – the direction a slope faces – is relevant as well: in the Northern Hemisphere, north-facing slopes are more shaded from the Sun and more exposed to Arctic winds, meaning that snow lasts longer, and the growing season is more limited. Consequently, the tree line winds down north-facing slopes and up south-facing slopes. Some slopes are additionally too steep or their soil too cold and shallow to support tree growth. Human activities like making fires and grazing livestock can have an impact, too. Alongside the role played by local wind patterns and other microclimates, which create patches of different conditions that either support or hinder tree growth, the overall result is a zigzagging rim or fringe of trees across the Earth's northern regions for over 13,000 kilometres, making the Arctic tree line the world's longest land-based ecological boundary.

In some places the Arctic tree line is easily discernible, but in others it is more of a diffuse transitional zone, stretching many kilometres, characterised by scattered krummholz (stunted trees, contorted by the wind due to their exposure), small shrubs and lichen. Nonetheless, there tends to be a shift from taller, densely packed coniferous trees at the edge of the boreal forest or taiga to the south, to the shorter, sparser, scrawnier vegetation bounding the tundra to the north. Eventually, the krummholz disappear. From here on the soil becomes less nutrient-rich, the wind increases in ferocity, and fewer and fewer organisms are able to survive.

Why is the Arctic tree line so important? Unlike pretty much everywhere else in the world, where the presence of trees is perceived positively and conservation involves protecting or planting them, in the far northern latitudes, evidence that trees are spreading is concerning. This part of the planet is particularly susceptible to climate change and even small changes here could have significant impacts elsewhere. It is the butterfly effect in action: a small increase in temperature may allow forests to advance northwards. The dark colours of trees – especially evergreens – and soil absorb far more of the Sun's radiation and heat than the reflective snow that covers tundra regions for much or all of the year. As a result, these areas warm even more, allowing further vegetation growth. The cycle proceeds as a positive feedback loop, albeit one that can be partially mitigated by cooling through increased transpiration.

This warming tendency additionally has implications for other species and natural processes. Small tundra shrubs risk being outcompeted for sunlight by tall evergreen trees like white spruce – whose growth has accelerated over the past century in line with general increases in annual and summer temperatures – and even deciduous species like larches, which conventionally prefer slightly warmer, wetter climates. Animals that rely on specific conditions for food and shelter may also either benefit or suffer depending on their habitat needs and preferences. Lynx, black bears and moose may be able to migrate northwards, but the existing inhabitants of what has long been a tundra region, such as musk oxen, red knots, ptarmigans and reindeer or caribou, will have to adapt to new competitors and predators and a dynamic environment. Indigenous populations like the Gwich'in (today living in Alaska, Yukon and the Northwest Territories), Inuvialuit

(Yukon and the Northwest Territories), Sámi (the Sápmi region of northern Norway, Sweden, Finland and north-western Russia) and Nenets (north-western Siberia), for whom these lands are not the inhospitable 'wilderness' of the southern imagination, but *home*, are also needing to adjust, with many revising their hunting, herding, harvesting and fishing strategies, itineraries and settlement patterns in response to changes in snow, ice and vegetation cover and animals' natural migration routes. In extreme cases, wildfires occur and invasive insects further damage fragile ecosystems, especially in more southern forests that are already relatively mild. Particularly concerning is that the permafrost of far northern latitudes is thawing, not only undermining the integrity of roads and building foundations, but also releasing the masses of carbon dioxide and methane stored here for thousands of years. There is now a legitimate fear that these greenhouse gases will accelerate temperature increases not just in the Arctic, but over a much broader area. And in doing so, they will – as part of a potentially calamitous self-reinforcing cycle – trigger further permafrost melting, in turn freeing even more carbon dioxide and methane into the atmosphere. The Arctic may seem distant to most of the world's population, yet the future of every place and every person is, even if indirectly, in its hands.

Of course, the Arctic tree line has never been fixed: the climate has always been dynamic and so the tree line has moved back and forth, although it has remained largely stable over the past 3,000 years or so. Nevertheless, the past 150 years have seen a clear warming trend following the end of the Little Ice Age which defined the middle of the previous millennium, directing attention to the poles. These places are not only sensitive to temperature increases, but can accelerate them through the melting and decline of reflective surfaces like ice and snow, in turn raising sea levels across the planet. Research is ongoing to determine just how sensitive trees here are to alterations in the climate: not only temperature, but also rainfall, wind, light and snow cover, and by extension variables such as soil, availability of nutrients like nitrogen, and presence of animals that could kill saplings. Working out how quickly trees respond is important, too, because the spread of trees following an uptick in temperature may not be immediate, especially in a region where tree growth is typically slow owing to the harsh and highly seasonal environmental conditions.

In this regard, the tree line provides a visible indicator of a separate, *invisible* line, marking the edge of where local conditions can accommodate tree growth. Indeed, the presence – or absence – of trees is based on variables that are less easy to distinguish visually, including the quality of the soil, temperature and wind. By the time tree saplings have managed to outcompete the tundra vegetation and grown large enough to be regarded as part of an advancing tree boundary, this invisible line may well have shifted. For this reason, the tree line expresses, belatedly, deeper processes, which occur out of sight until trees have had the time to mature. It represents a relatively convenient means of monitoring environmental changes, but with a delay.

This is not to say that observing the tree line is unimportant – far from it. Increased boreal forest coverage in far northern territories, a consequential finding of many studies, is a clear suggestion of a warming climate. Local dips in the Arctic tree line can indicate where forest fires and insects have ravaged areas that would otherwise thrive with vegetation. Both the presence and the absence of trees have a major impact on the lives of other species inhabiting this chilly region, including smaller shrubs and animals. And although it is less neat, the Arctic tree line forms a more distinct boundary than the invisible line of the Arctic Circle, which like the Antarctic Circle defines where the Sun does not set or rise on at least one day of the year and shifts with the Earth's tilt. As challenging as it may be, mapping the tree line can help us understand and attempt to mitigate some of the most severe impacts of climate change. In the future, the time delay between the invisible line indicating where trees can feasibly grow, and trees' actual emergence, may be clarified via the continued use of dendrochronology.*

Given trees' importance in supplying oxygen, providing habitats for wildlife, improving the soil, offering shade and cooling the air in hot climates, they play a vital role in determining the geography of life on our planet. Where they struggle to survive, other species tend to as well. By contrast, one insect's presence on the planet is almost universally perceived as a threat. Monitoring its geographical boundaries is thus essential to human lives, as we shall see next.

---

*This method, involving the dating of tree rings, can reveal how quickly trees are growing in a region. Warm, wet years tend to be represented by wider, denser rings than cool, dry years.

The Malaria Belt

Defeating malaria is absolutely critical to ending poverty, improving the health of millions and enabling future generations to reach their full potential.

Tedros Adhanom Ghebreyesus, director-general
of the World Health Organization (WHO)

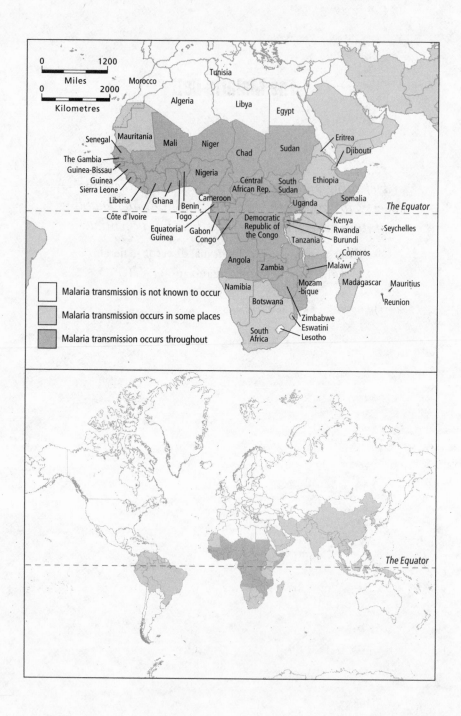

0   1200
Miles

0   2000
Kilometres

Tunisia
Morocco
Algeria
Libya
Egypt
Mauritania
Senegal
The Gambia
Guinea-Bissau
Guinea
Sierra Leone
Liberia
Côte d'Ivoire
Mali
Niger
Chad
Sudan
Eritrea
Djibouti
Nigeria
Ghana
Benin
Togo
Cameroon
Central African Rep.
South Sudan
Ethiopia
Somalia
Uganda
Equatorial Guinea
Gabon
Congo
Democratic Republic of the Congo
Kenya
Rwanda
Burundi
Tanzania
Seychelles
Angola
Zambia
Comoros
Malawi
Namibia
Mozam-bique
Madagascar
Mauritius
Reunion
Botswana
Zimbabwe
Eswatini
Lesotho
South Africa

The Equator

Malaria transmission is not known to occur

Malaria transmission occurs in some places

Malaria transmission occurs throughout

The Equator

I seem to have some sort of allergy to mosquito bites, because when I am bitten – which happens all too frequently, as apparently my blood is irresistible – I often end up with a bulbous, pus-filled dome, generally on an ankle, swelling over an inch from the rest of my skin. Not wanting to repel the reader, even if I recall a friend looking queasy on observing first hand this distinctive reaction during a camping trip, I make this point partially as a reminder to myself that it is nowhere near as severe as the symptoms that tragically afflict millions of these little rogues' victims every year. Although some people manifest few symptoms, if any, others experience consecutive 'cold' (chills, shivering) and 'hot' (fever, high temperature, vomiting, nausea, diarrhoea, body pain, headache) stages, followed by sweating and fatigue. Additional symptoms can include jaundice, enlarged spleen or liver, severe anaemia, hypoglycaemia, acute kidney failure, seizures, coma and hearing loss. Even those who recover may subsequently suffer relapse. Young children, who have yet to develop immunity, and pregnant women, whose immunity is compromised, are especially vulnerable. Spread by European colonisers to the Americas, possibly having killed both Alexander the Great and Genghis Khan centuries earlier, malaria is a disease whose geography is conspicuously dynamic, and has posed a greater threat to some of the most influential figures in human history than any of their rivals and enemies. In fact, it is probable that malaria is the most prolific killer of all time, with some estimates suggesting that half of the people ever to have lived ultimately died either directly or indirectly from this malady.

Even today, malaria is endemic in around half of the world's countries and threatens almost half of its population. Most cases are concentrated in a wide belt across the tropics, whose boundaries shift by season and with every success and failure in curbing the disease's spread. Around 90 per cent of the hundreds of millions of cases and upwards of 400,000 deaths per year occur in just one, albeit expansive, stretch of land: sub-Saharan Africa, most of which is generally understood to constitute the Malaria Belt. Why is this part of the world so susceptible when female *Anopheles* mosquitoes, which transmit the disease, live on every continent barring Antarctica?

First, two of the most efficient *Anopheles* species in spreading malaria – *Anopheles gambiae* and *Anopheles funestus* – are both common in sub-Saharan Africa, as they easily proliferate in the climatic conditions typical of tropical regions, comprising hot temperatures and high levels of rainfall and humidity, which provide numerous water bodies for them to breed and lay their eggs. Second, they are both anthropophilic: that is, they have a particular predilection for human rather than animal blood. Third, the deadliest of the five malaria parasites to infect humans, *Plasmodium falciparum*, also favours sub-Saharan Africa's heat and can develop rapidly within both *Anopheles gambiae* and *Anopheles funestus*. Thus, even though malaria is also a significant issue in India, Papua New Guinea and other countries that suffer from this combination of malaria-carrying mosquitoes (some of which are also anthropophilic) and parasites, sub-Saharan Africa is home to the most dangerous forms of both. The fact that areas close to the Equator experience little seasonality, due to the Sun being overhead for most of the year, only exacerbates the issue, as people there are vulnerable to these mosquitoes and parasites from January to December, as opposed to a period of several months, as is the case in relatively cooler and/or drier places further north or south.

Nevertheless, for many reasons it would be wrong to view sub-Saharan Africa as a single, monolithic entity, including the fact that not all parts of this region are equally vulnerable.* Some of its countries contain mountainous areas (which are cooler on average) and arid regions such as deserts (which, aside from around oases, are too dry for these mosquitoes to proliferate), nipping a map of the Malaria Belt with holes, where the disease is not a significant problem. Certain countries, especially those in the far south – South Africa, Botswana, Namibia and Eswatini (formerly Swaziland) – have proved more successful in controlling the disease, thanks to a combination of focused public health measures and the natural advantages offered by their landscapes (many of which are uplands or deserts) and seasonality. By contrast, in some rural parts of sub-Saharan Africa, many residents have expressed reluctance to adopt the strategies used in numerous cities in this part of the world, for reasons as diverse as costs, misunderstandings, a relative shortage of health clinics, and the need to harvest the fields during the dark, increasing exposure to mosquitoes. Consequently, a general urban–rural divide can be discerned in malaria cases and vulnerability as well. Any map of the Malaria Belt is nuanced by these variations and we should pay attention both to the factors that shape susceptibility and to the responses taken by different communities to mitigate the disease. However, even if it is possible to simplify and visualise the geography of malaria risk through maps, on the ground, the lines distinguishing one's relative vulnerability cannot be seen.

---

* After all, given its sheer scale as well as its geographic and cultural diversity, 'sub-Saharan Africa' is inevitably an imprecise way of describing this part of the world. The World Bank, for instance, includes forty-eight countries within sub-Saharan Africa, stretching from Mauritania and Sudan (much of which comprise parts of the Sahara Desert) to South Africa, as well as the island nations of Cape Verde, Comoros, Madagascar, Mauritius, São Tomé and Príncipe and Seychelles. This means that the Bank only considers six African nations *not* part of sub-Saharan Africa.

Intriguingly, another determinant of malaria risk is the very presence of humans: the malaria that affects us simply cannot exist *without* us. This is because a mosquito must have already become infected through taking blood from a person (or, in other types of malaria, an animal) containing an early version of the malaria parasite, at this stage called a gametocyte. Within the mosquito, the gametocytes develop into the next parasitic stage, sporozoites, before being injected into a human victim during feeding. The parasite finally matures in the liver and divides itself into merozoites, which invade and destroy the body's red blood cells. In this way, malaria transmission relies on three parties: humans as hosts; mosquitoes as vectors, spreading the disease without suffering from it; and parasites as causative agents. Therefore, places devoid of people – some areas of the desert or the rainforest, for instance – are also free of malaria.

Another interesting aspect of malaria is that despite being known for millennia – the ancient Greek physician Hippocrates described something akin to the disease* – it remains such a significant threat. Its name is derived from the medieval Italian for 'bad air', reflecting the long-time popularity of the now obsolete miasma theory, which held that poisonous vapours were responsible for various diseases; it was not until the late nineteenth century that Alphonse Laveran, Ronald Ross and Giovanni Grassi separately demonstrated that malaria is actually caused by parasites. Perhaps surprisingly, only in October 2021 was a vaccine recommended by the World Health Organization for children at risk, providing hope that the disease will soon – finally – be

---

* 'This disease is habitual to them [waters that 'are marshy, stagnant, and belong to lakes'] both in summer and in winter, and in addition they are very subject to dropsies of a most fatal character; and in summer dysenteries, diarrhoeas, and protracted quartan fevers frequently seize them, and these diseases when prolonged dispose such constitutions to dropsies, and thus prove fatal.'

consigned to history. Certainly, in contrast to the expedience with which several COVID-19 vaccines were developed and approved in many developed countries, it is striking how long this process has taken: a situation arguably indicative of a general lack of attention to the world's least advantaged places, even if the disease has a notorious ability to adapt to different treatments. An additional area of current research is on the degree of protection against the *Plasmodium falciparum* malaria parasite possessed by people with sickle cell trait, an inherited condition in which the red blood cells are crescent-shaped rather than round that is especially common among people with African ancestry, including millions in the Malaria Belt. The degree to which people who suffer repeated attacks of malaria develop partial – if not complete – immunity is also a crucial subject of contemporary scholarship. Increasing our understanding of malaria could prove key to improving (and saving) the lives of the hundreds of millions who live in at-risk areas.

After all, malaria's impacts are not only health-related. In addition to the costs necessitated by treatments and preventive measures, sufferers may miss numerous days of work and education. Families can be forced to pay significant fees for their loved ones' burials. Industries such as tourism are undermined when investors and travellers are unwilling to visit. Malaria can also exacerbate socioeconomic inequalities at the local scale, for those with means are able to live in areas that are less vulnerable: it is no coincidence that British colonists in India during the nineteenth century established hill stations in upland areas, where the climate was cooler and mosquitoes posed much less of a problem than to the poor local communities below.* Nevertheless, for those with less of a choice, the disease is not just physically harmful,

---

*Further, in their secluded environs, they originated what would become one of the world's most popular cocktails, adding their gin rations to the bitter tonic water they drank for its quinine's antimalarial qualities.

but tends to imply lower life chances and earnings than are possible beyond its boundaries. Imposing direct costs in excess of $12 billion on sub-Saharan Africa each year, malaria remains one of the most important inhibitors of development in some of the world's poorest societies.

And yet the modern fight against malaria was catalysed not by the disease itself, but by another source of death and suffering, to which the disease contributed. During the Second World War, American troops in the South Pacific found that their Japanese counterparts were not the only threat within this tropical theatre. Amid the bombs, the silent force of malaria slowly but surely debilitated the American forces, impelling the formation of the Office of Malaria Control in War Areas in 1942 to mitigate this and other vector-borne diseases. Established in Atlanta, near the country's largest body of malaria cases in the south-eastern United States, after the war the Office was succeeded by the United States Centers for Disease Control and Prevention (CDC). This federal agency has become key to tackling malaria and other diseases across the world ever since, including sexually transmitted infections, influenza, Ebola, Zika and, most recently, COVID-19. However, it is easily forgotten that its original purpose was to control and eradicate malaria in the United States, an objective that was achieved in 1951 (notwithstanding individual cases of migrants and travellers bringing the disease with them from abroad) through insecticides, wetland draining, the increased use of glass windows and window screens and improved treatments and monitoring.*

---

* Among older methods to control malaria, perhaps none was as creative as that patented by Dr Charles Campbell of San Antonio in Texas, a bacteriologist who in the first three decades of the twentieth century pioneered the development of bat roosts, recognising that bats happily chow down on mosquitoes and, with the right choice of sounds, can be coaxed to live in places where they are most needed. Although Campbell's

Efforts to tackle the disease have evolved considerably, especially as the traditional method of spraying dichlorodiphenyl-trichloroethane (DDT) has become both less effective due to some mosquito species' ability to develop resistance to it, and more controversial because of the damage it causes to people and the environment. Indeed, in most countries DDT is now regarded as a last resort, being relatively inexpensive but generally unpopular among the public, mainly owing to its adverse health impacts, as well as its tendency to discolour the walls of people's homes and even excite other pests including bedbugs. Instead, emphasis tends to be placed on malaria-control measures such as indoor residual spraying (IRS), whereby alternative residual insecticides are sprayed onto the interior walls of houses,* insecticide-treated nets (ITNs), which protect people as they sleep, and courses of antimalarial drugs, particularly targeted towards at-risk populations such as pregnant women and infants.

Still, preventing the spread of malaria continues to constitute a major challenge, especially in sub-Saharan Africa. For instance, whereas in parts of Europe and North America mosquito larvae have been comprehensively killed or controlled, through applying larvicides, or draining or filling water bodies like swamps and marshes where mosquitoes typically breed, in much of sub-Saharan Africa such areas can emerge quite suddenly due to heavy rainfall and it can be difficult to apply larvicides extensively. Given the slow onset of the disease (it has an incubation period

---

precise technique proved quite challenging to replicate, locally, malaria cases diminished, earning him a nomination from the State of Texas for the Nobel Prize in Physiology or Medicine in 1919. Nor were bats' important efforts overlooked: the City of San Antonio (in 1914) and the State of Texas (in 1917) both passed laws prohibiting the willful killing of these animals. Locally beloved, the urban bat populations of San Antonio and Austin are today a tourist draw, the latter city even hosting a 'Bat Fest' each summer.
*Note, though, that these are not suitable for all surfaces and, like with DDT, some species of mosquitoes can become resistant to them.

of anywhere from a week to well over a month depending on the parasite involved) and its many potential symptoms, misdiagnosis is common,* including in non-endemic countries, where the disease may be relatively unfamiliar. It should also be noted that malaria can be passed onto others through contaminated needles or syringes, congenitally from mother to child, or via blood transfusions and organ transplants. On some small tropical islands, like Anjouan and Mohéli in the Comoros, the mass administration of antimalarial drugs, ITNs and IRS programmes has generated optimism that the disease will soon be eliminated, but in continental areas and places where malaria transmission is high, the disease is understandably much harder even to control. To date, only one sub-Saharan African country where malaria was once a problem has been certified malaria-free by the World Health Organization – Mauritius in 1973 – a sobering reminder of how much has yet to be achieved.†

In response, solidarity and billions of dollars in funds are necessary.‡ Malaria has proved capable of bringing together public figures as diverse as Bill Gates, Bono, David Beckham and Helen Mirren, various United Nations agencies, the World Bank, the World Health Organization, a range of non-governmental organisations and more. In 2019, malaria experts set a target of 2050 for its eradication (that is, elimination *globally*), and given noteworthy reductions in malaria mortality over the

---

*Some diseases that are frequently misdiagnosed as malaria include pneumonia, typhoid fever, dengue fever and yellow fever, the latter two of which are, like malaria, spread by mosquitoes, albeit by different species.
†The French overseas department and region Réunion is the only other part of sub-Saharan Africa to reach this milestone, while Seychelles (an archipelago) and Lesotho (high-altitude) are considered countries where malaria has never been a problem.
‡In 2018, the World Health Organization set a global target of $6.6 billion per year by 2020 in malaria investments, but ultimately, 'just' $3 billion was spent that year. The target for 2030 is $10.3 billion.

past decade, this seems if not probable then at least possible. One of the main obstacles is likely to be climate change, as there is considerable uncertainty as to how malaria transmission will be affected. Whereas some areas of sub-Saharan Africa are expected to become drier and thereby less prone to malaria (although their risks of other issues such as desertification, drought, water shortages and starvation will likely increase in one of the world's worst trade-offs), others are liable to experience conditions conducive to the spread of this disease, such as higher average temperatures and a longer summer season. Deforestation, a major issue in several sub-Saharan African countries, can exacerbate the risk of malaria by increasing exposure to sunlight (thereby raising temperatures) and reducing the prevalence of insectivores (which could otherwise limit mosquito numbers). High-altitude areas that have henceforth been too cold to sustain mosquitoes, especially in East Africa, are among the places that are now at greater risk of this disease. Countries further from the Equator, such as in the Mediterranean region, could also be unwillingly embraced by the Malaria Belt, the disease potentially posing additional complications due to many people's lack of familiarity with it. Crucial too is the public's commitment to preventive measures; as additionally seen in the case of the COVID-19 pandemic, the efficacy of vaccines and procedures is at least partly contingent on people's willingness to trust them. As an industrial machinery distributor in Guinea apprised me:

> Malaria's still a big issue but it's much better now than it was before, I would say. Prevention has always been emphasised by the government as the best way to fight malaria . . . and a little knowledge and the right information has a huge impact, certainly on the prevention side it's had an impact . . . but I don't know if eradication's possible, because not everyone's going to take the vaccine, and not everyone is going to use the nets, even though they do not cost much.

For all these reasons, the boundaries of the Malaria Belt may expand outwards before any improvements in prevention, treatment and monitoring cause them to retreat. To date, only one disease to afflict humans – smallpox – has ever been eradicated, providing a hint of the challenges that we face over the next few decades.

The Malaria Belt demonstrates how fluid boundaries can be, fluctuating invisibly across time and space, and gradually bringing different groups of people within their sphere of influence. Yet the same boundaries can also prove resilient in their very existence, our understanding of them and what they envelop often being insufficient to their elimination, at least until sufficient (read: considerable) effort is made. The fact that residents of the Malaria Belt face challenges that extend far beyond the disease's main symptoms, from limited income sources to additional health expenses, additionally reflects how one geographically situated issue can spawn myriad others. This necessitates attention to the butterfly effect at hand: a small spatial advance in malaria transmission can pose a significant, further socioeconomic threat to formerly thriving areas that, due to the consequent risk of being stigmatised by the disease, is difficult to overcome.

Even so, it is important to recognise the value of drawing invisible lines here: by distinguishing areas that are particularly vulnerable to the disease, it becomes easier to prepare for and respond to outbreaks. Knowledge and understanding, as we have also seen in the case of Tornado Alley in particular, truly can be the difference between life and death. And with them comes the potential to enact change, to improve the world around us, perhaps.

How Invisible Lines Help Us Exert
Our Influence on the Planet

Humans have never merely sought to learn. The previous six chapters demonstrated how we can draw or imagine invisible lines to better understand the planet; but we also seek to gain some degree of control over the world around us, especially in the face of the considerable challenges we encounter. Invisible lines can be used in diverse ways for this purpose, as the following six chapters will show us.

It may be tempting to think exclusively or primarily of lines aimed at controlling the planet in an insidious sense, such as banishing those deemed not to belong. Exclusion is indeed a common aim or outcome of invisible lines, and one we shall see arise frequently. However, this part attends to lines that, although not always beneficial in their effects, have at least been intended to provide control for benevolent reasons. Typically, the main goal of such boundaries is to make somewhere more liveable, through responding to an inadequacy in current circumstances and, most notably, managing a real or potential hazard. The COVID-19 pandemic provides an excellent example. Within weeks of the first cases of this disease being diagnosed, a boundary separating Wuhan – the pandemic's 'Ground Zero' – from the rest of China was established. We all know what happened next. Over the following months, the majority of the world's countries imposed their own travel restrictions, stay-at-home requirements and other policy responses, with the effect of drawing invisible lines designed to contain the virus. Suddenly, our encounters with the world around us changed: commuters were compelled to work from home-office cocoons; students were divided not by rows of desks and chairs, but by computer screens; residents of care homes were hidden behind closed doors from their loved ones; essential workers were forced to become all too familiar with areas of particularly high risk. In many countries, brand-new boundaries emerged between those regions, counties or municipalities where internal travel was considered safe, and those where it was not. On a more micro scale, 'social distancing' practices created invisible boundaries separating ourselves from others, and even with the easing of lockdown restrictions, many continue to perceive such lines when choosing where to sit on public transport or in a restaurant or bar. Although coronavirus policies requiring the enforcement of boundaries have not always proved popular, they are indisputably an example of how we can use invisible lines to impose control in the face of disaster.

Thinking of travel restrictions specifically, such invisible lines can be perceived in reference to hazards other than disease, too. Government bodies create travel advisory maps that take into account dangers such as violent crime, inconsistent law enforcement, civil unrest, terrorism and armed conflict, in the process moderating their nationals' movement and directing their presence across the planet. The notion of invisible lines separating 'safe' and 'unsafe' areas can similarly be discerned in the case of no-fly zones, established to restrict or prohibit aircraft from operating over specific territories, which are not necessarily defined according to international borders. Often associated with territories in the midst of violent conflict, no-fly zones can alternatively be created in response to disasters such as the nuclear accident at Japan's Fukushima Daiichi Nuclear Power Plant in March 2011, which also saw the drawing of a 20-kilometre evacuation zone and a 30-kilometre exclusion zone for those on the ground.

We will first see how Kazakhstan's Kokaral Dam was constructed to tackle the catastrophic shrinking of the Aral Sea, with the effect of creating an invisible boundary between improved water quality and fish stocks to the north, and enduring despair to the south. Next, the Qinling–Huaihe Line represents an intriguing example of an invisible line that, having been drawn merely to describe China's north–south divide, was eventually used to determine the construction of subsidised district heating systems, with contrasting effects on winter warmth but also smog. In the United Kingdom, as people became cognisant of the need to reduce air pollution and other problems typically associated with cities, green belts were established as invisible boundaries to rampant urban sprawl. Elsewhere, human activity may be constrained to an even greater extent by the drawing of invisible lines: the Chernobyl Exclusion Zone in Ukraine, for example, was created as a necessary response to the world's worst nuclear disaster. A different kind of invisible line drawn to protect people from a hazard is a cordon sanitaire, one of the most historically noteworthy examples being the English village of Eyam's self-isolation from its neighbours following a bubonic plague outbreak in 1666. Wrapping up this part is the International Date Line, which since its establishment in 1884 has helped facilitate the standardisation of time across the planet.

The Kokaral Dam

We cannot expect charity from Nature.
We must tear it from her.

Joseph Stalin

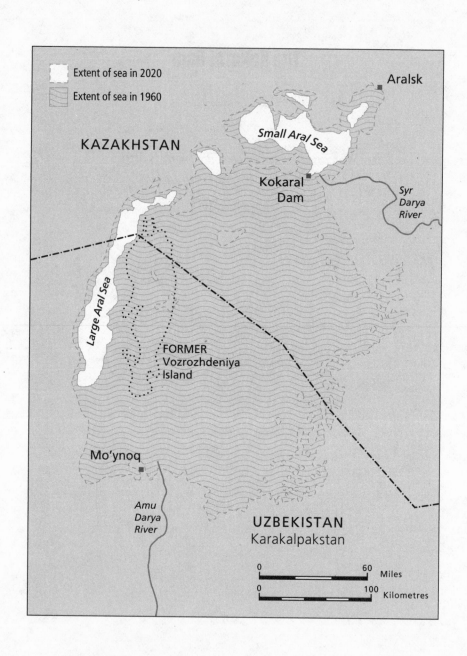

The intransigent Soviet dictator would doubtless never admit it even if he were still somehow alive today, but with the benefit of hindsight, we can safely say that Nature has always deserved a little more respect. Over seven decades after Stalin launched the Soviet Union's Great Plan for the Transformation of Nature, a grandiose project to increase the country's agricultural productivity, specific portions of the old country continue to wrestle with the legacy of his acolytes' over-zealous pursuit of material gain. Despite the manifold technological innovations developed throughout the millennia to improve human livelihoods, we are today unprecedentedly conscious of the compromises we must make with our planet, to prevent us from destroying that which feeds and accommodates us. However hard we may try, the natural world is not easily controllable, and nor is doing so always advisable. Can we reverse – or at least mitigate – the mistakes of the past? Can we find a middle ground between domination and subordination? Can we make amends with Nature?

The Kokaral Dam in Kazakhstan, the biggest post-Soviet state outside Russia and today the ninth largest country in the world, provides insights into the management of an environmental crisis, having been constructed in 2005 in response to the rapid shrinking of the Aral Sea since the 1960s. And crucially for our purposes, it encapsulates how invisible lines, drawn to take some degree of control over the planet, can prove to be a matter of life and death, hope and despair. How did this situation materialise?

Let's quickly rewind to the late 1940s. A combination of infrastructural damage during the Second World War, a severe drought in 1946 and imprudent economic policies had brought about a major famine in the USSR. In order to respond to this grievous situation, save face and defy its rivals in the West, the Soviet government initiated a range of projects aimed at remodelling the natural environment and significantly increasing crop yields. At this time, the moderately salty Aral Sea was the fourth largest lake in the world, naturally supplied by the Amu Darya and Syr Darya rivers. However, as part of their Great Plan for the Transformation of Nature, the Soviet authorities opted to divert water from these rivers to irrigate Central Asia's steppes and deserts instead.

For a while, this looked like an astute decision. Crops such as cotton, cereals, rice and melons all grew abundantly. The republic of Uzbekistan, situated to the south of the lake, became the USSR's foremost producer of fruits and vegetables and, eventually, the world's biggest exporter of cotton. But like with most aspects of Soviet life, the good times did not last long. Starved of river water and robbed by evaporation under the beating sun, the Aral Sea progressively shrank. Once-prosperous fishing settlements such as Aralsk were cleaved from their primary industries, with fishers needing to commute a hundred kilometres just to reach their previously local water body. Not that access was the only problem: the remaining water became more and more saline, especially given that salt water is denser than fresh water and thus less exposed to evaporation in the upper layers, killing the majority of the lake's fauna. By the time the USSR disintegrated into various independent states at the start of the 1990s, the Aral Sea had undergone a split of its own, into a northern Small Aral and a southern Large Aral Sea. Around a decade later, the Large Aral, whose name was quickly becoming highly ironic, was divided further into western and eastern parts; after another decade, the latter was mere desert. Having shrunk by 90 per cent since 1960, the lake's complete disappearance seemed certain.

This was not for a lack of trying. In 1992, the newly independent Kazakhstan to the north built a sand dyke and a canal
at the eastern end of the Kokaral peninsula, aimed at reducing
the flow from the Small Aral Sea to its larger, southern counterpart, which is largely bounded by Uzbekistan. (Reflecting how
quickly this region has changed, until the 1960s the peninsula
had been separate from the mainland as an island.) The dyke was
more successful in theory than in reality. Too flimsy to handle the
movement of the water, it repeatedly broke during the 1990s in a
paradoxical predicament: the more water the dyke controlled, the
greater the possibility of it being breached. And every time the
dyke washed away, the water level declined again. This frustrating cycle of construction and destruction was brought to an end
in the new millennium, when the World Bank stepped in with a
$64.5 million loan to support Kazakhstan in building a far more
stable dam alongside some other infrastructural adaptations,
at a total cost of $85.8 million. Water would no longer be able
to simply flow from the Small to the Large Aral. Since then, the
fresh water of the Syr Darya River has helped replenish the former
and reduce its salinity, with any excess (especially in the spring)
flowing through a sluice to the latter.

As a result, the dam has undoubtedly helped the communities
to the north, around the now stabilised Small Aral Sea. Various
invertebrate and fish species have reappeared or increased in abundance as the levels of salt in the lake have decreased considerably.
The most valuable fish is pike-perch, often exported to Europe and
known locally as 'gold fish' for the profits these sales can bring.
Carp, bream, asp and roach are also among the fish to return from
the Syr Darya and nearby water bodies, and especially near to
the dam there is considerable species diversity today. As the basin
continues to fill, albeit with some seasonal fluctuations, the old
fishing city of Aralsk in Kazakhstan has come to be located just
12 kilometres from the Small Aral, a suboptimal distance for a
fisher, yes, but a great improvement on just a couple of decades

ago. With commercial harvests improving rapidly, the profession is once again viable and for some quite lucrative. Nor are fishers the only ones to benefit: with increased yields, jobs are once again available in processing, transporting and selling fish as well.

The communities to the south in Uzbekistan would love to have the same fortune. The Large Aral has become just a narrow sliver, distant from traditional fishing communities. The once-thriving city of Mo'ynoq, for instance, is today increasingly reliant on disaster tourism instead. 'Sleeping with the fishes' has an entirely different meaning here: the port's old harbour is now advertised as a 'ship graveyard', located over one-hundred kilometres from the contemporary lake. The Large Aral simply does not receive enough water from the Small Aral and the drying, shrinking Amu Darya to overcome losses via evaporation. And even if the community still had the lake on its doorstep, it would struggle to benefit from it. The Large Aral Sea has continued to increase in salinity, with salt levels in some places far exceeding 100 grams per litre, compared to about 10 grams per litre in 1960 (by way of comparison, the world's oceans average out at about 35 grams per litre). Only the most salt-tolerant species – primarily a few species of roundworm, zooplankton and brine shrimp – can survive here. Even flounder, a highly salt-tolerant fish that was introduced in the 1970s, had become extinct in the Large Aral by the end of the 1990s, whereas it narrowly survived to the north and is now commercially caught. The natural gas reserves beneath the parched southern lake bed provide a glimmer of hope, and separately the community has shown great creativity by hosting the popular Stihia electronic music festival among its rusting trawlers, but sadly there are precious few other reasons to rave.

Certainly, the region to the immediate south of the lake – the autonomous Republic of Karakalpakstan within north-west Uzbekistan – has become exceptionally vulnerable to a number of serious issues beyond the loss of the fishery and the livelihoods that depended on it.* The pesticides used by the Soviet Union to increase cotton yields contaminated the lake with toxins such as DDT, while heavy metals have also accumulated here over time from industrial pollution. With the demise of the lake, these pollutants have become increasingly concentrated in the water that remains, with much of the rest creating toxic dust that is spread by the wind as suffocating storms. Many local communities are now susceptible to ingesting these toxins simply by drinking water and breathing the air, as well as by consuming local produce. The former Vozrozhdeniya Island – which, had it not disappeared into the desert, would sit on the border with Kazakhstan – is another cause for concern. For years it was a secret Soviet bioweapons laboratory used for the testing of anthrax, bubonic plague, smallpox and other agents, some of which have leaked into the soil and infected species that could spread them elsewhere. Various cancers, anaemia, respiratory illnesses such as tuberculosis, and eye and kidney problems are disproportionately common in this region. Although Karakalpakstan's infant mortality rate is now a fairly middling 10.6 deaths per 1,000 live births, in the mid-1990s various sources indicated figures in the fifties and, in some districts, above 100, among the highest rates in the world. Fortunately, significant improvements in maternal and neonatal health care, supported both by national and international organisations, have helped the maternal mortality rate drop to a level fairly typical for Central Asia, although concerns remain as to the large numbers of children born with abnormalities or at

---

*Unprecedentedly large protests against incumbent Uzbek President Shavkat Mirziyoyev's decision to downgrade Karakalpakstan's autonomous status, which saw numerous deaths, injuries and arrests and prompted the government to declare a state of emergency, saw the region gain belated international attention in July 2022. Mirziyoyev quickly dropped all his proposed changes to Karakalpakstan's status, which were intended as part of a larger constitutional reform designed to extend his term in office from five to seven years.

low birthweight.* Furthermore, the climate has become increasingly extreme, with enormous temperature fluctuations between summer and winter as well as less rainfall, typical of a more continental climate. Farmers find it harder to grow crops, especially with the wind periodically depositing salt as well as toxins from the former lake. There is little respite for a region that just half a century ago was full of optimism for the future.

This is not to say that the Uzbek government has failed to react, although to date it has been reluctant to adopt the same kinds of large-scale infrastructure projects seen in Kazakhstan, lest water be diverted from farmers elsewhere in the country. So far, most of the focus here has been on improving water management and quality, through the restoration of wetlands and the planting of salt-tolerant species on the former lake bed. In the coming years, Uzbekistan's appetite for major ventures may also be undermined by the horrific burst of the three-year-old Sardoba Dam in the country's eastern Sirdaryo region in May 2020, which resulted in six fatalities and severe flooding on both sides of the border. If any good can come from such a disaster, it is that the two countries' governments subsequently signed a joint roadmap for transboundary water management, providing some promise of improved international relations in the future.

Returning to the case of the Kokaral Dam, it is important to emphasise that this project did not create the problems to the south. At the same time, it is more than just a symbolic division between a convalescent north and a critical south: by controlling the flow of water from the Small to the Large Aral, it has effectively struck the final blow to the latter, while enabling the former's survival. It marks not only the boundary between two lakes, but also two very different futures. Although it is by no means regarded as

---

*Karakalpakstan's maternal mortality rate was 26.4 deaths per 100,000 live births in 2021. In 1995, it was as high as 120, far exceeding the average of the time for the Central Asia and Caucasus region, 68.

perfect to the north – there are plans to continue developing it to handle greater volumes of water, but progress has stalled in recent years – the dam has offered a lifeline. Fisheries are rebounding, people's health is improving and hope if not quite optimism is returning. The greatest risk today may be *over*fishing. By contrast, in the south, anguish as well as resentment – towards Kazakhstan's government for building a dam, towards Uzbekistan's for proving less proactive – are more common emotions. Greater cross-border collaboration seems necessary to ensure that the dam does not become a source of significant international tension, especially with climate change's erratic impact on water availability. There is no official divide between the northern and southern sides of the dam and their hinterlands, but it is indisputable that the two are separated invisibly in their prospects for the future.

In fact, large dams are often prone to entrenching environmental and socioeconomic inequalities and divisions. The colossal Three Gorges Dam in China is perhaps the most famous example: its construction displaced 1.3 million people in large part to provide electricity, especially for the major cities to the east. And more generally, thanks to government policy, China has seen a significant invisible boundary emerge between regions, which continues to shape lives and livelihoods to this day.

The Qinling–Huaihe Line

We will declare war on pollution and fight it with the same determination we battled poverty . . . Smog is affecting larger parts of China and environmental pollution has become a major problem, which is nature's red-light warning against the model of inefficient and blind development.

Li Keqiang, premier of the People's Republic of China

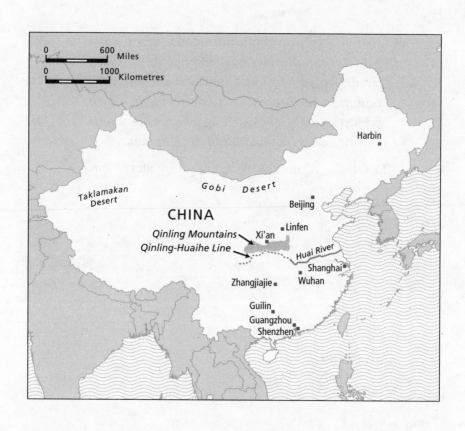

There is a noticeable chill in the air today, and a thin layer of frost dusts the fields. Thick blankets adorned with red roses are brought from their summer hiding places. Hopefully they will brighten up the gloom; the joyful festivities of Ghost Day, with its lotus-shaped lanterns and sweet incense, feel distant now. The summer may be muggy, but it's surely no worse than the long, bleak winter to come. It's that time of year again. Better wrap up warm.

Just a few kilometres to the north, the winter will be no less frigid, but the mood is different. Warmth pumps through the houses like a toasty hug. As the temperature drops over the next few weeks, there will be little fear of frozen pipes and icy skin. Still, nothing's perfect. While those to the south will be digging for layers, the residents here will be rummaging around for their facemasks. The problem is not disease – well, not the *primary* problem. The real issue is the smog that will soon envelop the town.

The Great Wall may be the most famous boundary in the world, snaking for well over 20,000 kilometres across northern China and parts of Mongolia in order to repel invaders. A more obscure (and invisible) boundary is the Heihe–Tengchong Line, which was drawn by a Chinese geographer named Hu Huanyong in 1935 to divide China diagonally from north-east to south-west into two portions with widely contrasting population densities. Even though appreciable population movements especially towards the south-east have altered Huanyong's figures in the interim, the line still represents an illuminating partition, with around 95 per cent of the country's population concentrated in a smaller area than their compatriots to the north-west. However, a different line plays a role which, although seemingly mundane, is even more significant in the lives of many of China's 1.4 billion inhabitants today. Running along the Qinling Mountains in the west before following the course of the Huai River,* in the 1950s it was used by the new communist leadership to distinguish between places that would receive a district heating system (to the north) and those that would not (to the south). With a small number of exceptions, generally where the cash- and energy-strapped government was reluctant to fork out for some of the communities on the northern bank of the Huai, this invisible line thus defines whether a person will be reliant on their own means for warmth, or whether they can depend on the government for this relative luxury.

The Qinling–Huaihe Line has a longer history than the Chinese Communist Party (CCP), having been drawn in 1908 by the future founder of the Geographical Society of China (GSC), Zhang Xiangwen, to demarcate the country's north–south divide, approximately along the northern 33rd parallel. In China, this partition takes several forms. For centuries, the north was more developed and is home to the majority of China's most famous historical sites, including the ancient capital Xi'an and its Terracotta Army, the Forbidden City of Beijing and, of course, the Great Wall. By contrast, the south has long been renowned for its natural landscapes (such as the shark's teeth-like hills of Guilin or the towering rock formations of Zhangjiajie, both of which inspired the film *Avatar*), although since the country's economic reforms of the 1970s it has become a key centre of high-tech and light industries and now includes three of the country's four

---

* *Hé*, as in Huaihe, is 'river' in Mandarin.

'Tier 1' cities: Shanghai, Guangzhou and Shenzhen (Beijing is the other). The climate also differs from north to south: the former is generally cooler and drier, whereas the latter is mostly character-ised by a hot, humid subtropical or tropical climate, depending in large part on one's proximity to the South China Sea. The Qinling–Huaihe Line relatedly marks quite accurately both the January 0°C isotherm (that is, the line distinguishing places whose average January temperature is below zero, and which are hence prone to freezing, from places whose average January tempera-ture exceeds this figure) and the 800 millimetre isohyet (the line dividing places where annual precipitation is below this amount, from those where annual precipitation is greater). Given crops' reliance on specific climate conditions, there are implications for cuisine, too, with wheat-based items such as noodles, steamed buns and dumplings common in the north whereas rice dishes have a longer history in the south. There are many countries with a north–south divide, but few if any pertain to as many subjects.

However, the CCP under the premiership of Zhou Enlai (1949–76) saw the potential for the line to be used to *determine* rather than merely *describe* difference. Whereas heating the north was deemed a necessity and a mere extension of the long-time culture of using a *kang* (a heated brick bed that doubles as a stove) in the coldest regions, the south was regarded as sufficiently warm to cope without a centralised system. In many places this is not unreasonable: the southern cities of Guangzhou and Shen-zhen, for example, have average minimum winter temperatures of around 10°C, quite comfortably above freezing. By contrast, each winter Harbin in the far north-east is cold enough to host an international festival of towering ice castles and mythological snow sculptures. The issue is that many communities near the line face a practically identical climate, but because of the simplicity of using such a boundary as a cut-off point, they are given vastly different resources to cope with it. When the temperature drops, complaints of inequality loom, as one south-sider told me: 'North of the line there is a centralised heating system but to the south of the line there isn't, yet it can be very cold in the south as well.'

This divide remains to the present day. Intriguingly, it is also less and less likely to be bridged owing to important changes in China's economy since the 1970s, as much of the onus has shifted from the state to the individual. Thus, whereas the enormous heating systems of the north were developed when the Chinese government prioritised major social projects with the support of the Soviet Union (and district heating is still the norm in Russia), today market-oriented solutions are sought, requiring households to pay for the heat they desire. Residents often remain compelled to find their own solutions on the coldest nights, including heat pumps, electric heaters and hot water bottles; many even visit bathhouses once or twice a week when it is too frigid to wash at home. Even in Shanghai, China's economic powerhouse, many of the poorest members of society are forced to encase themselves in coats and quilts as protection against the cold, for the simple reason that they live narrowly south of the Qinling–Huaihe Line and cannot afford a higher electricity bill.

However, it is not as if the residents to the north of the Qinling–Huaihe Line are without grievances. Although they enjoy the benefits of free or heavily subsidised heat, the most common source over the past half-century – the coal-fired boiler – produces considerable amounts of air pollution. The figures make for grim reading: almost all the most polluted cities in China are north of the line, with some having among the foulest air in the world. Accordingly, one person accustomed to travelling across the line emphasised how 'in the winter sometimes, if you fly from a northern city to a southern city, the improvement in air quality is easy to notice'. Admittedly, there are various reasons for the poor air quality in the north – many cities here are surrounded by mountains that prevent the wind from dispersing pollutants, while Chinese farmers often burn the straw in winter following the harvest, even though this has technically been illegal since the

1990s – but coal-powered heating is regarded as the biggest cause. As a result, during winter, smog is a severe issue, obscuring the view of all but the brightest neon signs in major northern cities. Occasional sandstorms from the Gobi and Taklamakan deserts provide a different glow, turning the sombre grey sky an eerie orange, but drastically aggravate the air quality in the process. Most seriously, the dangerous particulate matter both fine (PM2.5) and coarse (PM10) emitted in the north has increased residents' risks of cardiovascular and respiratory illnesses and has greatly contributed to an average life expectancy that is well over five years shorter than south of the line. One divide leads to another.

Faced with extreme cold and potentially toxic air, it is certainly preferable for many in the north to simply stay indoors, the boundary most important to them being the door separating their home from the outside. At the same time, their counterparts in the south look on with envy at the heating they enjoy by virtue of living on the right side of the Qinling Mountains and the Huaihe. Gradually, improvements are being made. Many northern cities, including Beijing, have transitioned to natural gas or electricity instead of coal, and new targets have been set to reduce particulate matter emissions. In cities such as Linfen, some residents have even been forced to go cold turkey as their traditional coal-burning stoves have been confiscated by local officials. Meanwhile, some southern cities like Wuhan have been trying to develop their own unified heating systems, although both economic and environmental concerns have often limited their expansion. Increasingly, renewable energy sources such as wind, solar and biomass are becoming commonplace in the south instead, in part to stymie frequent calls for the same types of district heating that have acted as a double-edged sword in the north.

Previous proposals to push the line further south have consistently been rebuffed on account of expense, but with recent interest in new energy sources, it may be that this boundary fades in relevance over the coming years. For the meantime, however, there is a distinct disjuncture in heating capacity between north and south, owing to a divide as simple as a line drawn from west to east. The case demonstrates how a boundary marked quite logically, using empirical data pertaining to the environment, can provide a convenient political mechanism by which to institute social difference as well. It also shows how even where we expect to benefit from the creation or employment of invisible lines which are intended to transform our engagement with the planet, there can be certain unanticipated consequences, impairing rather than improving the life chances of those on one side or the other. Still, in certain cases, invisible lines are envisaged as compelling means of *limiting* some of our detrimental impacts, including air pollution, on our surroundings. It's time to think green.

Green Belts

*Human society and the beauty of nature
are meant to be enjoyed together.*

Ebenezer Howard

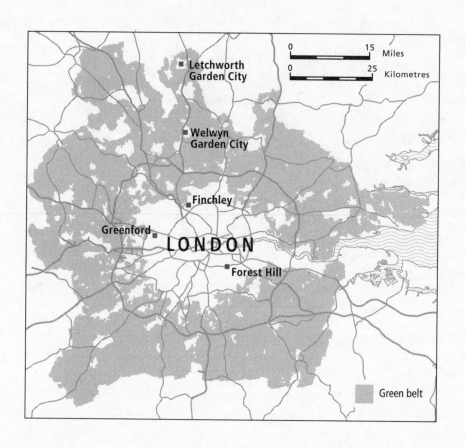

Miles: 0 — 15

Kilometres: 0 — 25

Letchworth Garden City

Welwyn Garden City

Finchley

Greenford

LONDON

Forest Hill

Green belt

When driving out from the centre of the United Kingdom's capital, London's suburbs can feel endless. Although this is in part a product of the traffic that continues to afflict much of the city, despite the successes of the city's congestion charge zone since 2003, even perceptibly there is a gradual rather than rapid transition from the grand Georgian, Victorian and Edwardian edifices and lavish parks that surround the city's core, to the interwar and modernist constructions that line the key thoroughfares a few kilometres out, and ultimately the sizeable semi-detached homes that adjoin seemingly every street in the outer suburbs. These neighbourhoods possess mere remnants of their former status as unique villages in their own right, having been swallowed up by the swelling metropolis during the nineteenth and early twentieth centuries. Names such as Finchley, Greenford and Forest Hill attest to a more rural history, while the historical county of Middlesex, most of which was officially incorporated into Greater London in 1965, remains only somewhat symbolically. Today, approximately 13.5 per cent of people in the UK live in a London borough, a percentage that can double depending on how widely one defines the commuter belt, encapsulating the city's gravitational pull. Yet what is remarkable is that compared to many of the city's counterparts in North America and East Asia, London's suburbs aren't really that extensive at all.

While this may be a source of disappointment to those who feel that biggest means best (or at least most important or noteworthy), it is worth reminding that *not everybody loves major cities*. Such a statement held particular resonance during the nineteenth century, when London's population grew from what now appears a modest 1 million in 1800 to approximately 6.5 million by 1900, and it held the rank of world's largest city for about a hundred years until it was finally overtaken by New York in 1925. It is easy for us now, seeing the pomp and circumstance, the painstakingly cool, the viridescent – really whatever we *want* to see – to overlook how intimidating London would have been to the new urbanites of two centuries ago, most having arrived from small villages, unprepared for the slums and factories that awaited them.

Certainly, for most, life in London and Britain's many other rapidly expanding Industrial Revolution-era cities would have been grim at best. It is no coincidence that Friedrich Engels developed with Karl Marx what we now call Marxism based on his experiences and observations of the impoverished slums of Manchester and Salford in north-west England. By the end of the nineteenth century, improvements in housing codes, food supply, wages, clothing, sewerage, medicine, washing facilities and more alleviated the disease and squalor with which London had become associated.* However, the city was still far from becoming somewhere one might consider desirable. The country's movers and shakers might choose to seek profits by working in the city, but few were so keen to actually live there. And so the suburbs expanded, enabled in large part by advances in public transportation and strategic pricing to prevent the masses from being able to afford those areas most coveted by the wealthy.

In the process, however, conflict over space started to emerge

---

*In 1858, for instance, the British Parliament was on the brink of moving out of the city due to the putrid stench of human waste and industrial effluent emanating from the River Thames. Conditions in the city's impoverished East End would have been even worse.

in new areas. As the middle classes relinquished much of the city to their less mobile working-class counterparts, they began to tread on the toes of those already living in the ex-urban outskirts. If we accept that not everybody loves major cities, then it is unsurprising that many of those living in the small towns and villages surrounding London (and elsewhere) feared the metropolis advancing menacingly towards them. Even the most carefully planned suburb brought unprecedented noise, traffic and pollution to places that had remained practically unchanged for centuries. Long-time residents feared that the 'character' of their unique settlements would disappear, that their health would become compromised, that they would be absorbed into the social, cultural and architectural homogeneity of which suburbs are still, albeit often unfairly, accused. How long would it take for London and other cities to expand across Britain's beloved countryside (which had incidentally become central to a sense of national identity given its supposed purity)?

Today, the green belt constitutes the invisible barrier to sprawl that many of these residents craved, ensuring a ring of green space around urban areas. It was a long time in the works. The concept is generally traced back to the urban planner Ebenezer Howard, who is best known for founding the garden city movement around the turn of the twentieth century, although older iterations existed in some ancient cities of the Middle East, and in an English context, in 1580 Queen Elizabeth I banned new constructions in a 5-kilometre ring around London in an effort to prevent the spread of plague. Howard's garden city idea championed the development of settlements that would combine the best of both the city (residences, cultural activities, job opportunities) and the countryside (fresh air, nature, agriculture, low rents). In this way, he sought to respond to the severe pitfalls of existing industrial cities, with their pervasive poverty, overcrowding, pollution and gloom. To prevent them from endlessly growing, Howard argued that his garden cities should be surrounded by a permanent 'belt' of farms and parks, and limited to just 32,000 people: beyond this point, a new settlement should be developed instead. Howard's idea thus also foresaw the risk of one city becoming far bigger than all others – as is in fact the case of London within the UK today – and attempted to mitigate this risk by providing a more appealing vision of what a city 'should' be.

The garden city concept never gained nearly as much traction as Howard, who envisioned it becoming the default for British urban planning, would have liked. In his lifetime, two garden cities (Letchworth and Welwyn) were established in Hertfordshire, the county to the north of present-day Greater London, although several other settlements across the world today bear at least traces of Howard's general proposal. By contrast, his more specific idea for green belts among settlements did eventually come to widespread fruition, being established not just around garden cities, but most of the country's major urban areas.

Indeed, from the 1920s, the green belt concept was advanced in policy circles and ultimately enacted as a means of guaranteeing open spaces and limiting sprawl, first around London in the 1930s, and from the 1950s around the key settlements of the West Midlands, South and West Yorkshire, and Cheshire and Lancashire, among others. Over time, many of these green belts have been widened to further resist pressure to build and ensure the protection of greater swathes of countryside.

On the ground, green belts may not be obvious, as they are rarely marked other than in occasional signs protesting against the possibility of opening up some green belt land for future development. However, when one considers why urban sprawl here eventually ends, the invisible line separating major urban areas from their rural surroundings becomes palpable. And even if the boundary does go unnoticed, the advantages provided by green belts can still be felt by urban residents. Many venture out to partake in various leisure activities impossible in major population centres, of benefit to their health and well-being. Green belts also ensure living space for wildlife, even if they have been criticised by some for limiting biodiversity through encouraging intensive agricultural practices and golf courses rather than being used as preserves. And to be clear, they are not without their drawbacks: development may simply occur beyond the green belt, compelling greater car use, while most significantly, they have been denounced for limiting the amount of space available for building and thus facilitating sharp increases in house prices, with London now one of the most expensive cities in the world to buy property. However, when one considers what it looks like to allow urban growth to proceed with few if any limits, green belts appear quite favourable in their provision of open space to urban residents. The Los Angeles conurbation (a word that encapsulates what happens when one settlement is allowed to merge with another) is a particularly famous example, covering over 1,200 square kilometres, but the likes of Phoenix, Dallas–Fort Worth and Oklahoma City cannot be overlooked. Notwithstanding differences in the amount of space available for development and the more significant role played by the automobile and zoning regulations in explaining most US and Canadian cities' distinctively low-density sprawl, British settlements are much less able to produce the kinds of near-endless suburbs typical across the Atlantic. It should also be mentioned that some North American cities (as well as settlements in several other parts of the world) have chosen to establish their own versions of green belts, or are required by specific state laws to develop them, indicating that their value is acknowledged beyond the UK. The Groene Hart separating the largest cities of the Netherlands is a particularly well-known example of a similar form of approach to land-use planning.

Green belts can thus be regarded as meaningful boundaries through their preventing one side from being consumed by the other, the product of an intentional decision to carefully plan out how land should be used. In this sense, they play an important role in ensuring that cities can be viewed as places that offer opportunities in their own right, rather than as places that merely take from and ultimately exceed their hinterlands. But they can also be established somewhat by chance: following the fall of the Iron Curtain, an incredible amount of biodiversity was discovered along the strip of land that separated Western and Eastern Europe. Having lain untouched for nearly half a century, this corridor is today being conserved as a 'European Green Belt', running from the Barents Sea in the north to the Black and Adriatic seas in the south. As we shall observe next, this is not the only instance of ecological hope springing from human trauma and struggle.

The Chernobyl Exclusion Zone

There are only three things you need to fear here. One: the drivers. Two: the wolves. Three: the radiation.

Ukrainian 'April Ludgate'

BELARUS

Polesie State
Radioecological
Reserve

Pripyat River

10-km zone

Chernobyl
Exclusion
Zone

Pripyat

Chernobyl
plant

30-km exclusion zone

Chernobyl
(city)

Dnipro River

UKRAINE

— · — · — · — Ukraine-Belarus border

0   30
                                          Miles
0   50
                                          Kilometres

Kyiv

My tour guide at the Chernobyl Exclusion Zone (CEZ), whose acerbic commentary convinced me that *Parks and Recreation*'s April Ludgate had decided to move to Ukraine, provided this warning on arrival at the first of two checkpoints that visitors must pass to see one of the world's greatest symbols of human hubris. Admittedly, I didn't need to be informed about the drivers: I had learnt to anticipate them within twenty minutes of leaving Kyiv Boryspil Airport, seeing a Škoda hurtle along the pavement in order to pass the rest of us chumps. The other two considerations, however, say a lot about northern Ukraine's divide, between the world that humans continue to mould, and the world that, perhaps irrevocably damaged, has been largely relinquished to nature.

The CEZ was established in the days after history's most severe nuclear disaster. From the early hours of 25 April 1986, engineers at Chernobyl Nuclear Power Plant's Reactor 4 conducted, as would prove highly ironic, a safety test, aimed at ascertaining how long the plant's turbines could produce sufficient power if an electrical outage were to occur. Over the next twenty-four hours, significant errors were made that drastically reduced the reactor's stability. At 1.23 a.m. on 26 April, an initial steam explosion shot a fireball through the roof and into the dark sky. As fires raged throughout the reactor, radioactive material spewed into the atmosphere, where it was quickly picked up by the wind. Most of the material was deposited in the surrounding area and immediately to the north, in the territory that just five years later would gain independence from the Soviet Union as the Republic of Belarus, although some was carried as far as Scandinavia and Western Europe, contaminating forests and farmland and creating widespread health concerns. In fact, had it not been for a radiation monitor at the Forsmark Nuclear Power Plant in Sweden flagging abnormally high levels of radioactive particles with a Soviet origin, it may have been years until the wider world learnt about the accident, as the USSR was desperate to cover it up. The number of human fatalities remains highly uncertain, not only because of ambiguities over the extent to which thousands of cases of diseases such as cancer represent secondary effects of the blast, but also because the Soviet authorities appeared to try to underplay the severity of the disaster in their record keeping. Estimates range between around thirty and a hundred deaths due to exposure to extreme radiation in the short term, and stretch well into the thousands when long-term health impacts are also considered.

The CEZ was originally drawn as a circle with a 30-kilometre radius around Reactor 4, all residents within this area being required to immediately evacuate under orders from the Soviet military. This circle also contained a smaller circle, extending 10 kilometres from the reactor in any direction, defining what was believed, not unreasonably, to be the area most severely contaminated by radiation. Over time, however, the CEZ's boundaries have been refined based on actual recordings of radiation rather than seemingly arbitrary distances. In particular, scientific tests aimed at monitoring the levels of radioactive isotopes such as caesium-137, strontium-90, iodine-131 and plutonium-238 and -239 in the soil have seen the exclusion zone mutate from a neat circle into a less elegant but more precise blotch on the map. Moreover, given the plant's proximity to the border between independent Ukraine and Belarus, these countries have established their own internal boundaries, resulting in the CEZ on the Ukrainian side, and the

Polesie State Radioecological Reserve abutting it to the north on the Belarusian side. Together, these two zones represent an area around 80 per cent larger than the original Soviet exclusion zone, roughly equally split between Ukraine and Belarus. Nevertheless, it is plausible that it will shrink in the coming years as the radio-activity of certain areas diminishes.

After all, even though there are areas of the CEZ that remain highly hazardous, there are other parts where the radiation has dropped to thoroughly normal levels. In much of it, in fact, the radiation is no worse than what one would encounter on an aero-plane; one enterprising company now even deems it safe to produce and sell 'ATOMIK' vodka made from local grain and water. However, radioactive dust has become concentrated in select hot-spots due to the elements and the actions of people, for instance through burying or segregating contaminated items, including the vehicles used by 'liquidators' in the clean-up operation. The dead pine trees that covered much of the CEZ acquired the name 'the Red Forest' due to their rusty colour after they absorbed consid-erable amounts of radiation from the explosion, and although most of them have since been buried, significant contamination still exists in the surface of the soil. Pripyat, the nearest settle-ment to the reactor, is perhaps the most famous ghost town in the world, a model Soviet city of 50,000 people that was abandoned in a matter of days.* Today, Pripyat's crumbling hospital, dusty swimming pool and unused amusement park (it was due to open just the next week, but instead became a certain contender for the *Un*happiest Place on Earth) all provide an atmosphere both eerie and wretched. It is hard to believe that this place of unkempt vegetation and broken glass was once thriving, and yet despite its sudden demise into a modern Pompeii, a Geiger counter here can

---

* Confusingly, the city of Chernobyl is actually a few kilometres further away from the power plant and, being far less contaminated, now acts as a modest hub for the CEZ's workers and visitors.

reveal enormous radiation discrepancies just metres apart. Consequently, throughout the CEZ, caution is required: guides seek to ensure that visitors do not travel off the beaten track or touch more or less anything; 'April' became animated only on recounting the story of a young woman who had to surrender her trousers because she had sat on a severely contaminated tree stump. The fact that crossing into the CEZ requires a visitor to present their passport and to undergo scans when entering and exiting its checkpoints as well as its canteen – whose food is brought, thankfully, from outside the zone – and must meet a specific dress code and refrain from smoking throughout their trip, further encapsulates the sense that this is a place distinguished from the rest of Ukraine.

As unusual as these experiences may be within a single country's borders, it is the scarcity of human presence over the past four decades that makes the CEZ so extraordinary. To the potential disappointment of science-fiction and comic-book fans, there is no Godzilla, Spider-Man or the Hulk to be found here, although several three-eyed fish discoveries around the world offer at least a small chance of a Ukrainian Blinky of *The Simpsons* fame freestyling in the CEZ's waters. The mutant deformities identified to date have generally been more modest than might be expected of such a momentous change in environmental conditions, including partial albinism in barn swallows, darker colouration in frogs and distinctive markings on certain bugs. There is the possibility that some of these are in fact adaptive responses to increased radiation, although much more research is necessary before iron-clad conclusions can be drawn. Also noteworthy are declining invertebrate numbers – potentially due to the fact that many spend long periods of their lives in the soil, much of which is especially contaminated – and the disproportionate susceptibility of some bird species to cataracts, tumours and sterility. Nevertheless, other species, especially large mammals, have benefited greatly from the significant reduction in anthropogenic influence since 1986. Populations of indigenous mammals such as deer, elk, moose, wild boar, brown bears, beavers, European bison, foxes and lynx have all multiplied over the past three decades. Grey wolves appear to be seven times more abundant in the CEZ than in nearby uncontaminated nature reserves. With all these animals ruling the roost, no wonder 'April' advised vigilance. Non-native Przewalski's horses, introduced in 1998 and temporarily endangered due to poaching, have also come to flourish thanks to robust protection measures against this activity as well as illegal logging and the salvaging of potentially contaminated metal. Today, it is impossible to simply dismiss the CEZ as a wasteland: it is almost unparalleled as a nature sanctuary, where many species, despite their radioactive environment, have proved able to reproduce at a rapid rate.

Some people also choose to live within the zone, even if there is no likelihood of it ever returning to its pre-disaster population of approximately 100,000 (plus another 25,000 in Belarus). The 'self-settlers' are known locally as *samosely* and are today believed to number fewer than 200, most of whom are elderly women. Although the Ukrainian government long sought to evict them, they have remained remarkably determined to cling onto the land they know best. Today, the authorities tend to acquiesce to the older *samosely*'s demands and a government agency ensures that doctors are able to visit them. By contrast, younger *samosely* are generally pressured to leave. It is worth noting that some of the latter were previously displaced by war in Ukraine's eastern Donbas region (ongoing since April 2014) and regard the CEZ as a place that is both cheap and only a hundred kilometres from the capital, Kyiv. A transient group that has come to be a source of aggravation are 'stalkers' (named after a Soviet-era science-fiction film), generally young trespassers committed to exploring the CEZ for fun, some even organising surreptitious raves among the ruins. Since the disaster, only one person is believed to have been born in the CEZ, in 1999, another atypical aspect of this part of

Ukraine, and one the authorities originally tried to cover up due to their embarrassment that they had been unable permanently to evacuate the area.

Still, certain human actions have been regarded more positively. In the immediate aftermath of the disaster, the evacuees were ordered to leave their pets behind at least temporarily, but most were never able to return and in some cases Soviet soldiers shot domestic dogs in order to reduce the spread of contamination. Today, however, the surviving pooches' wild descendants (as well as any dogs that may have wandered in from outside the CEZ) are spayed or neutered and vaccinated so that they can be adopted, their years in radiation-induced captivity finally at an end. Meanwhile, the remaining dogs, which are forced to compete for food and space with the zone's much larger and fiercer wolves, offer companionship to the CEZ's guards. Radiating love, many have even become mini-celebrities online.

The power plant has been undergoing a slow decommissioning process, catalysed not by the 1986 disaster but following a fire in Reactor 2 in 1991, soon after Ukraine's independence. Gradually each unit has been shut down and an enormous two-part, half-cylinder dome – whose mundane name 'New Safe Confinement' hardly does justice to its distinctiveness as a megaproject – has been developed to replace the hastily built 'sarcophagus' designed to contain the obliterated Reactor 4 and its radioactive contaminants. A solar power plant has also been constructed to provide both new power and new hope for the area. Reactor 4 is not expected to be completely dismantled until the 2060s, and the CEZ will remain in place for at least as long, in order to minimise people's exposure to contaminants as well as for scientists to continue monitoring the area largely uninterrupted. And yet other actions may cause the boundaries separating the CEZ from the rest of the country to disappear too soon. In 2020, the nearby Pripyat River started to be dredged for the purpose of establishing a 2,000-kilometre, Baltic-to-Black-Sea inland shipping route called the E40, raising concerns that radioactive sludge will poison millions of people's drinking water. In April of the same year, severe wildfires, which can spike local radiation levels, provided another reason for continuing to minimise human activity here in the long term. The fine line between helping and hindering such a delicate area needs to be detected and also respected.

Lastly, there is for the meantime at least a very different way in which the zone stands out from the rest of the country: its largely untouched evidence of Soviet history. In recent years the Ukrainian government has worked hard to 'decommunise' the country, banning communist symbols and calling for the removal of communist monuments and the renaming of certain settlements and streets, yet the CEZ has come to constitute an unofficial open-air museum of far-left politics, where the iron and sickle still stand, if not proud, then prominent. In particular, Soviet symbols and propaganda continue to adorn the walls of Pripyat, which would be unthinkable anywhere in Ukraine beyond the CEZ. A no less striking example of communist history is the enormous Duga missile-detection radar – nicknamed 'the Russian Woodpecker', for the repetitive noise it would produce on shortwave radio bands – which is poorly hidden in the CEZ's forests. Thus, the CEZ's boundaries may enable a form of communism to survive, albeit a static one. The fact that the financial compensation provided to victims following the disaster helped cripple the Soviet economy and contributed to the USSR's demise only makes the continued presence of its symbols that bit more ironic.*

Today, the CEZ's political future is highly uncertain, most

---

* According to the Communist Party Central Committee, in the immediate aftermath of the disaster, the USSR paid out $1.12 billion in compensation to 116,000 evacuees. Compensation has since been extended to nearly 7 million people in badly affected areas of Ukraine, Belarus and Russia, although the financial burden placed on all three independent nations has meant that some victims today receive as little as $5 a month.

obviously given Russia's invasion of Ukraine. Russian forces, entering via Belarus, captured the CEZ on 24 February 2022, the very first day of the assault, and although they were forced to withdraw from the area by the start of April (reportedly due to a combination of military losses and radiation exposure), while war remains ongoing in Ukraine, one can only conjecture what will happen here. So far, the widespread and very reasonable fear of the New Safe Confinement or the three other reactors being struck and releasing radioactive material has mercifully not come to fruition, although separate areas of concern are that the movement of Russian tanks and armoured vehicles has disturbed the soil, allowing radioactive dust to spread potentially beyond the CEZ's boundaries, and that Russia's assault is bringing us to the edge of a nuclear crisis. Previously, there was genuine hope that the zone would eventually be completely decontaminated and hence little different from its surroundings. However, given its newfound value as a site of conservation and tourist interest, it is possible that in one form or another it will be made permanent. In particular, its boundaries are distinctive in separating a world over which humans continue to claim predominance, from a world left to nature. Animals, it seems, are often more resilient to radiation than they are to people, and are only too willing to fill the void left by our withdrawal. But as we shall see next, disaster can also stimulate the development of boundaries among people – boundaries designed to protect one population from another.

Eyam

---

*To some the sermon simply brought home the fact
that they had been sentenced, for an unknown crime,
to an indeterminate period of punishment. And
while a good many people adapted themselves to
confinement and carried on their humdrum lives as
before, there were others who rebelled, and whose one
idea now was to break loose from the prison-house.*

Albert Camus, *The Plague*

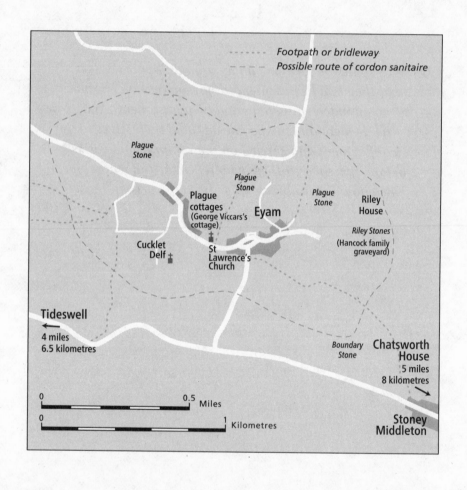

Footpath or bridleway

Possible route of cordon sanitaire

Plague Stone

Plague Stone

Plague Stone

Riley House

Plague cottages (George Viccars's cottage)

Eyam

Riley Stones (Hancock family graveyard)

Cucklet Delf

St Lawrence's Church

Tideswell

4 miles
6.5 kilometres

Boundary Stone

Chatsworth House

5 miles
8 kilometres

0   0.5   Miles

0   1   Kilometres

Stoney Middleton

A parent weeps. *Not again.* In a matter of days, the whole family has succumbed to the invisible terror that seems to pass silently from house to house. It is not as if there has been a lack of effort to prevent the spread of this fateful malady. The public are encouraged to wear masks. Money is treated with care. People meet out in the open – at most. *We haven't left the village for months.*

The notion of boundaries has gained particular resonance with the misery wreaked by the COVID-19 pandemic and the various measures implemented in response. In Europe, the Schengen area's policy of allowing free movement across national borders was at times suspended. Many countries even created internal borders to restrict movement between states and provinces. At a smaller scale, diverse social distancing procedures, including recommendations that implied an invisible line separating oneself from others, were put in place to minimise contact between people and thereby mitigate the spread of the coronavirus. However, in an already polarised context, protocols on tackling COVID-19 and even the very existence of the disease were fiercely contested. Scapegoats were sought. People and companies were judged. Whereas some willingly met in person, others preferred to insulate themselves from the wider world. The boundaries we saw during the height of COVID-19 were thus not just physical, but psychological, social and political.

The pandemic often felt like an unprecedented event in human history. In one way it was: its sheer reach, enabled by the global connectivity to which we have become so accustomed. Nonetheless, from its calamitous impacts to the procedures actualised in hopes of limiting its spread, there have been many antecedents: the Antonine plague of the second century CE, the plague of Justinian in the mid-sixth century, the Manchurian plague of 1910–11 and the 1918 influenza pandemic, to name but a few. When it comes to questions of boundaries, however, there is perhaps no better comparison than the bubonic plague ('Black Death') outbreak of 1665–6 and the particular case of Eyam.

Situated 50 kilometres south-east of Manchester, this small village in the English county of Derbyshire has long offered something of a learning opportunity for future generations suffering from the frightful impacts of contagious disease. The bubonic plague, which had intermittently devastated European populations since the thirteenth century, arrived in the village in late August 1665 via a parcel of cloth sent from struggling London to the local tailor Alexander Hadfield. On receiving it, Hadfield's assistant George Viccars noticed that it was damp and spread it out by the fire, unknowingly releasing the fleas that carried the disease. In a matter of days, Viccars was the first of the village's 257 victims.

It was not until June 1666 that meaningful action was taken to control the disease. The entire village was to be quarantined, a relatively obscure concept at the time. The term derives from the distinctive sanitary measure adopted by the Republic of Venice during a previous bubonic plague outbreak in the fourteenth century, which required ships to sit at anchor for forty days (*quarantena* in the Venetian language) before passengers would be allowed to disembark and cargo could be unloaded. For the following four months, Eyam would be disconnected from the outside world, withdrawing into an early version of a community-wide lockdown. What made the Eyam case even more unusual is that instead of this being a policy imposed from above, it was agreed through persuasion, led by the young parish priest William Mompesson and a former village rector, Thomas Stanley. When a few panicked residents tried to leave, Mompesson convinced them that doing so would endanger the lives of others. In the end, he barely needed to do the job of monitoring his peers. One woman, who took off to nearby Tideswell, was recognised as a resident of Eyam and was promptly chased from the village, all the while being pelted by rudimentary missiles and cries of 'The Plague! The Plague!'

Even though religious leaders tended to enjoy considerable public esteem at this time, with disease generally being regarded as God's punishment – and so following a priest's instructions could be viewed as a route to repentance – it is still remarkable how willing Eyam's population was to risk death in order to protect others, especially considering that the majority of the village's fatalities occurred in the months *after* the quarantine was introduced. In London, a curfew was imposed in 1666 whereby residents were required to be home by nine in the evening, but according to sources such as the naval administrator and diarist Samuel Pepys, who later that year would document the great fire that ravaged the old city, the acrimony with which it was policed provoked considerable antagonism: 'A watch is constantly kept . . . night and day to keep the people in, the plague making us cruel, as doggs, one to another.' Moreover, King Charles II and many of the country's lords were criticised for providing little in the way of aid during the Black Death and for instead retreating to remote country estates. By contrast, by taking matters into their own hands while being sure to elicit the views of the community, Eyam's clergy undoubtedly saved large numbers of lives on the outside, practising what they preached and filling the lacuna in leadership left by the country's political authorities. The plague overwhelmed the village throughout the summer of 1666, and yet people still acquiesced to the restrictions. Ultimately, and crucially, the quarantine's overall purpose was realised: the disease did not spread from Eyam.

A gritstone boulder, prosaically called the 'Boundary Stone' and located a short walk towards neighbouring Stoney Middleton, still marks part of the cordon sanitaire that was established to deter movement to and from the village. During the cordon's existence, it represented a subtle but in practice impermeable frontier, respected by those on either side of it. Many would never cross the fields surrounding the village again. Furthermore, the Boundary Stone and other boulders of its kind not only demarcated Eyam's perimeter to the benefit of the outside world, but also played an essential, practical role for those within. In a classic case of desperate times calling for desperate measures – and acting as a forerunner of the increased use of contactless payment in place of cash during COVID-19 – Eyam's residents would leave coins in the holes drilled into their surface, containing vinegar which was believed to disinfect them. In return, villagers from elsewhere would trade food and medicine. The Earl of Devonshire of nearby Chatsworth House, too, reportedly left much-needed provisions at Eyam's southern boundary, after Mompesson wrote to him requesting support during the village's self-isolation. In these ways, the movement of people was constrained, but goods could be traded with caution.

Beyond these boundary-drawing processes and (albeit temporary) shifts in methods of exchange, various other parallels can be drawn with the present day. Mask wearing became commonplace to ward off the plague, even if the prevailing view was that disease was caused by noxious miasma – therefore stuffing one's mask with herbs was believed to provide a degree of protection. Still, Eyam's clergy rightly suspected that enclosed spaces were hastening the disease's spread, and so just as Pope Francis conducted Mass outdoors to reduce the risks of the coronavirus spreading, Mompesson began to lead services not in St Lawrence's Church, but outside at a natural limestone archway called Cucklet Delf; a remembrance service is still held here every year on the last Sunday of August. Attendance at funerals, like those throughout the COVID-19 pandemic, was also greatly reduced, with individual families promptly burying their dead in fields and gardens rather than congregating at the village graveyard. Another similarity was that the bubonic plague appeared to kill quite randomly, one particularly distressing example being the story of Elizabeth Hancock, who was seemingly never infected but was forced to bury her six children and her husband in the space of only eight days. And just as many couples during COVID-19 were suddenly compelled to decide whether or not they felt safe meeting in person, two lovers, Emmott Sydall of Eyam and Rowland Torre of Stoney Middleton, opted to practise a precursor to what we would now call social distancing, keeping to either side of a nearby valley. After Sydall stopped appearing in April, before the quarantine had even been imposed, Torre hopefully persevered, travelling to their meeting place until Eyam's restrictions were lifted in the autumn. Only then did he learn that his betrothed had perished in the diseased village.

Quarantining would take a long time to become common practice, but Eyam's example is rightly used as a case study of disease prevention through social distancing and sterilisation. Just as importantly, adherence to the quarantine was impressive on both sides of the boundary, exemplifying the mutual respect, solidarity and reciprocity that these communities were able to develop. Today, this pretty village manifests several pieces of evidence of this traumatic period, from Viccars's cottage to Mompesson's open-air church. Its tale of torment and tenacity is told through tourist information placards and a museum dedicated to the village's distinctive history. Perhaps no site is as simultaneously poignant and inspiring as the remaining Boundary Stone, providing a reminder of our shared mortality, our potential for self-sacrifice and our capacity to draw lines to protect others. But invisible lines for the betterment of human existence are not only conceived and realised at the scale of the local or national; they can also be drawn through international collaboration, to accommodate our constantly evolving relationship with the planet. The following is a compelling example of how technological advances would necessitate a brand-new and ingenious way of perceiving and dividing the globe.

The International Date Line

Only the Krauses let him down, and that was
simply because they forgot about the International
Date Line and arrived twenty-four hours late.

Arthur C. Clarke, *Childhood's End*

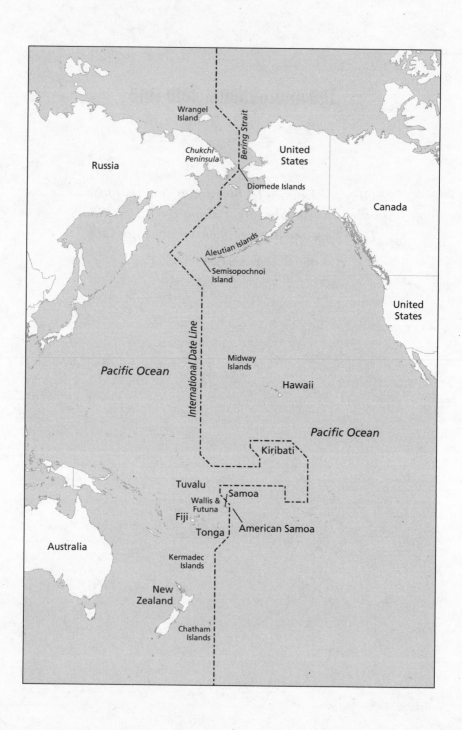

I first learnt about the International Date Line as a child through my grandfather, who for a time travelled quite frequently between Arizona and East Asia for business. On one occasion, he flew from Tokyo to the United States on his birthday, departing in the evening, yet landing approximately ten hours later, not on the next day, but again on his birthday. He claimed that this meant he had been able to celebrate twice on board the plane, with the flight attendants bringing two separate cakes to mark the occasion – or perhaps *occasions*. He was always an adept storyteller, and it is possible that he embellished the airline's generosity, but regardless, the tale captured my young imagination, and the line has intrigued me ever since. I finally crossed it for the first time in 2019, flying from Chicago to Tokyo on the way to Singapore, and experienced the commonly described confusion that comes with 'losing' an entire day, before making it up on the trip back. How is it possible for us to 'time travel' in this way, and what does this invisible line tell us about the importance of boundaries in the world?

First, it is important to recognise that the International Date Line is far from 'natural', even though it is based on the entirely natural rotation of the Earth as it orbits the Sun, which those of us not standing at either the North or South Pole see in the form of the Sun rising and setting each day. Rather, the line is fundamentally imaginary, running from north to south through the Pacific Ocean, roughly following the 180th meridian of longitude but veering away from it whenever it would otherwise meet a territory. The line marks the boundary between two calendar days, and so whereas it may be Thursday on the western side of the Pacific, it is still Wednesday on the eastern side. To make matters even more confusing, what we can regard as the geographical west of the Pacific, i.e. East Asia, Australia and so forth, is in time zone terms actually the east, because time zones, invisible lines in themselves, use the Prime Meridian (which runs through London) as the zero point and these places are to the east of this city. By contrast, the geographical east of the Pacific, i.e. the Americas, is in time zone terms to the west of London. As one can well imagine, London being on the zero line was a human decision, and by extension the International Date Line's placement at 180 degrees either west or east of it (being on the exact opposite side of the world) is the result of other human decisions. And human decisions do not end here. When the line reaches Antarctica, it seemingly disappears, rarely being drawn on maps; instead, a rather confusing system of time zones is used to mark the time here, primarily but not entirely based on different territorial claims. Moreover, any countries situated in the immediate vicinity of the line are unilaterally able to decide on which side of it they would like to be for time-keeping purposes. In these ways, the line is a somewhat fluid boundary, its positioning prone to constant change and still quite ambiguous in certain parts of the vast Pacific. But despite these idiosyncrasies, the line has a significant impact on countries' day-to-day practices and should thus be regarded as a highly pertinent demarcation of our Earth.

Before noting some examples of countries that have moved across it over time (pun not intended), it is worth considering how the line came to be. The concept of drawing horizontal lines of latitude and vertical lines of longitude (the Prime Meridian and the 180th meridian are both examples of the latter) on maps is far from new, having originated in ancient Greece, but the idea of drawing *time* onto maps is remarkably recent, dating back to nineteenth-century Britain. By the middle of the century, railways had become widespread here, but were proving very confusing to their users, as schedules presented the specific time at each stop, which differed whenever one travelled even a short distance either west or east. To solve the common problem of too many missed trains, standardisation was in order, with the time at the Royal Observatory in Greenwich, south-east London, selected as the necessary standard for the entire country.* Over the subsequent decades, other countries followed suit in standardising their time, to the particular benefit of the railways and their users.

Of course, a single time would not suffice in a country the size of the United States. Thus, on 11 October 1883, the heads of its railroad companies convened at the Grand Pacific Hotel in Chicago, where they agreed to replace the perplexing non-system of some fifty different standards – connected to any of the hundreds of separate local times available – with four coordinated time zones based on a place's distance west of Greenwich, an idea originated two decades earlier by a school principal from Saratoga Springs, Charles F. Dowd. Just over a month later, on 18 November 1883, much (although maddeningly, and perhaps inevitably, not all) of the US public consented to resetting their clocks to the new system.† This day would come to be known as the 'Day of Two Noons' among those who witnessed both the traditional solar noon (i.e. when the sun appears to be at its highest position in the sky) and the new 'official' noon, and who accordingly needed to reset their clocks by up to thirty minutes. Even so, the

---

*Even so, for a short period the clocks of some British towns even more bewilderingly displayed both the local time and the time in London, as can still be seen at the Corn Exchange in Bristol.

†For some, the idea of manipulating the time was 'unnatural' and thus to be resisted. Most notably, Detroit for decades saw disagreement over whether to continue using local time or whether to instead adopt the new standard time system, and if the latter, whether Central or Eastern time would be preferable.

US Congress only made these four time zones – plus a fifth for the quite recently incorporated territory of Alaska – official in 1918.

Still, a national system of time zones was of limited value in an increasingly interconnected world. Indeed, especially after the laying of permanent transatlantic telegraph cables in the 1860s, there remained the risk that without international agreement, confusion would occur. And so, following some pressure to establish a globally recognised Prime Meridian for the particular benefit of ships and railways, as well as a proposal for a worldwide system of time zones by the Scottish-born Canadian engineer Sandford Fleming, in October 1884 the International Meridian Conference was held at the request of the US President Chester A. Arthur in Washington, DC to determine the future of time. Ultimately, the forty-one delegates representing twenty-six countries resolved (among other things) that a Prime Meridian should be adopted and that it should pass through Greenwich. Only one country – Santo Domingo, now the Dominican Republic – opposed this plan, while Brazil and France abstained, the latter refusing to adopt Greenwich Mean Time (GMT) as the global standard until 1911 and calling it, rather contemptuously, 'Paris mean time, retarded by nine minutes and twenty-one seconds', until as late as 1978. Even though Fleming's proposal for time zones was dismissed on account of being beyond the conference's purview, his idea of dividing the world into twenty-four time zones (one per hour), each fifteen degrees of longitude apart (for a round world implies 360 degrees in total), would in essence come to fruition as more and more countries set their times on this basis, notwithstanding some adjustments based on national borders and inconsistencies in the adoption of daylight saving. China is a particularly noteworthy example of a country that instead uses a single time zone despite straddling over five thousand kilometres from west to east, the equivalent of five time zones elsewhere. Its border crossing with Afghanistan marks a time difference of three and a half hours! Australia takes the opposite approach, using six time zones spread across three hours for its mainland, either thirty or forty-five minutes apart. Perhaps most interestingly of all, for nearly three years, North Korea's Pyongyang Time (PYT) was intentionally moved back thirty minutes, showing how easily time can be manipulated, as well as the considerable role played by geopolitics.*

Meanwhile, in the process of marking the Prime Meridian through Greenwich as zero degrees longitude, the opposite side of the world – 180 degrees – was also determined. The main reasons for choosing Greenwich were as follows. First, Britain was at this time the world's foremost naval and commercial power, and accordingly, the majority of the world's navigators would use its admiralty charts and nautical almanacs, which would not coincidentally display Greenwich as the Prime Meridian. Second, the Royal Observatory was renowned for the quality of its data, and Britain in general enjoyed an excellent reputation for cartography, so Greenwich was deemed a suitably reliable option. And third, the United States, which by this time boasted the world's largest railroad system, had recently adopted a standard time system that was something of a derivative of Greenwich, meaning that its adoption internationally would imply fewer alterations

---

* Why, one may ask, did North Korea opt to move its time back rather than ahead? Here another geopolitical layer emerges, for the main target of Supreme Leader Kim Jong-un's decision was not South Korea, but Japan, which had as coloniser from 1910 to 1945 imposed its own time zone on the Korean peninsula. In an appropriately symbolic move, the short-lived time zone took effect on 15 August 2015, the seventieth anniversary of Korea's liberation. The resetting of PYT in 2018 was similarly emblematic, intended as an expression of reconciliation with the South. Another good example of geopolitics informing time zone choices is Spain, which despite being on the same longitude as the United Kingdom and GMT, uses Central European Time. This is because in 1942, under General Francisco Franco's command, it moved an hour forward to be aligned with Nazi Germany, and has never moved back.

than any of the other options on the table. As one can see, then, Britain's status as a key node in an increasingly connected world afforded it an enormous advantage. However, there was also a fourth, *indirect* benefit of running zero degrees longitude through Greenwich: doing so would ensure that the 180-degree line would largely run through the Pacific Ocean, meaning that the division between one day and another would affect as few people as possible. The resultant International Date Line is a rare example of a globally accepted standard that has never been officially defined by an international treaty, and yet is a subject of great, obvious relevance to people throughout the world.

This can be seen from the fact that the line has been adjusted over time at the behest of the countries most significantly affected by its positioning. As the line proceeds south from the North Pole, it winds first to the south-east to avoid Wrangel Island and the Chukchi peninsula of Far Eastern Russia, before running south again through the Bering Strait. Here it splits the Diomede Islands (one of which belongs to the United States, the other to Russia), which, despite being under four kilometres apart, consequently exist at different ends of the twenty-four-hour cycle. If it is conceptually possible to see a different day, then this is the place to do it. From here, the line makes an enormous detour to the southwest to ensure that all the Aleutian Islands sit on the Alaskan side of the boundary. Any Aleutian Islands west of the 180th meridian are east of the Prime Meridian, with the uninhabited Semisopochnoi Island of Alaska thus technically representing the easternmost land location in North America according to longitude, despite appearing to the west of the continent. The line subsequently returns to 180 degrees and remains there until reaching the Equator.

The island nation of Kiribati – which, despite having a land area similar to Bahrain, covers an expanse of ocean greater than the size of India – necessitates the next and most considerable swing, this time sharply to the east. After achieving independence from the United Kingdom and acquiring the Phoenix and Line islands from the United States in 1979, Kiribati found trading between its islands on either side of the International Date Line rather inconvenient, as only four days of the week were weekdays on both sides. Consequently, its eastern half skipped Saturday 31 December 1994 in order that the whole country would fall on one side of the divide from 1995. After winding somewhat awkwardly around Kiribati's easternmost islands, the line divides the independent nation of Samoa from the US territory of American Samoa. The two previously shared a time zone, but Samoa disliked being nearly a whole day behind its main trading partners Australia and New Zealand and its expatriate communities there, whereas American Samoa was happier being closer time-wise to the United States. Consequently, along with Tokelau, a territory of New Zealand, Samoa crossed the line at midnight on Thursday 29 December 2011, with the effect of deleting Friday 30 December as it jumped straight forward to Saturday 31 December overnight, ready to ring in the New Year first rather than last. The line then runs close to 172 degrees west in order to accommodate Wallis and Futuna (a French island territory), the Kermadec and the Chatham Islands (parts of New Zealand) and the independent countries of Tuvalu, Tonga and Fiji, which also all look primarily towards the countries to the geographical west for trade. Nevertheless, with at least one eye on its tourist appeal, Fiji has erected signs to mark the 180th meridian, which bisects three of its islands, even if the time is necessarily consistent on either side. Eventually, the line returns to 180 degrees, until it reaches Antarctica.

A final quirk pertains to international waters. All ships are requested to adhere to nautical time zones, which change with every fifteen degrees of longitude, similarly to Fleming's suggestion, unless they are within a country's territorial waters, where the nation's self-determined time zone also applies. A Nautical Date Line was recommended and established by the Anglo-French Conference on Time-keeping at Sea in 1917, running along the

180th meridian, with the exception of where land and territorial waters interfere. In these places, rather than veering away from this meridian in the manner of the International Date Line, the Nautical Date Line is simply left as gaps.

The International Date Line enables us to live in a globally connected world, even while it operates as a kind of boundary, not just between days, but to the realisation of trade and communication between those on either side of it. Before it was articulated as a boundary from the late nineteenth century, there was nonetheless understanding of the changing of the days and the possibility of gaining or losing time, as Phileas Fogg famously experiences in Jules Verne's novel *Around the World in Eighty Days* and Ferdinand Magellan much earlier observed while attempting to circumnavigate the world. The line is hence not completely a product of our imagination, but its location in the Pacific and its fairly frequent repositioning on the basis of different countries' political and economic interests show that it can be moulded, too. The gradual movement of the Earth's tectonic plates also requires that the line be adaptable, as landmasses slowly shift, compelling countries to redefine their relationships with the 180th meridian (far) in the future.

In these ways and like other boundaries across the world, the International Date Line is not simply a demarcation between two sides, but a dynamic and compelling representation of our relationship with the world. It is the result of convenience, yet a bringer of complication. Both alluring and elusive, it tells us a lot about humans' efforts to make sense of the planet, our challenges in mapping it, in identifying and visually portraying a constantly evolving globe. Change is our Earth's only constant, implying the movement of its boundaries and belts, and the emergence of new splits and sectors. The International Date Line perfectly exemplifies our desire to structure the future through the use of geography and take some control over the globe.

How Invisible Lines Allow People
to Claim Territory as Their Own

As we have seen already, invisible lines can enable humans to shape the planet in some way. However, given our varying interests and concerns, it is inevitable that in many cases, competition will arise over the control and use of a territory. Violent border disputes between two (and sometimes more) countries are the most obvious example, from Kashmir to Donbas and Nagorno-Karabakh to the West Bank. Additionally, there are territories which, despite an absence of bloodshed, are the focus of significant diplomatic discord, including Antarctica (parts of which are claimed by seven countries) and the Spratly Islands (claimed by six). Separatist movements across the world similarly perceive boundaries and as such desire borders that differ from the current state of affairs: Scotland, Catalonia, Transnistria, Somaliland, Western Sahara, Ambazonia and Kurdistan are just a few contemporary cases on which to keep an eye. Meanwhile, many in Belgium will be familiar with the battle cry 'Long live free Flanders, may Belgium die', as notably declared by a deputy from the Flemish nationalist party Vlaams Belang in 2010. The partitioning of Belgium along a linguistic line between Flemish-speaking Flanders and French-speaking Wallonia – although clearly complicated by the existence of bilingual Brussels and German-speaking Ostbelgien – has long been mooted, given contrasting claims to nationhood.

Still, claiming a territory as one's own is not an urge uniquely possessed by political leaders and their supporters. Shifting our attention from the national scale to more local, everyday contexts, we may note, for instance, the universal phenomenon of NIMBYism, characterising residents who only approve of or at the very least acquiesce to proposed developments such as housing estates, power stations, hospitals, railway lines and entertainment venues provided they are constructed sufficiently far from their homes. In this regard, not-in-my-backyarders imagine invisible lines separating places where such developments can be considered acceptable from those where they must be resisted. Relatedly, planning policies like zoning enable invisible lines to emerge, through either permitting or prohibiting particular developments, resulting in distinct clusters of single-family homes, high-rises, shopping centres, light industry and so forth. No surprise, then, that residents are often keen to have a say over zoning ordinances, to protect their visions of what can and cannot be built in their neighbourhood.* And sometimes, people subconsciously draw invisible lines defining what should be allowed in areas that are only speciously 'theirs'. One obscure example I think about inexplicably frequently is the octogenarian retired dentist Peter Maddox's yellow Vauxhall Corsa, which from 2015 attracted a shocking amount of ire among tourists to England's picturesque Cotswolds region (as well as, inevitably, social media users), one of whom even felt driven to scratch 'move' in its bonnet. By suggesting that Maddox's little car was a blight on the landscape and was consequently ruining their photographs, these visitors

---

*Zoning is common in many countries, including across most of the United States. The stark exception among major US cities is Houston, whose residents have consistently voted against the use of zoning laws. Although the city does have its own system of codes to govern development, parts of Houston are, thanks to the lack of zoning, characterised by a mishmash of building types: houses between factories and warehouses, mammoth office buildings looming over suburban homes and, in one case, a crematorium and mortuary in an otherwise residential area. For this reason, invisible lines can be harder to discern here than elsewhere in the country.

essentially implied that there is an invisible line separating beautiful from banal places – one that banana-coloured vehicles must not traverse. However, as hard as they might have tried to will it into existence, there were plenty of others unwilling to respect such a boundary. In a remarkable declaration of solidarity, a convoy of a hundred bright yellow cars was driven around Maddox's village in 2017, while a GoFundMe page, shared through the car's own Twitter profile, was created to 'Save Peter's Yellow Corsa'. In brief, it is unreasonable to expect everyone to concur with one's interests in a territory and how it should be used.

In this part, we will explore six examples of invisible lines being drawn or imagined by people or groups seeking to claim somewhere as their own. The Treaty of Tordesillas, negotiated and signed in 1494, is probably the most famous example, and certainly the one with the widest geographical spread: Spain and Portugal opted bilaterally (albeit with papal oversight) to carve up newly 'discovered' lands between them, and only them. A much less well-known case, but one that also involves privileged people in one part of the world tenuously seeking sovereignty over distant lands, is Bir Tawil, a place unusually rejected by the nation states with strong claims to it through their contrasting interpretations of its boundaries. Australia's Outback is another intriguing example of those living beyond a territory's (nebulous) boundaries somehow claiming it as their own, with the effect that the place is treated simultaneously as quintessentially 'Australian' and as the 'Other' to 'civilised' Australian society. Sometimes, however, boundary drawing for territorial purposes is a matter of necessity, the Inter-Entity Boundary Line in Bosnia and Herzegovina being a revealing example of an administrative line established to ensure peace and safety, following a brutal conflict which has left behind a landscape blighted by landmines. And elsewhere, where the different parties remain antagonistic, territorial claims can easily descend into violence, as we shall see in the cases of football in Buenos Aires, where diehard fans seek to defend their club's presumed boundaries, and street gangs in Los Angeles, which have long fought over portions of this teeming metropolis.

The Treaty of Tordesillas

No one can give away what he does not himself possess.

Hugo Grotius

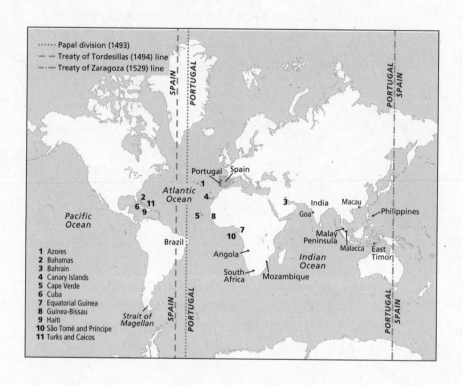

Papal division (1493)
Treaty of Tordesillas (1494) line
Treaty of Zaragoza (1529) line

SPAIN
PORTUGAL
PORTUGAL
SPAIN

Portugal Spain

Atlantic
Ocean

India Macau

Goa

Philippines

Pacific
Ocean

Malay
Peninsula

Brazil

Malacca East
Timor

Angola

Indian
Ocean

South
Africa Mozambique

Strait of
Magellan

SPAIN
PORTUGAL
PORTUGAL
SPAIN

1 Azores
2 Bahamas
3 Bahrain
4 Canary Islands
5 Cape Verde
6 Cuba
7 Equatorial Guinea
8 Guinea-Bissau
9 Haiti
10 São Tomé and Príncipe
11 Turks and Caicos

A few years ago, a team of researchers discovered that vultures are quite willing to travel extensively around Spain, but that when they reach the Portuguese border, their numbers decline drastically. The reason for this apparent disinclination to cross into Portugal is not necessarily that they prefer the ochre plains of Castilla y León to the sandy beaches of the Algarve, but that Spain has a much looser policy on the removal of cattle carcasses. Like any canny traveller, vultures are always conscious of where they might find a good meal. Their geography thus marks out an unofficial divide between two countries that have their own official border, one that has scarcely changed for over 700 years. However, the demarcation lines between Spain and Portugal are by no means limited to vultures, land administration and twenty-first-century protocols. In fact, back in the fifteenth century one of the world's longest lines was drawn to carve up these two countries' claims to the entire planet. While this boundary shows that humans, like vultures, are not averse to picking over places that take their fancy, its legacy is far more extensive.

The story, as with so many others, begins with Christopher Columbus. Having survived a shipwreck off the south-western coast of Portugal in 1476, Columbus, a seafaring entrepreneur who was originally from the long-established maritime and commercial power the Republic of Genoa in modern-day Italy, decided to move to Portugal's capital, Lisbon. The city had already become home to many of his Genoese peers, including mariners, merchants and cartographers like his own brother, Bartholomew, and Columbus recognised how he could help advance Portugal's aspirations to become a global empire. Indeed, thanks to the recent efforts and patronage of Dom Henrique ('Prince Henry the Navigator'), Portugal was already in control of much of the West African coastline, where it had started a trend that would deplorably be embraced by others in the centuries to come: the Atlantic slave trade. It was now looking further east, towards the potential riches available in Asia. Achieving this objective felt more palpable after Bartolomeu Dias became the first European to sail around the *Cabo das Tormentas* ('Cape of Storms') in what is now South Africa in 1488.* Columbus's bold target was India.

The itinerary he planned was highly unconventional. He devised a plan to sail west rather than east, expecting it to be quicker and easier. His idea was sound, except for two things. First, he underestimated the circumference of the Earth. Second, and relatedly, he did not anticipate the existence of a land between Europe and Asia when travelling west (what would later become known as the Americas, named after an Italian explorer named Amerigo Vespucci, who unlike Columbus believed that it represented an entirely new continent). Columbus presented his idea to the Portuguese King John II in 1484. To his chagrin, the king was not interested and preferred instead to continue pursuing an eastern passage past the southern tip of Africa.

Undeterred, Columbus went instead to Portugal's arch-rival, Spain, whose 'Catholic Majesties' Queen Isabella I of Castile and King Ferdinand II of Aragon were in the midst of a war with the Islamic Emirate of Granada, and had also initiated the notorious Spanish Inquisition to reinforce their religion while suppressing

---

* Although this point is not technically the southern tip of Africa, its subsequent renaming as *Cabo da Boa Esperança* or 'Cape of Good Hope' by King John II reflects how determined the Portuguese were to encourage ambitious explorers to travel even further.

Muslims and Jews. Again, Columbus's proposal fell on deaf ears. Not until 1492 did Columbus receive the assent of the Catholic Majesties, who, in the euphoria of finally defeating Spain's Muslims, recognised the potential for Columbus to accumulate further riches for Spain and spread their faith in the process. By travelling west, Columbus could establish new trading posts in the name of Spain,* rather than relying on the numerous outposts that Portugal had created along the West African coast. Perhaps he could even find a route to attack the Ottoman Empire, a growing Islamic force and one likely to be hostile to Spain following the Inquisition, from behind. And so, in 1492, the same year as the Inquisition came to a head with the Alhambra Decree which expelled the country's practising Jews, Columbus set sail with three ships, the *Santa María*, the *Niña* and the *Pinta*. Some have suggested that Columbus was himself Jewish or of Jewish descent – maybe a Marrano, a forced convert to Christianity who continued, dangerously, to practise Judaism in secret – and understandably quite keen to maintain some distance for a while.†

---

* Technically Castile, but de facto Aragon as well.

† A key advocate of the thesis that Columbus had Jewish origins (which is at least a century old) was the prominent Holocaust survivor and Nazi hunter Simon Wiesenthal, who maintained that Columbus's decision to sail west in search of a place where Jews could find refuge was inspired by biblical prophecy. Admittedly, the evidence available is only circumstantial, but various clues do offer some intrigue. For instance, Columbus originally planned to set sail on 2 August 1492, the very day that Jews were legally required to either convert to Catholicism, depart Spain, or face death; this date also happened to be Tisha B'Av, a solemn Jewish holiday commemorating the destruction of both ancient temples in Jerusalem. The fact that he later postponed his voyage by one day may indicate that he thought better of travelling on a date many Jews consider unlucky. Additionally, Columbus's distinctively triangular signature resembled familiar inscriptions on Jewish gravestones, while he consistently used the Hebrew letters ה״ב (*bet-hei*) in his letters to his son Diego, meaning *B'ezrat Hashem* or 'With God's help', a common Jewish blessing.

Columbus demonstrated his understanding of the Earth's wind patterns by initially travelling south to the Canary Islands rather than due west, as here he could exploit the strong northeast trade winds for the voyage across the Atlantic. Just over a month later, on 12 October, he and his companions spotted land, today believed to be either the Bahamas or Turks and Caicos, which he named San Salvador. Later that month he reached Cuba, which he first thought was Japan. Before returning to Spain with the *Niña* and the *Pinta* on 16 January 1493 (the *Santa María* ran aground on 25 December, a very bad Christmas present for the sailors), Columbus visited what is now Haiti, which he called *La Isla Española* ('the Spanish Island', now Hispaniola, a much better gift to the country that was supporting him). Still, he wondered if this was also part of Japan. With gold in his pockets and a small contingent of captives in tow,* Columbus had much to show the Catholic Majesties, even if his journey would be delayed by a brief period of detention in the Portuguese-controlled Azores, whose leader was suspicious of the Spanish fleet.

Before travelling to Spain to receive his due honours, however, Columbus simply could not resist boasting of his achievements to John II of Portugal. By doing so, he set in motion one of the world's greatest diplomatic crises. The king, unsurprisingly, was angry that Columbus had made his discoveries for Spain and contended that they were rightfully Portuguese due to a clause in the

---

* Quite how many people Columbus seized (and who did not then escape) during his first voyage is unclear, but a reasonable estimate is one to two dozen. All but six appear to have died before reaching Europe, and only two were still alive a year after being captured. In stark contrast to her hostility towards Jews and Muslims, Isabella demonstrated remarkable clemency towards the survivors, admonishing Columbus for enslaving people she considered her subjects and potential Catholics, and ordering that they be returned home, following baptism, of course. She did not waver from this stance, ordering Columbus's arrest in 1500 for his increasingly severe abuses against Indigenous people, and stripping him of his governorship.

previous 1479 Treaty of Alcáçovas – confirmed by the papal bull or decree *Aeterni regis** in 1481 – giving Portugal a range of exclusive rights in the Atlantic.

While Columbus was being lauded in Spain, John II, whose moniker *o Príncipe Perfeito* ('the Perfect Prince') was apparently not reflected in all his decisions, wrote to the Catholic Majesties threatening to send part of his far superior fleet to the lands claimed by Columbus. He did, however, offer the possibility of a compromise: an imaginary line running due west from the Canary Islands, which would divide the Atlantic into a northern Spanish portion and a southern Portuguese portion. With this move, the concept of a boundary running through the ocean was initiated.

Alarmed by John II's threat of war, Isabella and Ferdinand's first move was to speak to Pope Alexander VI, Rodrigo Borgia (born de Borja), who conveniently was from the Spanish Crown of Aragon. At this time, the pope wielded incomparable authority and the Catholic Majesties played on their shared faith and nationality as well as their commitment to expelling non-Catholics from their country, in order to convince him of their rights to the 'New World'. Their approach had the desired effect. On 3 May 1493, Alexander VI issued a new papal bull called *Inter caetera*,[†] granting Spain a number of exclusive privileges in territories that were not already controlled by a Christian leader; in return, Spain should convert these territories' populations to Catholicism. The following day, he provided a clarification, explicitly granting Portugal rights to territories in Africa, and Spain the same across the Atlantic. He also proposed a new straight line through the Atlantic – from north to south rather than east to west – arbitrarily along a meridian about 100 leagues west of the Portuguese-controlled Azores and Cape Verde. In this way, Spain would be able to claim all the lands to the west, and Portugal

---

* '[Clemency] of the eternal king'.
† 'Among other [works]'.

all those to the east. Moreover, the pope threatened to excommunicate any seafarer who travelled through the other country's waters without their monarch's consent. Even more contentiously, a further papal bull called *Dudum siquidem** appeared to give India to Spain despite being to the east of *Inter caetera*'s line. The Spanish leaders were duly thrilled.

Predictably, John II was dissatisfied by this plan. Although he would enjoy a monopoly in Africa and, if his fleets could make it there, most of Asia, he did not believe he should face any constraints. Portugal's naval strength and ability to navigate the world was unrivalled. His country was clearly leading in what would become known as the 'Age of Exploration' or the 'Age of Discovery'. Why should he stand down, especially when he interpreted the Treaty of Alcáçovas as being in support of his land claims in the 'New World'? Another grievance was that it would be almost impossible to adhere to the pope's boundary line, because even the best navigators travelling south to later take the eastern route to Asia would struggle to avoid crossing it here and there due to the power of the trade winds. It is striking how willing John II was to challenge the traditional authority of the pope over matters of sovereignty by pushing for a new diplomatic agreement, even if he feared personal excommunication. His Portuguese delegation thus suggested to their Spanish counterparts that *Inter caetera* could be used as a *starting point* in negotiations between the two countries.

These talks would not be easy. The future of the world was being determined. Territories both known and unknown would be carved up by the world's most powerful country and its most ambitious. From March to June 1494 the two sides deliberated in the small Spanish town of Tordesillas, not far from the Portuguese border, overseen by a papal representative as mediator. The resulting Treaty of Tordesillas, signed on 7 June, reaffirmed many of

---

* 'A short while ago'.

Inter caetera's conditions, but added some embellishments, like a joint expedition (which never happened) to mark the course of the invisible line by establishing boundary towers in places like Cape Verde, and a straight channel for Spanish ships to pass freely through Portuguese waters, necessary for travelling to and from the Americas. The most important aspect of the treaty, however, was its moving of the boundary line further west, to the meridian 370 leagues west of Cape Verde, or a little under 2,000 kilometres. Instead of passing through the centre of the Atlantic, it would now run roughly halfway between Cape Verde and Columbus's discoveries for Spain.

Seemingly unknown to the negotiators, this invisible line would also cut through the eastern part of Brazil. When Pedro Álvares Cabral reached this territory on the way to India in 1500, he was consequently able to initiate its colonial period. To this day, Portuguese is the official language of Brazil, the only country in the Americas to have any part of its landmass east of the line. By contrast, through the actions of Hernán Cortés, Francisco Pizarro and other *conquistadores*, the vast majority of this part of the world would come to speak Spanish. Although Portugal had already assumed control of many places to the east of the line, it is noteworthy how many places can be found here where Portuguese is still either the primary or secondary tongue, including Cape Verde, Guinea-Bissau, São Tomé and Príncipe, Angola, Mozambique, East Timor and Macau, and historically also Goa and Indonesia. Today, just one country speaks Spanish east of the line, Equatorial Guinea (formerly Spanish Guinea), which was ceded to Spain in 1778 after Portugal became convinced that it was merely a place of disease and disorder. However, the Philippines and several Pacific islands have also listed Spanish as their official language in the past. This brings us to the final part of the story.

Columbus never managed to make it to India on his second (1493–6), third (1498–1500) or fourth (1502–4) voyages. Instead, travelling in the opposite direction, his Portuguese rival Vasco da Gama became the first European to reach India by sea in 1498, enabling his country to claim control over much of the Indian as well as the Atlantic Oceans. Still, another milestone remained to be achieved: a complete circumnavigation of the globe. The Portuguese explorer Ferdinand Magellan had already travelled to the Malay peninsula, by the first two decades of the sixteenth century a coveted destination for explorers because of its abundance of spices, which could be sold for considerable profits abroad.* However, he wanted to become the first person to travel to the Moluccas, appropriately nicknamed the 'Spice Islands' and now part of the Maluku archipelago of Indonesia, via a new route heading west. The catch was that he could not gain permission from the Portuguese King Manuel I, John II's successor, and fell out with him so badly that he was subjected to public humiliation in his own country, despite his previous achievements. Like Columbus before him, he looked to Spain for support; after all, he would have to start by travelling through Spanish-controlled waters anyway. Spain's teenaged King Charles I – or Charles V of the Holy Roman Empire – agreed in 1519, and with a fleet of five ships Magellan set out for what he expected to be a two-year journey.

Over a year later – Magellan was slowed by a serious insurrection in Patagonia – he finally passed from the Atlantic to the Pacific via a narrow strait near the tip of South America, which he called *Estrecho de Todos los Santos* ('Strait of All Saints'). Its current name, the Strait of Magellan, was given to it later by King Charles in his honour. Not knowing the size of the Pacific, Magellan was surprised that what he assumed would be a journey of just a few days from this point actually took nearly four months.

---

*Later, in the mid-seventeenth century, the nutmeg island of Run was traded by England for the Dutch-owned Manhattan following a protracted conflict, exemplifying the region's desirability to Europeans.

In March 1521 he finally made it to Asia, becoming the first European to lead a voyage across the Pacific. However, he would not make it to the Spice Islands for the second time in his life; he was killed on the island of Mactan in the Philippines after attempting to convert the population to Catholicism. Nevertheless, his colleague Juan Sebastián Elcano eventually assumed control of the mission and managed to lead one of Magellan's original five ships, the aptly named *Victoria*, all the way back to Spain via the traditional route, making him the first person to circumnavigate the Earth.

Why is this all important? Because if somebody could circumnavigate the world, then just one boundary was insufficient. Where does east become west and west become east? Both Spain and Portugal claimed that the valuable Spice Islands were on 'their' side of the boundary, Portugal by pointing to its traditional eastward routes, Spain to the westward passage found by Magellan and Elcano. Further, by travelling across the planet, had Elcano not illegally passed through a significant portion of 'Portuguese' waters? The fact that he voyaged in a westward direction was surely irrelevant. A conference was organised in 1524 across two cities – Badajoz in Spain and Elvas in Portugal – bringing together the brightest minds, including cartographers and navigators, to draw an anti-meridian, ideally one that would give the two countries equal halves of the world. Reportedly, although probably apocryphally, the simplest solution was proposed by a small boy, who on seeing the delegation brandished his backside and suggested that they draw the line through the crack. It was not until 22 April 1529, partially aided by the international marriage agreements for which royals are so known, that a treaty was signed in Zaragoza, Spain, positioning the anti-meridian 297.5 leagues or a little more than 1,700 kilometres east of the Moluccas. The existing line defined by the Treaty of Tordesillas would not change. Even more intriguing than the fact that Portugal was granted substantially more of the world than Spain is that the

Philippines, which would soon become a Spanish colony, are actually far to the west of the line and thus in 'Portuguese' territory. Despite this misdemeanour – and Portugal's own transgressions in South America as it pushed the borders of Brazil further and further west – the two countries largely respected the two meridians defined by these treaties in the subsequent decades.

And that was that, or at least it could have been had there only been two countries in the world. As the *conquistadores* found in particular, just because a treaty suggested that they could claim most of the lands in the Americas did not mean that these places' inhabitants would acquiesce. Time also saw the emergence of new maritime powers – England, the Dutch Republic and France – that felt no need to respect treaties that pertained only to two countries. This is reflected in their use of letters of marque authorising privateers (effectively pirates with paperwork) to attack and steal from Spanish and Portuguese ships. At least as important as these physical assaults was the publication of the Dutch jurist Hugo Grotius' treatise *Mare Liberum* (1609), which popularised the principle of 'freedom of the seas', the forebear of the United Nations Convention on the Law of the Sea's 'freedom of the high seas' (effective since 1994) and a foundation of modern international law.* Addressing this work to the 'Rulers and to the Free and Independent Nations of Christendom', Grotius directly challenged the papacy's authority to determine sovereignty and ensured that Spain and Portugal's monopoly of the world's main waterways would henceforth become a matter of international controversy and concern. For all these reasons, the two meridians that had been drawn to split the Earth into two were quickly

---

*Even so, Grotius wasn't averse to brute force: his reputation was built on his earlier and excruciatingly comprehensive legal defence (titled *De Jure Praedae*, or 'On the Law of Prize and Booty') of the 1603 seizure of the Portuguese *Santa Catarina* in the Singapore Strait by his cousin, Jacob van Heemskerck.

rendered outdated; future treaties, especially in South America, would amend specific borders rather than modifying two overarching lines that had become impossible to police.

Yet this is not to say that the Treaty of Tordesillas and the subsequent Treaty of Zaragoza had no long-term impact. Spain became phenomenally wealthy from the precious metals it secured through its colonies, enabling it to wage wars on multiple continents and bring once-powerful civilisations – the Maya and Incas – to their knees. Relatively speaking, Portugal tended to be less interested than Spain in pressing inland to seize new territories, and instead preferred to continue exploiting its competitive advantages in the lucrative and efficient maritime trade, controlling numerous ports in the Indian Ocean, from the island of Mozambique to Malacca in modern-day Malaysia, and from Bahrain to Macau.* Until the Dutch became a formidable competitor in Asia in the seventeenth century, Portugal was effectively able to enjoy exclusivity over this vast region's riches for a good hundred years. And in the past century, Chile and Argentina have invoked the Treaty of Tordesillas to defend their land claims in Antarctica and the Falkland Islands (Islas Malvinas), respectively. The Treaty's implications today may not always be obvious, but their existence cannot be denied.

Finally, what of the pope? The Treaty of Tordesillas's signatories committed merely to requesting his acknowledgement of their agreement, which was made without his presence and input. It was only in 1506 that Pope Julius II officially sanctioned the resulting boundary through the papal bull *Ea quae pro bono pacis*.† The papacy's authority to delimit countries' boundaries would continue to diminish over time, especially as more and

---

* Incidentally, the English name for the language of south-eastern China – Cantonese – is derived from the Portuguese name for the Guangdong region, Cantão, providing another legacy of sorts.
† 'Those [agreements] for the good [i.e. promotion] of peace'.

more countries, influenced by the Reformation, looked for new sources of guidance and leadership. Over the following centuries, the notion of dividing the world into two to the benefit of just a couple of nations became increasingly difficult to justify politically, legally and philosophically. And yet, despite the numerous and diverse land claims we can identify across the world, there is one place in particular that is actively rejected by the countries that could take it with little complication. How has this unique situation developed?

Bir Tawil

This is your chance to become an honorary Princess, Knight or Court Jester or even get the King to do your bidding.

Jeremiah Heaton

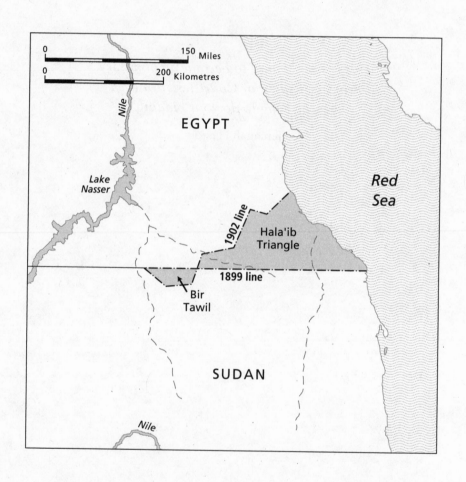

Since 2014, a diplomatic crisis has brewed online. Political leaders veer between measured correspondence and passionate reproach. Sometimes negotiations take place quietly, through private messages; at other times, the internet becomes a public medium for the key actors to challenge and debunk each other's claims. The focus, as is typical of political wrangling, is territory. But little else in this case is conventional.

In fact, Bir Tawil's circumstances are among the oddest in the world. A modest (about 2,000 square kilometres) wedge of land between Egypt and Sudan, it could quite easily be claimed by either nation. Instead, it is shunned by both. This unusual situation has attracted the interest of those with lofty ambitions, with three men in particular claiming ownership of the territory. First up is an American farmer named Jeremiah Heaton, who in 2014 made himself King of North Sudan, his chosen name for the region, in order that his seven-year-old daughter Emily could be a real-life princess; one must ask whether his other two children's demands are more humble. Second, an Indian IT entrepreneur called Suyash Dixit in 2017 titled himself King of Dixit, in hopes that putting himself figuratively on the map would ensure a personal legacy. The third key claimant is Dmitry Zhikharev, a Russian radio operator who asserts that Heaton and Dixit both lack evidence for their respective claims and that his visit to the territory in 2014 makes him the true King of Mediae Terrae, in homage to J. R. R. Tolkien. Notwithstanding a variety of other internet-based claims, including for a Kingdom of the State of Bir Tawil (which almost immediately underwent a 'civil war', documented online), an Emirate of Bir Tawil (whose claim cites the Qur'an), a Grand Dukedom of Bir-Tawil (which issues its own currency), a State of Birland (which produces its own stamps) and a Confederated Empire of Bir Tawil and Territories (whose national anthem is 'fifteen men on a dead man's chest'), these are the three main actors in a bloodless conflict over a place that barely causes a ripple in its own region. Cases are made and promptly disparaged. International interest waxes and wanes. And in the midst of this dispute, the lives and interests of those who actually live in and around Bir Tawil are consistently overlooked.

How did this unusual situation arise? As with so many other disagreements over territory in Africa, Bir Tawil's predicament has its roots in colonialism. And like many of the other examples considered in this book, it involves the drawing of at least one boundary line. In 1899, a treaty signed by the United Kingdom and Egypt specified that the territory south of the twenty-second parallel – a straight political boundary from west to east – would henceforth be jointly administered as Anglo-Egyptian Sudan. However, in 1902 the UK drew a new administrative boundary, which, in a rare demonstration of the empire trying to take local needs at least somewhat into account, followed the ways in which the local ethnic groups were distributed across the region. Thus, whereas the nomadic Ababda around the mountain of Bartazuga were more strongly connected to Egypt to the north and should be under its jurisdiction, the Beja people of Hala'ib by the Red Sea were to become part of the Sudanese quasi-colony to the south, with whom their culture was deemed more similar.

When Sudan gained independence in 1956, it claimed that the 1902 line was the true border between it and Egypt to the north. By contrast, Egypt argued (and still argues) that the 1899 line is correct, stating that the 1902 line as an administrative boundary cannot be used to establish sovereignty. The main reason why the two countries perceive their borders differently pertains to the Hala'ib Triangle, a portion of land along the Red Sea, which according to the 1899 political boundary belongs to Egypt, being located north of the twenty-second parallel, whereas the 1902 administrative boundary indicates that it is part of Sudan, as the line wiggles to the north-east. Far larger, more fertile and coastal, the Hala'ib Triangle is coveted much more highly than the arid, landlocked Bir Tawil, which is located to the south of the former line (making it part of Sudan) and north of the latter (making it part of Egypt). In an elegant but frustrating catch-22, claiming sovereignty over Bir Tawil would imply acceptance of whichever line means relinquishing one's claim to the Hala'ib Triangle. As a result, Bir Tawil remains unloved by the two countries that have a legitimate claim to it. This is where the aforementioned claimants step in.

Recognising this quirk, Heaton, Dixit, Zhikharev and several others all claim to have visited the territory, making their respective marks through raising their own flags (and in Dixit's case, planting some sunflower seeds as well). However, it is difficult to prove one's visit to Bir Tawil: whereas much of the border between Egypt and Sudan is defined and patrolled, at Bir Tawil the situation is as ambiguous as one might expect. Moreover, southern Egypt has a number of checkpoints (and advance permission from the Egyptian army is required even for travel near the border), but these do not correlate with the location of Bir Tawil. The general area also lacks landmarks by which to prove one's visit, and guides have been known to declare that their visitors have reached Bir Tawil when a GPS says otherwise. On the ground, the territory's lines are truly invisible. This has only fuelled doubt and discord, now not only between two nation states, but also between individuals, who regularly assert that their rivals never visited Bir Tawil at all.

Thus, despite an absence of official borders here, certain boundaries exist which shape people's engagement with the area.

Most prosaically, we can see how differently two lines on a map may be interpreted, with the two states holding the strongest claims to Bir Tawil – Egypt and Sudan – sidestepping the possibility of a mutually agreed border, lest it imply their renouncement of territory elsewhere. Instead, two hastily drawn boundary lines remain, leaving the possibility for a loophole in sovereignty claims to be exploited. In the process, a second, more conceptual sort of boundary emerges: one between the tangible and the virtual worlds. Where else can an individual make even the semblance of a legitimate claim to territory than over the internet? There is no easier way for a person to engage in a diplomatic dispute regarding a territory that they may not have ever visited. Facebook and even LinkedIn have become sites where political claims are made and defended. Competing visions for the future can be marketed to an interested – and sometimes perplexed – audience. There is something quite charming about the juxtaposition of utopian and often quirky descriptions of how the territory's apparent potential could be harnessed, and the gridlocked reality negotiated by the nation states of Egypt and Sudan.

However, there is also a more insidious disjuncture that is rarely acknowledged by the region's aspiring rulers: that they do not have the same interests in and understandings of the territory as those who actually use it on a regular or semi-regular basis. Rarely if ever are the concerns of Bir Tawil's nomadic groups, who still use it for grazing and shelter, taken into account on the blogs and websites created by those who battle over it online. Indeed, the foreign claimants' plans for the territory, however well intentioned and whether meant seriously or in jest, tend to demonstrate a profound lack of concern with what the region's itinerant residents are inclined to want. For instance, Heaton's desire to turn Bir Tawil into a centre of high-yield agricultural production and innovation, solar energy, digital currency and free information exchange seems unlikely to appeal to the Ababda and Bishari (a subdivision of the Beja) people who are accustomed to moving across the general region with minimal interference, who rely on its mineral resources and whose trading practices are far more tactile. Further, Heaton and Dixit's idea of basing the territory's economic system on powerful computer technology appears especially implausible given that temperatures in the area frequently exceed 40°C. The notion of creating an untaxed, libertarian paradise for foreign investors in a hot, dusty, remote part of the desert is ambitious, to say the least. No wonder such agendas have been met with a combination of mystification and mirth among those familiar with the area. And they are not the only ones: Heaton's crowdfunding campaign to raise $250,000 to establish the state stalled at just $10,638, despite an offer to choose for oneself an honorary title. Clearly others are sceptical, a feeling not helped by the fact that several years later, some investors are publicly suggesting that the plans were all a hoax.

As the history of Africa as a whole demonstrates so well, there is a danger in casually applying strict borders – as would presumably be implemented were Bir Tawil ever to become an independent country – in a region that is so poorly understood by those involved in divvying it up. After all, and regardless of how innocuous one's claims are to Bir Tawil, there is a much more serious precedent that cannot be ignored. The long-distance claimants regularly assert that they are anything but colonialists, but clear parallels emerge whenever foreign individuals browse world maps in search of territory they can proclaim as their own, while ignoring the existence and rights of Indigenous populations. (Disney pulled out of turning Heaton's story into a film following a backlash on social media for this reason. Even in nation-building, the internet both giveth and taketh away.) No land is genuinely *terra nullius*,* as the would-be kings argue; we cannot simply assert that there is nothing there. On the ground in Bir Tawil, tensions exist. Armed gangs, gold miners and smugglers

---

* 'Nobody's land'.

cross through the area – raising the question of what constitutes an illegal act in a place with no laws. They have their own routes and they do not take kindly to outsiders visiting their territory, as adventure tourists who have been forced to look down the barrel of an AK-47 can testify. Among the Ababda people, too, I was informed by one such traveller, who has direct experience of liaising with this community, 'The worst-case scenario is Westerners coming there trying to claim their land. They are of the opinion this is their land and they are generally not welcoming of tourists.' Simply put, there are always boundaries, recognised by locals, if not by those looking at a computer screen. So what happens when new arrivals' perceptions are at odds with existing understandings of the land? The following case demonstrates how invisible lines, located abstractly in the imagination, can fuel discord over consequential questions of territory and citizenship.

The Outback

Australia lives with a strange contradiction – our national image of ourselves is one of the Outback, and yet nearly all of us live in big cities. Move outside the coastal fringe, and Australia can feel like a foreign country. I don't think I'm the only Australian who feels vaguely guilty about that, as if we're all going along with a story that isn't quite true.

Kate Grenville

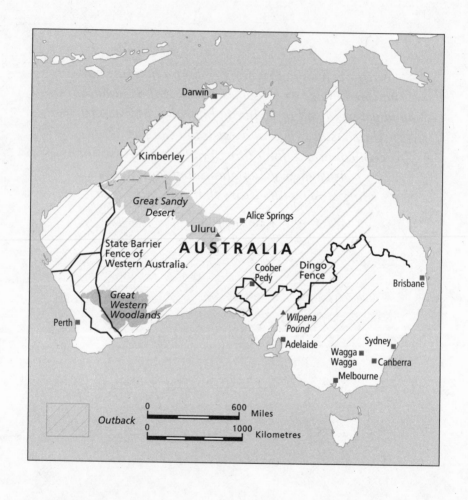

Darwin

Kimberley

Great Sandy
Desert

Uluru

Alice Springs

AUSTRALIA

State Barrier
Fence of
Western Australia.

Coober
Pedy

Dingo
Fence

Brisbane

Great
Western
Woodlands

Perth

Wilpena
Pound

Adelaide

Sydney

Wagga
Wagga

Canberra

Melbourne

Outback

| 0 | | 600 | Miles |

| 0 | | 1000 | Kilometres |

Bring out the A to Z of phobias! Insects, lizards and snakes. Wide open spaces. Temperatures exceeding 40°C. Abundant stories of UFO sightings and alien abductions. It's fair to say that a trip through Australia's Outback is not for the faint-hearted. Nor can one expect an experience quite like it elsewhere on the planet. With just three people per square kilometre, Australia is the world's third least densely populated country (after Mongolia and Namibia), and towards the centre of the country one can travel for hours without seeing as much as a single vehicle. This is a place where home-schooling is often a matter of necessity, rather than preference. Medical services and mail deliveries are regularly provided by air. Most farms – or 'stations', as they are called here – have their own airstrip, and possession of a recreational pilot licence is relatively common. The Eyre Highway, one of the country's longest roads, proceeds towards the horizon without a single bend for nearly 150 kilometres. The red rocks of the Outback's interior present an otherworldly landscape, and observers of the changing colours of Uluru, Australia's iconic, glowing sandstone monolith, often describe it as providing spiritual rejuvenation and a separation from the banality of everyday life. All this considered, it is easy to see why travelling through the Outback is frequently compared to crossing a frontier.

Yet where this frontier is to be found is highly ambiguous. The name 'Outback' appears to have first been used in print in 1869 to describe the lands west of Wagga Wagga, New South Wales's largest inland city and by most countries' standards already very remote.* This would make the vast majority of Australia part of the Outback, based solely on geography. Nonetheless, the numerous definitions of 'Outback' and maps produced over the years to distinguish this area from the rest of the country tend to place the boundary somewhat further to the west, based on a range of more specific criteria.

For instance, according to many, the Outback is defined by its low population density, even by average Australian standards. However, even the more populous eastern coastline, which is seldom considered part of the Outback, has significant stretches with few inhabitants. Nor is distance from the sea an especially effective criterion: Alice Springs, the Northern Territory's third largest settlement, is Australia's most geographically central town, but with 26,500 inhabitants and a population density of approximately eighty people per square kilometre it seems to have less of a claim than the desolate Great Sandy Desert, which stretches to the Indian Ocean. Aridity shows a lot of promise as a criterion and, as with tree lines, there can be a discernible boundary between the country's relatively lush forests, especially in the east, and its drier woodlands, scrublands, shrublands, savannah and other grasslands, all of which tend to fall under the 'Outback' umbrella along with deserts. Nevertheless, the Northern Territory's capital, Darwin, is sometimes defined as an Outback city, despite having a tropical climate (comprising distinct wet and dry seasons) and being surrounded by eucalypt open forest and small patches of rainforest. To many people in Darwin, these facts prohibit it from being part of the Outback at all, whereas others regard it as such because it is so isolated within Australia that it is far nearer to

---

* Various stories exist attempting to refine the history of the term, along with similarly evocative names like 'Never-Never' and 'the Red Centre', which together provide a sense of being in a poorly known and potentially inhospitable back-country.

various major cities in Indonesia than it is to Brisbane, Adelaide or Perth. Complicating the matter further is the sheer scale of the Outback, being over two-thirds the size of the forty-eight contiguous states of the United States put together. Even a relatively small section of it, like the Great Western Woodlands – the world's largest temperate woodland, situated a relatively modest 500 kilometres east of Perth – is bigger than England and Wales combined. Consequently, locating the boundary of the Outback is like finding a needle in a haystack.

As may have already been observed from the above, part of the difficulty pertains to the diverse landscapes that are considered to constitute the Outback, each with their own distinct climates and species. For instance, Wilpena Pound of the dusty, Martian-like Flinders Ranges looks like a cross between a volcanic crater and a giant tree stump, and yet is regarded as 'Outback' in the same way as the Kimberley region, with its deep river gorges, towering waterfalls and white sandy beaches. Perhaps the most effective way of discriminating the Outback is therefore subjectively, as a vast area of 'wilderness', this region being globally recognised as one of the largest 'untouched' places on Earth. It brings together a range of places that share a paucity of human activity, unlike the urban development and intensive agriculture found in the more temperate and fertile regions to the south-east especially. Indeed, despite the presence of a few settlements within the broadly defined Outback that are important mining centres – like the partially underground Coober Pedy – as well as human interference in the form of non-native species, fire and irrigation, the bulk of this vast region is used for livestock grazing at most, the very definition of low-intensity land use.

Thanks in large part to this general remoteness, the Outback is home to a wide variety of endemic animal species across its diverse ecosystems. These include marsupial moles, monjon (a species of rock-wallaby), rough-scaled pythons, Spencer's burrowing frogs, thorny devils and the world's most venomous snake, the inland taipan, as well as the majority of Australia's red kangaroos, emus, Stimson's pythons and large monitor lizards called sand goannas. As an aside, widely abhorred creatures such as spiders and crocodiles tend to be more common *beyond* the Outback. As regards flora, mulga trees and desert oak are reasonably well distributed across areas that are often associated with the Outback, and barely anywhere else. In these ways, one may discern a boundary between the Outback and the rest of Australia based on the species encountered.

There are other dividing lines in Australia that traverse parts of the Outback, too. Perhaps the most noteworthy is the 'Dingo Fence', which was constructed in the 1880s to protect the flocks of sheep in south-eastern Australia from the dingoes to the north and west. At 5,614 kilometres, it is the world's longest fence and is the main reason why dingoes are rare in much of the country's south-east. The second longest fence is also in Australia: the State Barrier Fence of Western Australia. This was built twenty years later to prevent rabbits, emus, foxes and other so-called pests from entering pastoral areas, and has since been supplemented by two additional barriers to animal movement. Rabbits had been introduced in 1788 to provide English settlers with a reminder of their homeland as well as some hunting fun, but even the best marksmen were unable to keep up with these animals' ability to proliferate. Myxomatosis in the 1950s represented a far more effective population check for these animals, although their numbers have partially recovered in the decades since.

An additional semantic challenge pertains to 'the bush', another term that is familiar to Australians in name and yet scarcely defined or definable. Some describe the bush and the Outback interchangeably, whereas others view them as separate but poorly specified regions. The bush, for instance, is sometimes used to refer to a wooded or shrubby rather than forested area, where the soil is of relatively but not prohibitively poor quality and accordingly the population is rather small, while the Outback is even more remote. Today, both terms are regularly used quite nostalgically to describe the abandonment of contemporary conventions and the search to (re)connect with nature. There may be dangers involved in travelling so far from 'the big smoke' – the city – but the experience, according to the cultural narrative, promises to be exciting, energising and uplifting. In these ways, the Outback and the bush are not merely or even primarily geographical place names: they are emotionally charged *concepts*.

This can be seen best in how the Outback is often said to be both unknown and, ironically, familiar. As a concept, the Outback is instantly recognisable in its obscurity. People across the world have some notion of it, enabled in part by films like *Crocodile Dundee*, *Mad Max* and *The Adventures of Priscilla, Queen of the Desert*, which consistently portray tropes such as endless roads crossing endless desert, deadly animals in unnamed places, and rugged, forthright residents, many of whom are on the move. Furthermore, despite being home to just 4–5 per cent of the country's population (depending on how the region is defined), and so a marginal place by most measures, it is widely perceived as fundamental to Australian national identity.

Clearly, then, there are certain paradoxes at play. Historically, the principle of *terra nullius* was used by settlers to legitimise the seizing of Indigenous lands across Australia. Inspired by tales of courage and conviction, the Outback came to be regarded as a hostile place that only the boldest men – for this tended to be a masculine exercise – dared confront. By overcoming its varied challenges and in the process naming its places with more innuendoes than the randiest adolescent,* white males were regarded as the conquerors of the Outback. Eventually, the Outback's natural

---

* One enterprising company has even produced a map of crude Australian place names, including Bumbang Island, Spanker Knob and Mount Buggery. As an innocent soul, I nevertheless prefer the candid Useless Loop, Mount Mistake and Nowhere Else.

beauty, combined with its remoteness, saw it reimagined as a land that could be enjoyed even by those living in urban and suburban communities elsewhere in the country, albeit temporarily. Few people actually wanted to live in the Outback, but they could still claim these lands beyond the frontier as part of their birthright as Australians. Moreover, the Outback came to represent the combination of resilience, practicality and lack of pretension that continue to be seen as stereotypically 'Australian' traits, with the images of the stockman (the Australian equivalent of the American cowboy) and the unkempt bushman as their quintessence, harkening back to a simpler time and personifying Australians' deep-rooted pioneering spirit. The country's 'unofficial national anthem', 'Waltzing Matilda', encapsulates the significance of the bushman as a refreshingly uncomplicated, independent and thus profoundly *Australian* character, an itinerant worker who carries his backpack or sleeping bag (his 'Matilda') from job to job. By contrast, despite living here for over 50,000 years, Australia's Indigenous communities have long been exoticised and disparaged and their claims to the land regularly ignored. They have accordingly struggled to enjoy the same status as citizens as those with much shorter connections to the country, and who often retain more than just an emotional bond to a second 'home' elsewhere in the world.

In the past three decades, this debate has come to a head. Most notably, since the High Court's ruling in the *Mabo v. Queensland* case of 1992, which specifically pertained to Mer Island between Australia and Papua New Guinea, Indigenous Australians have progressively won greater recognition of their land rights. In the broadly defined Outback, they have achieved particular successes, such as exclusive possession native title in much of Western Australia, which allows these groups to possess and occupy an area to the exclusion of others, as long as they can prove that they have a continuous connection to it. Admittedly, many of these areas are less coveted by other citizens and so there has tended to be less displacement of Indigenous people than in (generally coastal) locations earmarked for intensive agriculture and urban development. But when one considers the ugly history of colonisation on these lands, with violence and disease (most notably smallpox) threatening to extinguish these populations for ever, such advances are noteworthy. Today, Indigenous groups represent at least 25 per cent of the total population of what one might consider the Outback, whereas their populations are *relatively* smaller (although their absolute numbers are greater) and their rights far fewer elsewhere. Here is thus another distinction between the Outback and the rest of the country.

A relevant dispute pertains to Uluru, which has long been marketed as an Australian icon under the English name Ayers Rock, but has deeper significance to the local Anangu people. This community regards it as sacred and disapproves of those who come from outside the Outback to climb it, an act akin to climbing over a church or mosque. (More scandalous episodes have seen the rock formation treated as a film set, a strip venue, a golf course and a toilet.) On 25 October 2019, ascending Uluru was permitted for the final time, the impending ban stimulating a mass influx of Australians seeking to complete what had become regarded as something of an Australian rite of passage, a means of 'proving' one's national identity. Now that scaling Uluru is forbidden, it is possible that new ways of engaging with the Outback will be sought by those who choose not to live in it but deem it central to a feeling of being Australian. So far, many Australians have been thoroughly supportive of the ban and are seeking to become more educated about Indigenous rights and culture. For their part, Anangu, I was informed, are delighted to offer a range of 'respectful activities' such as guided walks, talks and presentations to their 'visitors' or 'guests', these choices of terms providing a gentle reminder that ultimately, this land is 'their home, their identity and their responsibility to care for'. Accordingly, some hope the national park in which Uluru stands will eventually be managed solely by Anangu, rather than jointly with the Australian government, as has been the case since 1985. Until that time comes, though, there remains the risk of disagreement between members of the country's Indigenous and majority populations concerning the use of this land, and by extension who really 'owns' Australia more notionally.

For these reasons, the fact that the precise boundary of the Outback is ambiguous is somewhat immaterial. More salient is that such a boundary is perceived at all, enabling those who enjoy greater privilege by virtue of their unquestioned citizenship and their settlement of lands on the 'civilised' side to define 'Australian-ness' on their own terms. Hence, depending on the situation, the Outback can be viewed as either central to one's national identity (because it both exists within Australian territory and is supposedly uncorrupted by external influence), or as wild lands beyond a frontier (thereby implicitly denying or diminishing Indigenous communities' claims to 'modern' Australian identity and territory). Over time, the repeated invocation of a boundary, however spurious, can enable one to emerge, wrapped up in contested discourses of belonging and ownership. The boundary may not be exactly mappable or appear physically in the form of a fence or sign, yet its presence – *somewhere* – is largely unquestioned.

Interestingly, population shifts from the Outback to the south-east in particular over the past few decades have left behind dwindling numbers of people to oversee the former. There is today concern that environments that have for millennia been subtly managed by Indigenous communities will be disrupted by the departure of their guardians. In response, rather than viewing the Outback as somewhere untouched, greater attention is now being paid to actively – discreetly, but still actively – conserving its fragile ecosystems, such as by seeking to control its wildfires, feral animals and noxious weeds, drawing on both modern and traditional expertise. Instead of perceiving the region quite simplistically as a place where enterprising minds can profit from its pastures, mineral reserves and tourism potential, consideration is being given to its distinctive needs and how best it can be safeguarded in the face of a changing climate. The Outback's boundaries may be difficult to define, but the region continues to be of great interest and importance to many, and there is considerable determination to ensure that it remains something of a wilderness. By contrast, there are parts of the world where invisible lines operate not as shifting boundaries across which a potential threat exists to distinctive places and their inhabitants' rights and dignity, but as more fixed frontiers marking out a palpable hazard to human life. Next follows a cautionary tale of how severely we can scar our surroundings for generations.

Landmines and the Inter-Entity Boundary Line

---

*The political union of the Yugoslavs
was always before my eyes.*

Gavrilo Princip

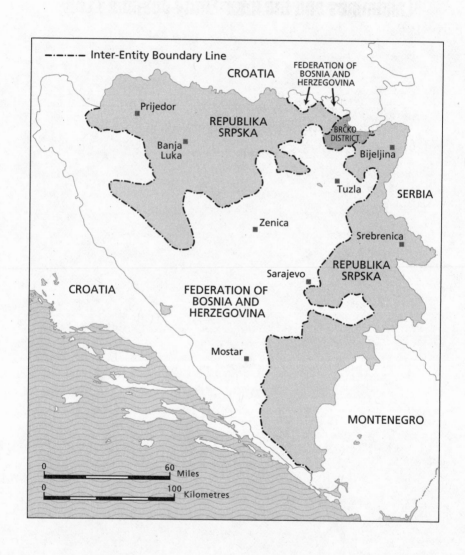

Inter-Entity Boundary Line

CROATIA

FEDERATION OF BOSNIA AND HERZEGOVINA

Prijedor

REPUBLIKA SRPSKA

Banja Luka

BRČKO DISTRICT

Bijeljina

Tuzla

SERBIA

Zenica

Srebrenica

Sarajevo

REPUBLIKA SRPSKA

CROATIA

FEDERATION OF BOSNIA AND HERZEGOVINA

Mostar

MONTENEGRO

0   60 Miles

0   100 Kilometres

At the corner of the Appel Quay and the Latin Bridge,* there is both a museum and a plaque marking the spot where one of history's most famous misfits took aim, not knowing precisely how his actions would catalyse the twentieth century. After hitting his primary target – Archduke Franz Ferdinand of Austria – and by accident the archduke's wife, Sophie of Hohenberg, Gavrilo Princip swallowed a cyanide capsule, believing his job to be done. Unfortunately for him, the poison had oxidised, leaving him fully conscious during the pummelling he subsequently received. Too young to receive the death penalty by a matter of weeks, Princip spent the rest his life in prison at Terezín, a place that would later assume notoriety as the Nazi concentration camp of Theresienstadt. Today, Princip's legacy is highly disputed: he is viewed by many Serbs as a national hero who challenged the despised Austro-Hungarian imperial authorities, but elsewhere as a terrorist whose actions helped plunge Europe into the First World War. As a Bosnian Serb, Princip's identity encapsulates the challenges in discriminating social boundaries in this famously intricate part of the world, and through his actions at this street corner he brought himself and his country international attention. Bosnia and Herzegovina, or BiH, has hardly become any less newsworthy since.

In fact, BiH has stood prominently at a crossroads for far longer than just one century. For over 400 years it was one of the

---

*Today Obala Kulina bana and Latinska ćuprija, respectively.

Ottoman Empire's most important territories in Europe, and the country still generally enjoys warm relations with Turkey thanks to their strong historic and cultural ties. In cities such as the capital, Sarajevo, it is not unusual to find medieval mosques just metres from churches of various denominations, and the continued commingling of the Islamic call to prayer and church bells makes palpable this country's complex history of coexistence and competition. However, while its central location within the Balkans has enabled BiH to adopt many of the best aspects of Europe and Asia, not least in its cuisine, it has also rendered it vulnerable to assault. The goal of expelling external powers and thereby enabling the unification of BiH and Serbia was a major reason why Princip and his fellow Serb conspirators of the Black Hand secret society – whose official name *Ujedinjenje ili smrt* translated more menacingly to 'Unification or Death' – felt driven to assassinate Franz Ferdinand. Their larger objective was realised following the First World War, but long-standing grievances and tensions between communities in this conspicuously diverse region would not be muted for long. During the brutal wars that saw the disintegration of the Yugoslav federation in the 1990s, it was almost inevitable that BiH, with its heterogeneous population and its geographic positioning between the main warring parties of Croatia and Serbia, would become the battleground for most of the worst nationalist and ethnoreligious violence. Crucially, the lines that were drawn here at this time have not so much disappeared, as evolved.

During these wars, Croatian Catholic and Serbian Orthodox communities were targeted both in BiH and in more mixed areas over the borders, by the Army of Republika Srpska (the Bosnian Serb Army or VRS) and Serb paramilitaries on the one hand, and the Croatian Defence Council (HVO) on the other. However, no group was victimised as much as Bosnia's Muslim ('Bosniak') population, as the Bosnian Serb forces in particular sought to extinguish this long-established community in order to 'ethnically cleanse' the territory and bring it under the control of a 'Greater', homogeneously Orthodox Serbia. Concentration camps provided an uncomfortable reminder that the persecution of minorities had not ended in Europe half a century earlier, while torture, gang rape and sexual enslavement all became commonplace. Massacres of Bosniaks, including at the United Nations 'safe area' of Srebrenica, live on in infamy.

The Bosnian War (1992–5) had numerous consequences, including casualties potentially exceeding 100,000, permanent disabilities, trauma, material and economic damage, and the displacement of almost half of BiH's population either internally or internationally. Several of the protagonists, including the Bosnian Serb leaders Radovan Karadžić and Ratko Mladić, have been convicted of war crimes, genocide and other offences; others, like the current president of the far-right Serbian Radical Party, Vojislav Šešelj, have been acquitted, to no little controversy.* One of the most important legacies of the conflict appears in the form of lines, or, to be more specific, two types of lines that, for good reason, closely follow one another. These are the remaining lines of landmines from the war, which nearly thirty years later still pose grave danger to many inhabitants, and the Inter-Entity Boundary Line (IEBL), drawn to subdivide BiH into two administrative parts.

The latter may sound relatively inconsequential, but it plays an important role in distinguishing BiH between the generally Serb-populated Republika Srpska (RS) and the largely Bosniak and Croatian Federation of Bosnia and Herzegovina (FBiH), a condition of the Dayton Accords of 1995, the peace agreement that ended the Bosnian part of the Yugoslav wars. Thus, BiH mostly operates as two separate, autonomous entities – or rather

---

*By contrast, in 2006, the Serbian President Slobodan Milošević died of a heart attack while in prison, just weeks before the scheduled conclusion of his trial.

three, when one also considers the small, multi-ethnic and fiercely contested Brčko District in the north-east of the country, which is officially shared by the FBiH and RS but operates as a self-governing unit and effectively splits RS into two. Further complicating matters is the fact that at any one time, BiH has *three* presidents, one of whom must be Serb, one Bosniak and one Croat. The former is elected in RS, whereas the latter two are elected by their respective communities in the FBiH. All three rotate the position of chairperson every eight months, in the order Bosniak → Serb → Croat. And of course, they can only claim one of these three identities, regardless of their family history. A person who identifies differently – Jewish or Roma, for instance – is instantly ineligible.* Moreover, a Serb living in the FBiH, or a Bosniak or Croat living in RS, enjoys no political representation among their own group. Thus, although the Dayton Accords managed to put an end to the intentional bloodshed, they crystallised the country's ethno-religious divisions in its political system.

Sparing a thought at this point for all those schoolchildren in BiH wrestling with what must be the most convoluted political system in the world – and I have not even mentioned the roles of the Parliamentary Assembly and the cantons in the FBiH – the IEBL today acts like a county or state boundary between RS and the FBiH. There are no military or police checkpoints, for example. Instead, the line on the ground is merely marked by road signs at the appropriate points. However, it is a different line that has remained the greatest subject of concern both domestically and internationally. This is because the IEBL was drawn along the front lines at the end of the Bosnian War (with some slight

---

* Members of these communities, supported by the international non-governmental organisation Human Rights Watch, have long highlighted their effective exclusion from the country's politics, yet despite several favourable rulings by the European Court of Human Rights since 2009, to date, ethnic discrimination remains entrenched in BiH's constitution.

adjustments, especially around Sarajevo), where the warring parties had planted more than 2 million landmines and other explosives, not only to mark what they viewed as their territories, but more importantly to physically keep others away. During the peace process, a 2-kilometre 'Zone of Separation' was created on either side of the IEBL to demarcate the ceasefire area and, by extension, the rough area containing the majority of minefields. The issue today is that even though the hostilities are now in the past, the landmines are not aware of this fact. Since the end of the war, more than 600 people have been killed and over a thousand more injured by landmines, especially PROM-1 anti-personnel bounding fragmentation mines, which are designed to spray projectiles in open areas. Approximately 15 per cent of post-war landmine casualties have been children.

Since 1996, the United Nations Mine Action Centre (UNMAC), later the Bosnia Herzegovina Mine Action Centre (BHMAC), alongside a range of government agencies, non-governmental organisations, military contingents, commercial companies and other domestic and international actors, has worked hard to identify and clear the landmines. This is an unenviable task, usually a manual process requiring the safe inspection, collection, detonation and subsequent verification of live explosives, often on steep, rocky mountainsides or in thick vegetation, where venomous snakes pose an additional hazard, while carrying heavy equipment in potentially sweltering conditions. Adding to the challenge, many mines are made primarily of plastic and so cannot be recognised by metal detectors. Heartbreakingly, many de-miners have lost their lives through their necessary and principled work. A further predicament is the fact that the precise locations of the landmines are often uncertain. Indeed, although minefields were mapped fairly meticulously at first, towards the end of the conflict their planters' record-keeping became more haphazard. In many cases, the details of their geography were lost or destroyed. Nevertheless, the IEBL has provided a useful starting point, the vast majority of landmines being concentrated along or near to this line. New technologies, such as drones with remote sensing capacities and mobile phone apps that allow for information to be crowdsourced, have helped to identify dangerous areas, improve the mapping of landmines using geographic information systems (GIS) and reduce landmine-related accidents.

The severe flooding and associated landslides that afflicted much of the country in May 2014 have exacerbated the challenge of identifying and clearing the remaining landmines, as many were moved closer to residential areas, in some cases over 20 kilometres away from their original position. Constrained by this event as well as funding shortages, an ambitious target set in 2008 to clear all the country's landmines by 2019 was not met and has since been extended to 2027. Recent estimates suggest that there may still be 180,000 mines scattered across the country, contaminating as much as 2 per cent of the country's total area and threatening over 15 per cent of the population, especially in rural parts of north-eastern FBiH. And it is not even as if the Bosnian War was the only conflict to present challenges: on occasion, unexploded munitions from World War Two are uncovered as well. Even though great progress has been made since the 1990s, with an estimated three-quarters of once-contaminated territory now deemed safe, BiH remains one of the most severely mine-affected countries in the world.*

The remaining landmines mark one of the world's most meaningful urban–rural divides. Thanks to concerted de-mining efforts around urban areas, these tend to be the safest places, with the

---

* At least sixty countries across the world still hold landmine-contaminated territories, including China and Russia, both of which are, like the United States, permanent members of the United Nations Security Council but *not* signatories to the 1997 Ottawa Treaty for the prohibition and elimination of anti-personnel landmines. With a scarcely conceivable 23 million, around a fifth of the global total, another non-signatory – Egypt – is today contaminated by more landmines than any other country, particularly near its borders with Libya and Israel.

Sarajevo metropolitan area declared landmine-free by the humanitarian, non-profit organisation ITF Enhancing Human Security in May 2021. But not far into the surrounding countryside, significant danger can persist. Forested areas may be particularly perilous, as landmines here are both difficult to see (especially as most of them are green) and prone to being triggered or moved by erosion, temporary streams, animals and previous explosions. Agricultural areas, too, can prove hazardous, especially where mines were placed randomly rather than in clusters, and many farmers – representing the largest proportion of victims since the war – remain reluctant to tread beyond the fields they know best, surrendering what may actually be safe, productive land. Some rural areas that were once known intimately by older generations have now been abandoned for nearly thirty years.

Education has helped build landmine awareness: the United Nations and the Red Cross are among the organisations to lead various programmes for different age groups, especially on International Mine Awareness Day (4 April). In 1996, DC Comics even collaborated with the United States government and United Nations International Children's Emergency Fund (UNICEF) to create a free *Superman* comic book dedicated to promoting landmine awareness among children in the former Yugoslavia, while new playgrounds have been developed to direct children away from mine-contaminated areas. Both fatalities and injuries have shown a clear declining trend over time, but a new fight is now being waged against complacency, as some people have started to explore dangerous areas for a hike or to forage, on the assumption that they have been entirely de-mined. A related challenge pertains to whether minefields should be marked. Many are now explicitly labelled with fences (often made of barbed wire) and signs, of great value during the Pokémon Go craze of 2016, when some players followed their phones into hazardous areas in hopes of 'catching' a rare creature. However, some argue that promptly de-mining rather than first designating these areas is preferable, especially given the risk that people will assume that any *un*marked zones are safe. Evidently, demarcating landmine boundaries is not infallible, and errors or oversights can have fatal consequences. Keeping to known and official trails and roads is essential to staying on the right side of an invisible line dividing safety from catastrophe.

The continued existence of landmines has also stunted BiH's development. The repair of much of the country's war-damaged infrastructure has had to wait until local de-mining has been completed, and with money often short, many buildings even in urban areas still show battle scars such as bullet holes. Health facilities continue to be strained and disability payments for victims may prove limited. In contrast to neighbouring Croatia, which is also in the process of de-mining and where more than 200 people have lost their lives to these devices since the end of the war, BiH remains severely stigmatised by these explosives, limiting the considerable tourism potential offered by its rugged Dinaric Alps, Ottoman-era villages and the rare primeval forest of Perućica. The optimism of the 1984 Winter Olympics feels distant today.

The case of BiH demonstrates the extent to which boundaries can alter lives. More than being mere administrative lines, boundaries can quite literally mark the difference between life and death. In this instance, they are also expensive, constraining a country's economy through harming formerly productive workers, reducing the utility of the land, deterring investment, complicating transportation and directing money away from other domains. As a consequence, such invisible lines need to be mapped with appreciable precision. But whereas landmines are physical objects that can conceivably be located with a certain degree of precision, there are other types of boundaries of a more perceptual sort, whose geography is inevitably subjective and often highly contested. Invisible lines do not have to rely on entities as hazardous as landmines in order to be discerned: in many cases, these divisions are produced and reproduced through the use of colour, sound and performance.

Football in Buenos Aires

I'm from the craziest gang of all,
Which conquered four blocks walking through La Boca,
To run off River you need to show more balls,
*Balls that the Rojo and the Bosteros don't have.**

River Plate supporters' chant

---

* Yo paro en una banda que es la más loca de todas,
La que copó cuatro cuadras caminando por La Boca,
Para correr a River hay que poner más huevo,
Huevo los que no tiene el Rojo tampoco los Bosteros.
(Note that *el Rojo* refers to Independiente, *Bosteros* to Boca Juniors.)

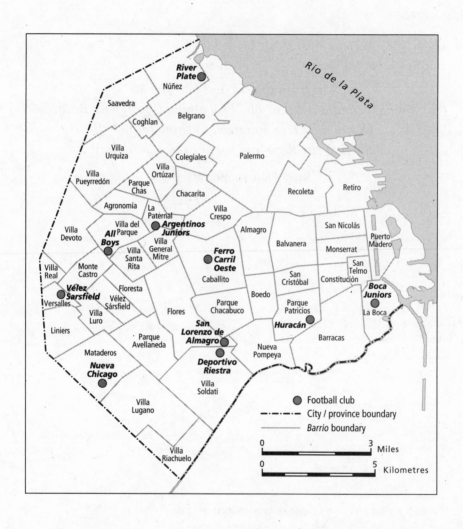

River Plate
Núñez

Saavedra

Coghlan

Belgrano

Río de la Plata

Villa
Urquiza

Colegiales

Palermo

Villa
Pueyrredón

Villa
Ortúzar

Parque
Chas

Chacarita

Recoleta

Retiro

Agronomía

La
Paternal

Villa
Crespo

Villa Devoto

Villa del
Parque

Argentinos
Juniors

Almagro

San Nicolás

Puerto
Madero

All
Boys

Villa
General
Mitre

Villa
Santa
Rita

Balvanera

Monserrat

Villa
Real

Monte
Castro

Ferro
Carril
Oeste

San
Telmo

San
Cristóbal

Constitución

Boca
Juniors

Villa
Versalles

Vélez
Sarsfield

Floresta

Caballito

La Boca

Vélez
Sársfield

Flores

Parque
Chacabuco

Boedo

Parque
Patricios

Liniers

Villa
Luro

Huracán

Mataderos

Parque
Avellaneda

San
Lorenzo de
Almagro

Barracas

Nueva
Chicago

Deportivo
Riestra

Nueva
Pompeya

Villa
Soldati

Villa
Lugano

● Football club
─·─·─ City / province boundary
───── *Barrio* boundary

0 ———— 3 Miles
0 ———— 5 Kilometres

Villa
Riachuelo

Growing up in the United Kingdom, football was a prevalent force, whether in the media or in the playground. However, I never saw quite how territorial it could be (the feeling that every other person in south-eastern England supports Manchester United may have been a factor in this regard) until I visited Belgrade on a field trip during my twenties. I was staying in the district of Dorćol, not far from the old city, and was immediately struck by how many murals had been created honouring Partizan Belgrade, one of the city's two biggest clubs. Some portrayed club legends, but others depicted a variety of more internationally popular figures who in some way are regarded as sharing the team's values, including musicians, authors and actors, generally in Partizan's iconic black and white. As someone who wears a lot of black, I felt quite at home, but I was spurred to wonder if I would feel as comfortable wearing red, the colour of Partizan's fierce rivals, Red Star Belgrade. Matches between the two – the 'Eternal Derby' – frequently descend into violence, and I must admit that this aspect of the city filled me with some trepidation, even if the clubs were not playing each other that week. Different parts of the city include scrawls of graffiti admiring the two teams, reflecting the respective geographies of their fan bases, but also implying how a person should engage there: whether they can be open in expressing a preference, or are advised to conceal it.

Belgrade is not unusual in hosting at least two football clubs that hate each other's guts: São Paulo, Rio de Janeiro,

Montevideo, Glasgow, Milan, Athens, Istanbul and Cairo are just a few of the cities that claim to have the world's biggest derby. In my opinion, however, it is Buenos Aires. Like the protagonists in each of these matches, Buenos Aires' clubs represent different sections of society – whether in terms of religion, class, ethnicity or politics – grounded in specific neighbourhoods, which fans devotedly assert as their own. But Buenos Aires is no typical football city. For a start, it has twenty-four professional football teams; by comparison, London has sixteen, Rio de Janeiro nine and São Paulo seven. As a result, there are derbies across the city. Yet sheer numbers alone are not enough to distinguish Buenos Aires. Football seeps into the city's politics and social relations to an extent that is likely without parallel anywhere else on the planet. Supporters are quite regularly killed on account of their fandom: the period from March 2008 to December 2018 saw 103 football-related deaths in Argentina, the vast majority in Buenos Aires province. Meanwhile, the government and the police often look the other way. The quasi-religious intensity of football in Buenos Aires, combined with fans' fierce and widely legitimised defence of 'their' *barrios* (neighbourhoods), is where the city really stands out.

Certainly, perhaps more than anywhere else in the world, Buenos Aires' football clubs are profoundly associated with specific neighbourhoods, to the extent that sporting the 'wrong' team's shirt can arouse far more than the heckling heard elsewhere. Lines – invisible, yet perceptible – have been drawn to delimit supporters' ownership over particular territories within the city. Crossing them can require a willingness to 'pass' as a member of that *barrio*'s club. Tourists to Buenos Aires often put a visit to the stadium of one of the biggest clubs, Boca Juniors or River Plate, towards the top of their bucket lists, but they are warned against wearing the rival team's colours while in its vicinity: blue and yellow for Boca, red and white for River. As evidence of how strongly particular colours are associated with particular clubs, Boca managed to convince Coca-Cola, perhaps the most recognisable brand in the world, to advertise in black and white around their stadium, Estadio Alberto J. Armando (more commonly known as La Bombonera), for the simple reason that the corporation's usual hues, however internationally recognisable, would be perceived by fans as those of River. Murals and graffiti in the clubs' respective neighbourhoods reinforce supporters' claims to these areas, generally utilising the team's colours, along with images of popular players and the lyrics of fans' chants.

This tying of football clubs to *barrios* is no accident: it is the result of over 100 years of Argentina's unique social and political dynamics. Enabled by liberal immigration laws designed to build a strong agricultural and industrial labour force, around the turn of the twentieth century Argentina became home to one of the most significant immigrant populations in the world. By 1914, 30 per cent of the country's population was foreign-born, over double the corresponding proportion in the United States. Fifty-eight per cent of people were either immigrants or the children of immigrants. And in Buenos Aires specifically, as much as 70 per cent of the city's population was foreign-born. In this fluid context, football clubs and other civic organisations were often perceived quite politically, as effective means of building a sense of citizenship and local *barrio* identity among the country's immigrants, most of whom were arriving from Italy and Spain. With the electoral system undergoing major reforms in 1912, political candidates saw the potential to build strong blocks of voters through identifying themselves with or lending support to these organisations. This was an astute decision: clubs typically attracted young males, who were the biggest vote-holding demographic in the city at this time due to immigration being far greater among men than women, and in any case women's suffrage was not achieved here until 1947. Moreover, *socios* (members) were already familiar with the democratic power they enjoyed through electing their clubs' officials. Political candidates thus aimed to appeal to this population in a number of ways, not least by finding them places where they could play.

It is worth mentioning that these clubs did not just provide football: many offered opportunities to dance, box, swim or play basketball, bocce, field hockey or tennis. Some offered non-sporting pursuits, too, including cookery classes, films and even legal consultations. Tangos were created to honour clubs' successes and to emphasise their relationships with their *barrio*. In short, football clubs became communities in about every sense of the word, albeit ones in which football remained paramount, with politics perhaps second. Clear winners and losers emerged: the majority of clubs eventually folded as they struggled to compete with those that could afford to purchase higher quality amateur players and build better grounds. If they did not yet have the support of a budding political figure or businessperson, they almost certainly would soon, as they were increasingly deemed sure-fire means of attaining contacts and influence. By the 1920s, most *socios* attended clubs to spectate rather than play, with the largest clubs raising considerable funds through their gate receipts. The contemporary football landscape of Buenos Aires, with Boca Juniors, River Plate, San Lorenzo, Racing Club and Independiente as its biggest clubs, emerged within a decade.*

A sense of *barrio* identity became particularly important as the city continued to grow: its population practically doubled from 1.5 million around 1910 to almost 3 million in 1930, a third of whom were European immigrants. Public transportation enabled the city to sprawl, with residents seeking community and identity in their *barrios*. Over time, most of Buenos Aires' clubs have either moved to or been developed beyond the city's core, in large part because of difficulties in finding sufficient space in central locations. Even Boca Juniors, which have since their establishment in 1905 been

---

*Today, the latter two are both based in Avellaneda, the city to the immediate south-east of Buenos Aires, albeit still part of Buenos Aires province.

associated with La Boca, a working-class area by the city's docks, briefly played in the suburbs between 1912 and 1914, but moved back after most of their members quit, being either unwilling or unable to commute. In contrast to many of its predecessors, which often had British roots, the club was founded by members of the neighbourhood's Italian community, the majority of whom had arrived from Genoa; the team's fans still call themselves *Xeneize* (Genovese) in tribute to them. Enabled by this rooting in La Boca (even as their support base continues to expand internationally as well as nationally) and the club's maintenance of a working-class identity, Boca's supporters like to portray themselves as the team of 'the people'.

River Plate, with whom Boca contest the city's biggest derby, the *Superclásico*, present a different dynamic, having also been founded in La Boca in 1901 through a merger between the existing clubs La Rosales and Santa Rosa, but moving to the wealthier north in the 1920s, after bouncing around in search of a permanent home. Since 1938, the club has been based on the border between the leafy, residential *barrios* of Belgrano and Núñez, although it has held onto its name, derived from the English for *Río de la Plata*, which was often seen stamped on imported crates in La Boca.* Otherwise, River's fans have more or less entirely relinquished their club's modest roots, today regarding themselves as the club of the upwardly mobile, even if in reality they represent a much wider demographic. To this end, they nickname their club *los Millonarios* ('the Millionaires') for its history of paying

---

* Why not translate the name into Spanish, though? The director who suggested it simply liked how the English looked and sounded, and managed to convince enough of the rest of the board to agree. Various other clubs in Argentina have English names, too, often as a symbolic nod to the sport's place of origin. And by the way, if River's story seems like a rather banal way of naming a football club, consider that Boca Juniors chose to wear blue and yellow because of a proposal to mimic the colours of the first ship to pass by. It was Swedish.

premium prices for coveted players, and still often taunt their Boca counterparts as *chanchitos* ('little pigs') and *bosteros* ('manure collectors') because they deem La Boca dirty and smelly. In one game in 2012, River fans even flew an inflatable pig wearing Boca's colours over their rival's section of the stadium. In response, River are often called *gallinas* ('chickens'), on account of their collapse against the Uruguayan team Peñarol in the final of the most prestigious club tournament in South American club football, the Copa Libertadores, in 1966. Having raced into a seemingly comfortable lead, River capitulated, to the particular amusement of fans of their next opponent, Banfield, who immortalised the club's new, purported reputation for cowardice by chucking dead chickens onto the pitch. Given their class-based roots, stylistically the two teams tend to differ as well, with Boca fans expecting their players to be tenacious and industrious, whereas River supporters prioritise skill and seek to be entertained. Matches between the clubs are prone to descending into mass brawls, even during the ironically named 'friendlies'.

But it is off the pitch where much of the action occurs in Buenos Aires. Nowhere is this more evident than in each club's *barras bravas* – hardcore fans with a proclivity for violence – who practise a number of choreographed rituals to welcome and support their team, while intimidating others. Giant flags and banners, smoke bombs, firecrackers and chants, regularly to the tune of popular and folk songs and accompanied by brass bands and drums, all provide an atmosphere that is evocative and intense. Fights with rival fans are not uncommon and regularly spill over into the surrounding *barrio*. Police officers looking to suppress them are additional targets for representing a different kind of 'enemy'. Within the *barras bravas* there are also often factions, which compete for power and space. They are highly organised, sometimes to the point of military precision, and regularly wield guns and knives in their confrontations with others.

How has this situation been allowed to occur? Violence is

anything but a new phenomenon at Argentine football games. At the turn of the twentieth century, pitch invasions, vandalism and gunshots were fairly commonplace, to the extent that in 1924 barbed-wire fences were erected around pitches. However, the violence became far more organised from the 1950s, not coincidentally at a time when some of the most prominent political figures in the country controlled several of the major clubs and sought to increase their authority further. Many incumbent or nominee club presidents started to incentivise the *barras bravas* for their presence and incitement at political events as well as matches. Even today these groups are often rewarded either directly in the form of payment (sometimes a percentage of the transfer fee when a player is sold) or indirectly through a blind eye being turned to their involvement in illegal activities such as reselling tickets and merchandise, monopolising the sale of parking spaces and, most seriously, trading drugs. Violence and intimidation have become a lucrative business, and for many members their only income.

As one might expect, then, the lyrics of each club's chants are often highly political. Supporters regularly assert their preferred candidates for office with equal gusto to vivid narrations of their virility – football here remaining male-dominated and central to *machismo* – and drug and alcohol abuse, standard ways of coping with their team's failures and affirming their unconditional loyalty. Other lyrics describe a desire to kill or violate one's rivals, or at least to disparage their claims to the city and country: describing the opposition as foreigners in order to repudiate their status as Argentines is particularly common.

What makes this issue even more interesting is the fact that many *barras bravas* have become cleaved from the *barrios* that they claim to represent as extensions of their clubs. Indeed, many members of *barras bravas* live far beyond their club's neighbourhood and only visit it on match days. For instance, Boca Juniors' *barra brava*, known as La Doce ('the twelfth man'), primarily draws on individuals not from La Boca or even the surrounding area, but from distant *barrios* and suburbs. More importantly, whereas Boca Juniors invest in the local *barrio* and employ many of its inhabitants, La Doce are seen as a key factor behind La Boca's continued stigmatisation as an impoverished, crime-ridden neighbourhood with a large immigrant population, a representation that its residents strongly refute. Consequently, La Boca's residents often now regard La Doce as external mercenaries or mafiosi who solely seek financial gain through 'their' club, rather than being genuine fans. Even more intriguingly, rival *barras bravas* tend to view La Doce as archetypes of La Boca and thus as exactly what the *barrio*'s residents seek to deny.

A consequence is that the geography of the city follows a patchwork of football clubs, each representing not only a particular *barrio*, but also a political and social position. Unofficial boundaries exist within the city defining which club – and in many cases which politician – is the local preference. Wearing the opposition's colours in a rival *barrio* may garner unwanted attention and in some cases has seen innocent people attacked and even killed. Yet to many fans, this is an honourable practice to be admired. It is a way of standing before 'the enemy' in their own neighbourhood, a demonstration of what is locally called *aguante*, comprising endurance, tenacity and a willingness to use force to defend a club's reputation. It is central to a form of belligerent masculinity and is thus deemed not just admissible but desirable. Trophy-seeking forms an important aspect of this type of engagement with urban space, as fans often search for, steal and flaunt their rivals' flags, shirts, drums and banners in the manner of warfare. After all, such items represent a club and its very reputation, so taking them provides symbolic evidence of one's conquest of a rival *barrio* and by extension one's own power. As a result, fans regularly protect them even more zealously than their bodies, increasing the potential for violence. Murders over football paraphernalia are not unknown.

Buenos Aires, which is often compared to Paris for its beauty and culture, thus holds a sinister underbelly through its rich foot-balling history. Football provides the most significant boundary lines in the city. Boundaries are drawn and reinforced through per-formative practices, communicating to others who really 'owns' a particular area, thereby making what are often mere administra-tive lines at best feel visceral and intense. Consequently, visitors are compelled to make a decision about how to behave, depending on whether their aim is to conform or to contest. More than being 'just' districts, football clubs' *barrios* can serve as self-policed enclaves whose boundaries need constantly to be strengthened in order for them to survive. Such boundaries may be drawn or legitimised by figures of authority, but they are realised from the bottom up.

Through their use of identifying markers and fervour in dese-crating their rivals' *barrios*, *barras bravas* have much in common with gangs. However, gangs have many of their own means of engaging with urban space and claiming territory for themselves. Their boundary-drawing practices provide the focus of the next chapter.

Street Gangs in Los Angeles

When you in the hood, joining a gang it's cool because all your friends are in the gang . . . It's more a family than anything, and it's easier to become family than it is to get a job.

Snoop Dogg

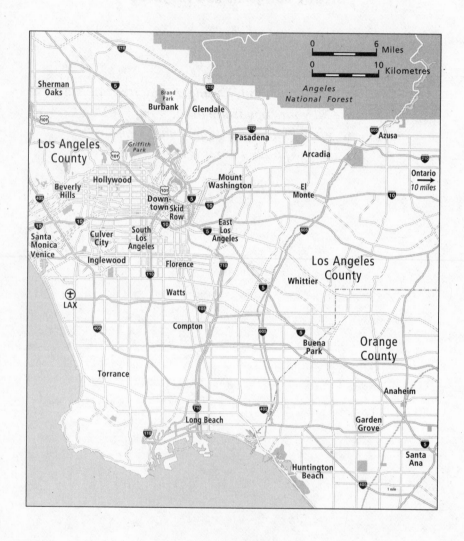

Although 'Muck City' (Belle Glade, Florida) and 'Port of Missing Men' (Aberdeen, Washington) give it a run for its money, 'the Gang Capital of America' may be the most inauspicious city nickname in the United States. Los Angeles, a city that brings up associations with Hollywood and food, sandy beaches and a balmy climate, is also notorious for its sinister underbelly, a complex and shifting terrain of alliances and rifts, racism and violence, widely romanticised in music, video games, TV and more: today one can even participate in a 'gang tour' to explore what are often little-known parts of this sprawling metropolis. And yet many gangs operate right under the noses of the city's tourists. Parts of the city that in the daytime are regarded as leisurely *neighbourhoods*, with popular cupcake bakeries, pricy boutiques and hip coffee shops, at night become menacing *hoods*. Other districts are less fortunate: even in the light they are perceived as 'dark', mysterious spaces, familiar only in name and seen solely in news reports.

Those who inhabit areas of the city that are prone to street gang activity are acutely aware of the intricacies of their local geography and the boundaries that divide 'safe' from 'unsafe' spaces. In some ways, these boundaries are marked, albeit quite subtly, in graffiti tags and murals intended to claim territory for themselves or their gang. This is a risky business that can trigger violent retribution; the boundaries between territories are particularly fraught. Some territories are delimited by obvious physical obstacles such as a freeway or other major road, railway tracks or the Los Angeles River. However, most boundaries are learnt through experience – often a deeply *negative* experience. Many boundaries are as subtle as two sides of a two-lane residential street, 'our side' and 'their side'. Locals must therefore develop a mental map of where they can and cannot go without transgressing a fiercely defended yet invisible line.

In such turbulent spaces, residents need to make careful decisions every day in order to keep themselves safe. As with Buenos Aires' *barrios*, sporting the 'wrong' colour or sports apparel, for instance, can have fatal consequences. A person affiliated with a gang may need to travel far to purchase groceries or petrol, if nearby amenities are in neighbourhoods claimed by a rival. Their routes may also have to change on a regular basis, in accordance with shifting gang boundaries. Consequently, what should be a short walk can become an intricate, circuitous journey through an invisible labyrinth. Even a person who has no gang affiliation at all may be caught in crossfire, with children as young as nine among those killed in shootings in recent years. Not without good reason, many residents are reluctant to speak to the police, lest their intervention become known to the gangs they fear. With all these risks involved, it is little wonder so few 'outsiders' ever see these places, unless they are passing over them on one of the city's paradigmatic freeways. They may as well be on a different planet.

Los Angeles' history of gang crime – and hence its history of social bonds and breakages – dates back to the first decades of the twentieth century, when Mexican American street gangs such as the symbolically named White Fence were established to defend Hispanic communities from racist attacks by their white neighbours.* However, gang activity was thrust into wider public

---

* In the United States, white picket fences are frequently associated with suburban single-family homes. However, given the controversial mid-twentieth-century history of discriminatory mortgage lending and 'white

attention during World War Two. The Sleepy Lagoon murder trial of 1942, in which five members of the Mexican American 38th Street gang were convicted of killing a twenty-two-year-old farmworker named José Gallardo Díaz without sufficient evidence, galvanised much of the Mexican American community in opposition to the bigoted discourse surrounding the case. The following year, sparked in large part by continued negative media reporting of this population, mobs of white US servicemen attacked any young Mexican American who was wearing the fashion of choice, a zoot suit, a baggy and flamboyant attire that many white Americans regarded as a profligate use of rationed textiles and thus an indicator of a person's lack of patriotism. The police mostly watched on as Mexican American *pachucos** as well as a number of Black and Filipino people who were not even wearing this resented get-up were violently beaten. Some decided to participate in the assaults, too, before arresting the victims rather than the perpetrators. The scene was thus set for decades of mutual suspicion and violence, between those said to be protecting and serving on the one hand, and thousands of minority ethnic and racial youths on the other. Even today, the wearing of a zoot suit is illegal in Los Angeles on the basis of constituting a 'public nuisance'.

After the war, much of the focus of street gang activity expanded from East Los Angeles to South Central Los Angeles, where not only Hispanic but also Black gangs were rapidly being established. In low-income neighbourhoods such as Watts, already suffering from overcrowding and unemployment, young Black males were frequently attacked by their working-class white peers

---

flight', to many this means that they are additionally emblematic of a middle-class 'American Dream' lifestyle accessible exclusively to white people. The following chapter on 8 Mile will provide further details.

* The name given to the distinctive Mexican American youth subculture associated with zoot suits as well as a hybrid slang called *caló*.

from nearby Compton in an attempt to force them from the area. This unwelcome was also apparent in the (lack of) opportunities available for Black adolescents to find comradeship and identity, being banned from many Boy Scout chapters and other organisations available to their white counterparts, and seeing around them severe discrimination in the labour and housing markets and the education system. The first Black gangs, such as the Slausons, the Businessmen and the Gladiators, were established to fill the vacuum. In contrast to the Mexican American gangs of the time, which were already competing for control over neighbourhoods, these Black gangs' territorial boundaries were predominantly defined by local schools and their immediate surroundings, where Black students sought to defend themselves against aggressive white youth gangs such as the flagrantly racist Spook Hunters. However, as white people increasingly moved to the suburbs, an option almost impossible for Black families, some Black street gangs started to turn on each other instead. In particular, divisions started to emerge on socioeconomic lines, with the Westside gangs of South Central Los Angeles generally looking down on their Eastside rivals. Territory and territorial boundaries began to become more important. Still, there was at this time little of the violence for which street gangs are now infamous. Most of the fighting was limited to hand-to-hand combat and in the most extreme cases knives and other metal implements. Murders were very rare.

Nineteen sixty-five saw old racial divisions reappear, after a physical confrontation between white officers and a Black man named Marquette Frye, plus his mother and stepbrother, exploded into six days of battling the Los Angeles Police Department (LAPD) and the National Guard in Watts. A short pause in gang activity commenced as many members instead joined the Black Panther Party and the US Organization, two Black Power groups committed to confronting police harassment and brutality. The newfound solidarity among Black people in South Central

Los Angeles did not last long, however, as the two organisations, intentionally provoked and subverted by FBI propaganda, came to see each other as competitors for recruits and authority. Members began to engage in shootings, especially in Southeast Los Angeles but most notoriously on the campus of the University of California, Los Angeles (UCLA) on 17 January 1969, resulting in the deaths of two Black Panther leaders, Alprentice 'Bunchy' Carter and John Huggins. Serious fractures within communities were emerging and violence was increasingly taking place on the streets.

With the US and the Black Panthers severely weakened and nationally influential Black leaders such as Martin Luther King Jr and Malcolm X assassinated by the end of the 1960s, new systems of authority and resistance were sought. And so a second phase of Black street gang formation was initiated, including the two most nationally renowned gangs, the Crips and the Bloods. The origins of the Crips are debated, but various sources suggest that they were founded by two teenaged members of rival South Central Los Angeles gangs, Raymond Washington and Stanley 'Tookie' Williams, who were looking to confront their more established rivals and assume de facto control of local neighbourhoods.* Infuriated by Crip belligerence, an assortment of smaller gangs soon opted to unite in response as the Blood alliance. For many young people, especially men in impoverished and deindustrialised inner-city areas, these gangs have since offered the clearest route to achieving status, camaraderie and, crucially, money, not least via the lucrative crack cocaine market from the 1980s. Facilitated by the drugs trade, the gang members of both groups have since been able to spread far beyond their original boundaries in South Central Los Angeles, attracting thousands of new

---

*Here is a fact which although not exactly 'fun', is certainly interesting: Williams holds the unusual distinction of both being nominated for the Nobel Peace Prize due to his subsequent anti-gang advocacy, and being executed following a death penalty sentence.

members, absorbing numerous smaller street gangs and causing inconceivable amounts of pain in most major cities in the United States, plus Toronto and Montreal in Canada.

It is important to recognise that in spite of their shared gang culture and 'Blood' or 'Crip' name, these groups in reality constitute loosely connected networks, rather than a single, hierarchical organisation. In addition, some of these sets are no longer racially homogeneous, instead welcoming members and making alliances with gangsters from different backgrounds. However, the majority of Los Angeles' gangs continue to be associated with a specific racial, ethnic or national identity, their names often providing a giveaway to their membership base and/or geographical origins, as is true for instance of the Sons of Samoa, the Asian Boyz and Armenian Power. Many Hispanic gangs' names incorporate the name of the area in which they originated and which they still claim as theirs, like the predominantly Mexican El Monte Flores (EMF), Florencia 13 (F13), Ontario Varrio Sur (OVS), the Avenues, Azusa 13 (A13) and Venice 13 (VS13), and the more multi-national 18th Street. As one can see, the number thirteen appears frequently; it refers to the applicable letter of the alphabet, 'M', for 'Mexican Mafia'.* The origin of the name of another Los Angeles-based gang, Mara Salvatrucha (MS-13), is less certain, but a common theory is that it derives from Salvadoran (i.e. *Salva*) slang for 'gang' (*mara*) and 'alert' or 'streetwise' (*trucha*). MS-13 was initially considered a 'stoner' gang – Hispanic and/or white gangs known for getting stoned on dope and listening to rock bands like

---

* Also known as 'La Eme' or 'La eMe', the Mexican Mafia has since 1957 grown from a humble band of Mexican American inmates seeking to protect themselves from violence at the Deuel Vocational Institution in Tracy, California, into a major criminal organisation, specialising in drug trafficking. Since 1992, it has required that Hispanic gangs in Southern California pay a percentage of their earnings to it, ostensibly in exchange for protection for any members in prison now or in the future. Refusal risks retribution.

the Rolling Stones – but its members, most of whom had fled the Salvadoran Civil War (1979–92), quickly realised that they would need to fight fire with fire if they were to survive on LA's toughest streets. Within a little over a decade, the largely harmless MS of the early 1980s had morphed into the brutal MS-13, notorious for drug, arms and human trafficking, extortion, murder and more. Many of its members were deported to El Salvador following the end of the country's civil war, but via various trafficking pipelines, the gang's activity has only spread throughout parts of Central and North America ever since.

It is also essential to note that the streets are not the only incubator of street gangs: particularly since the 1960s, the prison system has spawned some of the most dangerous groups on either side of the bars.* The landmark Civil Rights Act of 1964 outlawed discrimination on the basis of 'race, color, religion, or national origin' and ended legalised racial segregation throughout the country, prompting some inmates in newly integrated prisons to band along racial lines. Subsequently, the widespread adoption of 'tough-on-crime' policies in the 1980s and 1990s – designed to throw behind bars even those committed of a relatively minor, non-violent offence like drug

---

* There are also other types of gangs in Los Angeles that, although not street gangs, the focus of this chapter, are worth mentioning in brief. Some are part of international organised crime networks, such as triads based in Hong Kong and Taiwan, yakuza from Japan, and the Sinaloa Cartel established in Mexico. Others, like the Chosen Few and the Galloping Goose, are motorcycle clubs called 'one-percenters', referring to an alleged insinuation by the American Motorcyclist Association following a rowdy event in Hollister, California in 1947 that this proportion of motorcyclists are outlaws. And facilitated by the internet, the twenty-first century has seen the widespread emergence of alt-right, white supremacist groups, one particularly militant example being the Rise Above Movement (RAM) from Orange County, which became infamous for instigating violence and assaulting counter-protestors at the deadly Unite the Right rally in Charlottesville, Virginia in 2017.

possession or a technical violation of probation or parole – made California's prisons incredibly overcrowded. In such intimidating, unsettling facilities, it is little wonder that racially motivated gangs were able to grow and grow, using violence to settle disputes, discipline members and frighten others into joining them. Interracial violence became so severe in Californian prisons especially that the state opted to apply an unofficial policy of racially segregating what it deemed to be its most dangerous inmates. Even though the US Supreme Court ordered California to effectively cease this arrangement in 2005, some of the highest-security prisons still believe that separating certain prisoners is necessary to prevent them from fighting (and killing) those from different backgrounds. For their part, even where their prison is technically integrated, many inmates choose to stay separate in common spaces like the mess hall, believing that in order to survive, one should only congregate with peers of the same race.

Interestingly, too, among Hispanic gang members, a significant geographical divide provides the basis for some of the worst violence. Specifically, on entering the prison system, many set aside their street gang labels and unite with other Hispanic gang members as either Sureños, or 'Southerners' in Spanish, with origins in Southern California, or Norteños, 'Northerners', from Northern California. This territorial division emerged in the 1970s as the two groups professed contrasting loyalties to the Southern Californian Mexican Mafia on the one side, and the Northern Californian Nuestra Familia on the other. Most Hispanic prison and street gangs in the state now align themselves with either the Sureños or the Norteños, roughly according to an invisible west–east line along the lower end of California's Central Valley.

White supremacist gangs have long constituted a particularly severe problem in the prison system, often adopting the name 'Peckerwoods' to refer to their pugnacious subculture. The moniker derives from a nineteenth-century African American slang word for poor white people, which, despite originally being intended as derogatory,* was eventually reappropriated by racist white inmates looking to unify during the turbulent 1960s. The oldest of the major white supremacist prison gangs is the Aryan Brotherhood (AB), which emerged soon after the passage of the Civil Rights Act in direct opposition to the Marxist-Leninist Black Guerrilla Family (BGF), at the San Quentin State Prison near San Francisco in Northern California. Paranoid, defensive and bigoted, the AB developed an exceptionally severe initiation practice called 'making one's bones': assault or murder a rival gang member, an inmate of another race or a corrections officer. Here commenced the intractable race war that would in almost no time spread to penitentiaries across much of the rest of the country.

Peckerwoods have over time proliferated not only in the prison system, but also on the streets, not least in Southern California. Never successfully rehabilitated, released prisoners now engage in almost any type of criminal activity imaginable, from murder-for-hire to identity theft, and armed robbery to methamphetamine manufacturing. Generally driven more by avarice than ideology, despite their penchant for classic neo-Nazi symbols like swastikas and the number eighty-eight,† these groups tend to seek out the most profitable endeavours available, even if it means having to create business alliances with gangs constituted by members of another race, with the general exception of Black.

---

* It effectively means the same as 'white trash', and was inverted from the name of the woodpecker, which in the Southern states was sometimes believed to signify white people, in contrast to the 'African American' blackbird. To this day, many male white supremacists who want to be identified with Peckerwoods will tattoo themselves with a woodpecker, while female members, known as Featherwoods, will often choose a feather.
† This number is often used by white supremacist groups as code for 'Heil Hitler', the letter 'H' being the eighth letter of the alphabet. Other symbols widely favoured and co-opted by white supremacist groups include runes, Celtic crosses and shamrocks, all of which they deem historic emblems of white power, 'purity' and sacrifice.

Indeed, although the war they fight is now primarily about profits, race does still matter to white supremacist gangs: some members are committed to harassing and threatening Black families in an abominable effort to force them to relocate, in much the same manner as seventy years ago, while race-hate rhetoric continues to be employed in the prison system to attract and absorb new members. Still, one white supremacist gang is quite unusual in the welcome it has historically offered to those who have Hispanic ancestry, as long as they also identify as white and profess loyalty to the white race. Established in 1978 by John Stinson, an inmate at the California Youth Authority near Sacramento, the Nazi Low Riders (NLR)* grew quickly through its prison-based alliance with the AB. Around this time, many of the AB's leaders were being locked in solitary confinement, limiting the gang's influence. In prisons across California and soon elsewhere as well, the NLR filled the gap, operating as an intermediary or proxy of the AB in its broad criminal network, while recruiting young skinheads seeking protection and keen to avoid being tarred as direct associates of the more established and heavily scrutinised AB. Shortly, a street gang portion of the NLR emerged, too, comprising both former inmates and those attracted to this hostile subculture. To this day, the NLR cultivates a reputation for committing various racist, homophobic and sometimes fatal hate crimes against members of the public.

Unfortunately for almost everyone, even the official classification of the NLR as a prison gang and the conviction of leaders

---

* A lowrider is type of car that has been customised to be 'low and slow'. In the 1940s, they became particularly popular among many Mexican Americans in Los Angeles looking to distinguish themselves from white Americans and their general preference for another form of adapted car, the speedy hot rod. The NLR's decision to name itself after the former was thus highly symbolic, seizing a significant aspect of local Mexican American culture.

including Stinson (as well as some of the AB) around the turn of the century proved only moderately effective in stemming white supremacist gang activity. Some of the remaining NLR and AB inmates opted to unite – to no little controversy – with another local white supremacist group, Public Enemy No. 1 (PENI or PEN1), which traces its origins to the hardcore punk music scene in Los Angeles' Long Beach. Named after (but not endorsed by) the 1980s British anarcho-punk band Rudimentary Peni, the peculiarly middle-class PENI is infamous for committing white-collar crimes such as identity theft and fraud, although many members additionally engage in violent crimes under the guise of 'defending' white youths from other street gangs. Today PENI is a hybrid skinhead–street–prison gang, and the ability of its members to constitute a triple threat, acting as racist thugs, mercenaries and hustlers depending on the situation, allows them to flourish in prison yards and wealthy suburbs alike.

The blurring of distinctions between Peckerwoods and racist skinheads, some of whom additionally adopt elements from other local subcultures such as extreme sports, is gradually becoming more commonplace across parts of Southern California more broadly. Even so, most racist skinhead groups remain a distinct category, typically combining an interest in territory, in the manner of street gangs, with far-right politics. Admittedly, the latter point was not always the case: the skinhead subculture that originated in London in the 1960s was very broad and not necessarily racist. However, by the late 1970s skinheads had here and elsewhere in Western Europe come to include a far-right nationalist wing opposed to immigration, whose neo-Nazi ideologies and symbols would inspire the rise of various American racist skinhead organisations (some of which would additionally reappropriate Christian or Pagan iconography for their own ends) not long later. Today, most racist skinhead gangs or 'crews' are relatively small, operating locally or regionally and typically independently of one another. Quite unusually among gangs, they tend not to be motivated by money and instead prefer to threaten minority communities and their institutions, whether through vandalism (such as drawing swastikas on Jewish community buildings) or violence ('boot parties', when assailants kick and stomp a victim with steel-toed boots, being one of their calling cards). As a consequence, in certain generally suburban areas of Greater Los Angeles, it is overtly racist skinhead gangs like the Reich Skins that pose the greatest threat to local residents.

Befitting of a 'Gang Capital', Los Angeles is thus highly distinctive both in the pervasiveness of gang activity and in these groups' collective diversity, rendering gang crime alarmingly *normal*. Conservatively – for various uncertainties and gaps exist in its crime statistics – more than 5,000 violent gang crimes, including homicides, felony assaults and rape, take place just in the City of Los Angeles every year. What's more, this highly pressurised situation has been intensified by various incidents of police brutality against gang members as well as innocent bystanders, a particularly noteworthy example involving the LAPD's Community Resources Against Street Hoodlums (CRASH) unit, which was censured for framing large numbers of civilians for a range of crimes during the 1980s and 1990s in order to justify beating, shooting and imprisoning them. Racial profiling has further eroded confidence in law enforcement and teenagers are regularly arrested simply so that they can be fingerprinted and photographed for future reference. Even more scandalously, the Los Angeles County Sheriff's Department (LASD) has a long history of employing 'deputy gang' members – that is, cliques of police officers who covertly engage in typical gang activities such as shootings, assaults and sexual harassment.

For decades, new legislation and policies have been written and rewritten to tackle gang activity, and yet still law enforcement find themselves in a dilemma that is seemingly impossible to solve. The Racketeer Influenced and Corrupt Organizations (RICO) Act of 1970, which was initially aimed at organised criminal groups like the Italian Mafia, has over time enabled prosecutors to charge conspirators in gang crimes and put them in high-security federal prison. However, strict penalties face fierce resistance, not just from gang members, but from whole communities. One insightful example is the Street Terrorism Enforcement and Prevention Act (STEP) of 1988, which made participation in gang activity a criminal offence, but its strict implementation – including 'enhanced' penalties where a crime is associated with a gang – has long been criticised for limiting the possibility of rehabilitating individuals as young as fourteen. Another controversy pertains to civil injunctions, which were first introduced in the 1980s to constrain gang members' rights to assemble in specific neighbourhoods, while giving law enforcement new stop-and-search powers. Originally the hope was to prohibit activities as innocuous as congregating in groups of two or more and staying on the street for more than five minutes. However, due to these infringements of *everybody's* civil liberties, injunctions were modified to ban more obviously anti-social practices such as vandalism, trespassing, harassment, intimidation and public urination and defecation, plus the use of gang colours and hand signs.

Despite some successes in reducing serious crimes such as assaults, injunctions have continued to prove contentious. The maps produced to mark gang territories and their boundaries are publicised online, which risks these areas becoming further stigmatised by the extraordinary police attention they receive. Indeed, local communities have long argued that injunctions disgrace whole neighbourhoods – especially those predominantly inhabited by Black and Hispanic people – and subject them to exorbitant levels of police surveillance and harassment, including wrongful arrests. Civil liberties groups have long fought to prevent the police from blanketing large parts of the city with injunctions and have also sought to ensure that individuals, many of whom no longer live in the area or are associated with a gang, can dispute their gang designation in court, achieving a break-through in December 2020.

Furthermore, before the twentieth century was over, a state-wide database called CalGang was developed to compile intelligence on anyone suspected of gang activity or of coming into contact with gangs. However, large numbers of Hispanic and Black males are listed despite minimal evidence of gang affiliation, including gang interventionists whose job it is to liaise with gang members. Even babies, based on the ages of the individuals in question at the time of entry, were found to be included during a state audit in 2016. And as soon as a person is present in CalGang, even a minor crime can result in an excessive sentence. In summer 2020, the LAPD opted to no longer refer to this database in an effort to increase its accountability and trust among community members.

California locks up a disproportionate number of Black men and women, a reflection of systemic racism in the judicial system and US society more broadly.* Co-operative strategies involving religious leaders, parents, educators, former gang members and youth programmes are rightly praised for their role in reducing homicides, but unfortunately, gang crime has tended to fluctuate rather than proceed on a downward path. Truces – including that agreed between Bloods and Crips in 1992 – have briefly offered hope that the bridges between these groups will one day be mended. But it is not uncommon for gang members, especially younger individuals, to turn back to what they may view as the only opportunity available to them.

Gang crime tends to be self-reinforcing. Not only do local

---

*Here are two particularly alarming statistics: for every 100,000 Black adults in the United States, 1,501 are in prison, a figure that has actually *declined* over the past decade; in California specifically, Black people represent just 6 per cent of the state's total population, but 28 per cent of its prison population.

residents often feel compelled to join in search of socioeconomic mobility, status and safety in numbers, but businesses are also regularly forced away by the risks of violence and vandalism, leaving fewer alternative income opportunities for the community, less tax revenue to 'clean up' the area and more abandoned spaces for gangs to occupy. Gang crime, despite the potentially vast sums of money that circulate among members, is therefore *expensive*. It restrains afflicted neighbourhoods in a cycle of engineered disorder and channels all attention towards it. Even though gentrification has made many people more willing to visit or live in certain downtown and inner-city neighbourhoods – as well as parts of long-stigmatised South Central Los Angeles, which in 2003 dropped the 'Central' from its name in a cosmetic but surprisingly effective move – pockets of gang activity remain. Parks, for a long time dangerous, unmonitored spaces, have certainly become safer, but there remains a sense that the intensity of street gang crime in Los Angeles can never be eradicated. In the downtown neighbourhood of Skid Row, people experiencing homelessness have regularly been targeted and abused by gangs, while as certain northern suburban areas have found to their cost, gang crime can simply migrate. Today, the Los Angeles Police Department estimates that there are more than 450 gangs and 45,000 gang members just in the city, discounting the much larger metropolitan area, which is home to an estimated three to four times more of each. Differences between the LAPD's and the LASD's patrol boundaries, policies and practices further complicate policing in the city.

Gang crime also continues to evolve. Today, there are many gangs that, despite their street origins, operate in part from private spaces such as the home, especially via the internet, which is closely monitored by law enforcement. However, the traditional competition to claim territory has not disappeared: an argument on social media or a disputed drug sale on the darknet can quickly shift momentum back to the street. In turn, the LAPD has adopted geographic information systems (GIS) in the past two decades, enabling it more effectively to map criminal activity and thereby identify the locations where police resources are most needed. Unlike injunction maps, which imply that street gangs' boundaries are static, these maps enable the police to respond to criminal activity in real time. In many cases they are able to anticipate gang activity before it becomes dangerous, but they are constantly needing to keep up with what has become a fluid way of life.

Perhaps no group is more acutely aware of the difficulties of distinguishing gang members and pursuing a life beyond the gangs than those who leave their peers to carve out a new lifestyle. This is not simply a matter of relinquishing membership. There have been cases where a former street gang member, with no intention to cause trouble, has been attacked and killed simply because they have been recognised as an old enemy of a local rival. Others continue to be approached and arrested by members of law enforcement. The stigma of a criminal record can greatly limit their employment opportunities.

Former street gang members' engagement with space hence tends to remain greatly shaped by their time in neighbourhoods that are violently delimited and contested in the manner of warfare. If they have the chance, many leave and never return. In their place, new gang members are socialised to preserve their groups' boundaries through force, while compelling the authorities to play catch-up. Whereas these lines are unlikely to appear on official maps, for local residents they have an impact that can be more substantial than any other kind of boundary within the city. Being able to identify and visualise boundaries can determine one's behaviour – if not survival – in contentious places.

How Invisible Lines Allow People to Divide 'Us' From 'Them'

So far we have witnessed how lines operate as a simplifying device, enabling us to make our complex planet that bit more comprehensible. We have also observed that lines can be used to take control over the world (or at least a portion of it) and to claim it as one's own. In this part, we will explore how all three of these functions can coalesce, as lines can be used to divide one group of people or places from another. Sometimes these lines are rooted in economics. The Brandt Line, for instance, drawn by the West German chancellor Willy Brandt in 1980 to divide the world into a wealthy North and a poor South based on gross domestic product per capita, is, despite major changes in various countries' economies over the past forty years, still influential in shaping how we view the 'developed' and 'developing' worlds.* At the national

---

*It is important to mention that Brandt did not envision this line as a tool of division, but rather as a means of highlighting global inequalities and stimulating greater international cooperation, so that the gap between 'North' and 'South' could be closed. Although his Independent Commission on International Development Issues made various proposals to this end, the Brandt Line remains remarkably applicable even today. Also worth pointing out is that Brandt conceived this line as a more objective division than the older, three-part geopolitical segmentation into 'First' (capitalist), 'Second' (communist) and 'Third' ('exploited' and non-aligned) worlds, which is generally attributed to the French demographer Alfred Sauvy. The fact that over thirty years after the end of the Cold War, many still refer to a 'Third World' (albeit generally as an economic rather than an ideological

level, commonly perceived dividing lines between, say, north and south (England, Italy, India) similarly tend to be grounded in distinct economic as well as social and political disparities, although they may additionally comprise more imprecise divisions based on culture. More locally, lines can be associated with some kind of social difference. Consider for instance the boundaries of so-called ethnic enclaves and gay villages, neighbourhoods which tend to emerge in large part as a result of exclusion, via discriminatory housing and employment policies and practices and/or the threat of violence elsewhere, but which may come to be seen more positively, through allowing individuals to feel like they belong here exclusively. With respect to religion, clothing is regularly subject to invisible lines, whether to keep those in religious attire out of specific places (one may note the various countries that in recent years have banned the wearing of certain types of Islamic headscarves in specific public spaces and institutions) or, conversely, to ensure that only those in garbs deemed appropriate by a religious institution can enter. Perhaps most obviously of all, race is quite frequently central to efforts to distinguish between 'our' places and 'their' places, with particularly deplorable examples including the development of ghettos in Nazi-occupied Europe and the comprehensive apartheid system of racial segregation in South Africa and South-West Africa (now Namibia), which operated for most of the second half of the twentieth century. And don't think that such distinctions are always made to define one's access to land. The Chicago chapter of the notorious 'Red Summer' of 1919, a several months' affair of racially motivated violence across much of the United States, primarily committed by white mobs and white supremacists, was ignited when a Black teenager named Eugene Williams, hoping to enjoy a visit to the beach on a sweltering July day, was stoned by a white man until he drowned.

---

descriptor) further underlines how resilient such concepts and their dividing lines can be.

His 'crime'? His raft had drifted ever so slightly across an invisible line dividing the waters of Lake Michigan by race. In short, then, invisible lines can be far more than just descriptive: they can operate as consequential mechanisms of division, shaping our access to and perceptions and experiences of different places.

As we shall see, 8 Mile in Detroit exemplifies how racial segregation has been realised and reinforced in the United States through a combination of discriminatory mortgage lending policies and an imagined sense of difference between a predominantly Black city and largely white suburbs. Although they have evolved quite distinctively, Paris's *banlieues* present certain similarities in terms of the stigmas associated with deprived neighbourhoods on the other side of an imaginary, invisible line. Also worth considering is that, over time, perceived differences can be made physical through the construction of barriers, as we shall see in the case of the peace lines in Northern Ireland. And, even where a tangible barrier is removed, evidence of variation and disparity can endure in the long term, the Berlin Wall providing a compelling example of the continued power of invisible as opposed to visible lines. Apparent, then, is the power of our imaginations, and the assumptions and prejudices therein, in defining the boundaries between different places. This point is further illuminated by the final two cases in this part – on the Ural Mountains and the Bosphorus – exploring the popular but rather problematic belief that 'Europe' and 'Asia' are distinct continents on the basis of culture, despite the fact that continents are typically defined by the far less subjective criterion of landmass.

8 Mile

---

*I issue a warning now to all dope pushers,
to all rip-off artists, to all muggers: it's time
to leave Detroit. Hit 8 Mile Road!*

Coleman A. Young

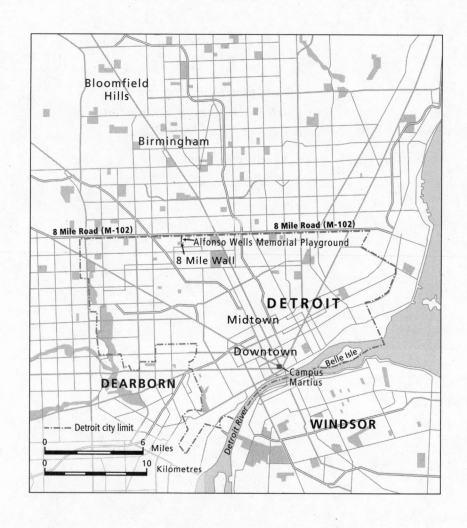

Bloomfield
Hills

Birmingham

8 Mile Road (M-102)   8 Mile Road (M-102)

←—Alfonso Wells Memorial Playground

8 Mile Wall

DETROIT

Midtown

Downtown   Belle Isle

■Campus
Martius

DEARBORN

Detroit River

WINDSOR

—·—· Detroit city limit

0   6 Miles
0   10 Kilometres

Humans have been experts at building barriers for millennia. In large part reflecting an intrinsic distrust of others, from Greece to China, defensive reinforcements such as walls have been fundamental to distinguishing between groups and protecting 'us' and 'our' resources from 'them'. Robust barriers can largely or entirely inhibit movement and interaction; breaking or repurposing them therefore has both a practical and a symbolic quality, proving one's ability to sabotage and potentially suppress the opposition. Perhaps this is one reason why the biblical story of the Battle of Jericho, in which marching Israelites managed to bring down what may have been the world's first significant defensive walls using just their voices, ram's-horn trumpets and sheer resolve, has continued to hold such allure to millions despite being historically unsubstantiated: who would be interested in the destruction of barriers lacking the formidability of stone and brick? Even today, it takes no time at all to find recent examples of countries erecting physical barriers as a means of buttressing territorial claims and defining belongingness, along with countermovements to damage or eliminate them. They encapsulate much of the human experience: identity, ownership and power. And in this sense, they provide not only a physical form of segregation, but also an invisible, psychological one.

In the context of the United States, racial segregation tends to be most readily associated with the Southern states, which, following the American Civil War and the abolition of slavery in

1865, enacted a range of discriminatory 'Black Codes' and sub-sequently 'Jim Crow' laws to continue disenfranchising Black people. However, white prejudice has prevailed far more exten-sively. It is true that many white people in the North condemned the segregation of the South during the mid- to late nineteenth century, which was enforced in spaces as diverse as public schools, public transportation, restaurants and graveyards and was even legitimised by the landmark US Supreme Court decision *Plessy v. Ferguson* of 1896,* whereby racially segregated facilities were ruled constitutional as long as there was no difference in quality. The resultant 'separate but equal' doctrine was in reality a cruel irony and prompted further state-sponsored segregation. Nevertheless, by most measures there has for a long time been an overrepresentation of Midwestern and North-Eastern cities among the country's most racially segregated places. Detroit, the one major US city to be situated directly north of the Canadian border thanks to the meandering of the city's namesake river (the band Journey's reference to 'South Detroit' in 'Don't Stop Believin'' is presumably Windsor, Ontario), regularly appears in first or second place. And controversially, in 1941 it even built a wall to divide white and Black communities.

---

*The case centred on Homer Plessy's clever experiment testing the impracticalities of Louisiana's Separate Car Act of 1890. Plessy was of one-eighth Black ancestry and thus classified as Black under the state's law, but had fair skin and thus raised little suspicion when he sat in a 'whites-only' car. After disclosing his racial identity to the conductor, Plessy was arrested and charged with violating the Act. His petition, which ultimately reached the US Supreme Court, was founded on the argument that as a US citizen, a resident of the state of Louisiana, and of mixed descent, whose Black ancestry could not easily be discerned, he was entitled to the same rights and privileges guaranteed by the Constitution to white citizens. However, only Justice John Marshall Harlan, who had already established a reputation for championing the civil rights of minority groups, dissented from the final 7–1 decision against Plessy.

The 8 Mile Wall is just one instance of a physical barrier erected in the United States for the purpose of separating racial groups. Numerous freeways across the country were intentionally routed to physically divide people of different races, from Los Angeles to New York and Milwaukee to Atlanta. In Chicago, for instance, the Dan Ryan Expressway helped separate the white Bridgeport neighbourhood – home of the city's mayor at the time, Richard J. Daley – from Black Bronzeville. Other major thoroughfares were used to bulldoze Black districts, in some cases without ever being connected to an exit, the abandoned I-170 in West Baltimore being a classic example. Protesting on freeways against racial injustice, as became commonplace in the aftermath of the infamous killing of George Floyd, a Black man, by a white police officer in Minneapolis, Minnesota on 25 May 2020, thus has a certain symbolic quality. Any freeway that forms a partition between different racial groups – or for that matter any railroad, giving deeper meaning to the phrase 'the wrong side of the tracks' – can be regarded as an all-too-common boundary in US society.

However, the developer of the 8 Mile Wall was particularly brazen in its efforts to profit from racial discrimination. The Home Owners' Loan Corporation (HOLC) from 1935 created what it called 'residential security maps' to display how secure a real-estate investment could be considered in nearly 250 US cities. These maps led to the term 'redlining', as the colour red was used to mark so-called hazardous areas, the poorest of four designations. If just 15–20 per cent of its population was Black, a surveyor would mark the neighbourhood in red, regardless of its amenities and upkeep. As a consequence, these maps helped build race into urban space: a neighbourhood would be reduced to its racial population and the moral judgements and stereotypes that people in a position of power applied to it. Old racial hierarchies were reinforced, with areas whose residents predominantly originated in Northern Europe being regarded as the most desirable and as having the lowest level of risk for mortgage lending. The mere presence of Black people, by contrast, was treated as a threat to white real estate. Having been denied a loan from the Federal Housing Association (FHA) to build an all-white neighbourhood on the basis that the local area of Detroit was described as 'hazardous' by the HOLC, the aforementioned developer asked whether a dividing wall separating the new estate from the existing Black community would change the Association's decision. Its offer was accepted. A wall 6 feet (1.8 metres) high, 1 foot (0.3 metres) thick and three blocks long from north to south was erected in Detroit's Eight Mile Wyoming neighbourhood, and the loans and mortgage guarantees the developer sought were duly made available.

It says a lot about the pervasiveness of racism in the middle of the twentieth century that a wall – and a very modest one at that – was all that was needed to turn a neighbourhood from maligned to coveted. Further, this wall was certainly not the only instance of developers seeking to attract white residents while denigrating their Black counterparts. Across the country, real estate agents stirred fears that Black people were about to move into historically white neighbourhoods in the inner city. This created a frenzy: the new residents would increase crime and bring down property values, so went the narrative. White families were incentivised by the government to make the most of the New Deal's generous subsidies and buy a brand-new single-family home in the suburbs, with, appropriately enough, a *white* picket fence, a garage and plenty of space for the quintessential 2.4 children. 'White flight' was underway. Many real estate agents then made enormous profits by selling white people's old inner-city homes to Black buyers at exorbitant prices, reflecting the latter's desperation to leave poor, overcrowded districts and the lack of housing stock available to them. After all, they could rarely move to the suburbs with their white counterparts: restrictive covenants were widely used to ban anyone who was not 'white' (definitions of which varied) from such sought-after areas, and most Black people were paid insufficiently to afford these homes. Many speculators rented inner-city properties to Black people, offering few protections despite the high costs they charged, to the point that it became impossible for residents to save money and effectively upkeep their homes and neighbourhoods. Starved of investment and services, these areas could only deteriorate. And whenever most white people saw them, they assumed the residents were culpable, solidifying their discriminatory perceptions. The concept of the 'ghetto' and its association with Black residents had come full circle.

By contrast, suburbia, which fittingly for the 'Motor City' was built on the assumption that (wealthy white) people would have cars, became the gold standard for twentieth-century living. The 8 Mile Wall provided an additional layer of supposed security for white people in this part of Detroit, as realtors boasted of how it would 'protect' them from the Black population on the other side and how it would ensure that their properties would not decline in value. More generally, it reinforced the emerging distinction between city and suburb, one that in the US context would come to acquire less-than-subtle racial connotations. The wall continued to represent a racial divide until the white community in its vicinity decided to move further from the city, especially in the aftermath of the major racial disturbances that rocked Detroit in 1967.

Today, there is no legal possibility of separating white and Black people in such a way: the Fair Housing Act of 1968 outlawed redlining by prohibiting discrimination in the sale, rental and financing of housing based on characteristics such as race, religion, nationality and sex. Black people are now theoretically able to live wherever they want.* The 8 Mile Wall no longer provides an official divide, but it does continue to exist, a reminder

---

*Subtler equivalents of redlining are, however, still having to be challenged, such as a tendency in some places to withhold lending from neighbourhoods lacking in banks, which is more likely to be the case in the inner city than in the suburbs.

of the country's history of racial segregation and discrimination even outside of the Southern states. Artists have adorned an exposed chunk of it in Alfonso Wells Memorial Playground with murals that encapsulate both the area's residents (for instance, children blowing bubbles, fair housing protests) and significant figures in African American history (such as the civil rights activist Rosa Parks). An enterprising non-profit helps under- and unemployed locals make and sell glass coasters that showcase the murals. Scaling the wall has become a rite of passage for many of the area's young residents. Schools organise field trips to use the wall as a teaching tool, and in March 2021 it was added to the National Register of Historic Places due to its significance. It is today used as a symbol of community rather than disunity. All it really divides are people's back gardens.

However, this does not mean that the area has become racially integrated. Enduring division, on the ground and especially in the psyche, is most clearly expressed through the road one block north, which gives the wall its name. Whereas the tiny 8 Mile Wall is just 0.8 kilometres from north to south, 8 Mile Road – whose official highway name is M-102 – is a major thoroughfare running over 33 kilometres from east to west. Its name derives from the fact that it is situated eight miles (13 kilometres) due north of the hub of the Motor City's wheel, Campus Martius. Unlike the freeways noted earlier, 8 Mile Road was not constructed or oriented with the express intention of dividing or displacing Black residents; rather, surveyors used this former dirt road as the baseline for distinguishing between counties across the southern part of Michigan's mitten-shaped Lower Peninsula. Nevertheless, it has come to be perceived as the divide between a poor, predominantly Black city to the south and the wealthy, largely white suburbs to the north. Given the history of redlining and white flight in the United States, it is not alone in forming such a boundary, but it is almost certainly the country's most famous example. As the country's poster child for urban decay – a place widely but not always fairly associated with empty plots, abandoned buildings, violent crime and a disappearing auto industry – Detroit is sharply juxtaposed with its flourishing suburbs, some of which, like Birmingham and Bloomfield Hills, are among the most expensive places to live in Michigan. The well-maintained homes and busy strip malls here stand in stark contrast to the dilapidated structures and shuttered stores across much of Detroit's Wayne County. Politically, too, a far greater proportion of conservative voters can be found north than south, while the median family income is considerably higher and the poverty rate much lower.

In these ways, there is empirical evidence of a divide between the northern suburbs and the southern city, but a widespread *impression* of difference has proved even more compelling. For many, the road demarcates where they feel like 'insiders' and where they feel like 'outsiders'. A fear of being deemed 'out of place' is no trivial matter in a country where both violent crime and racial profiling remain all too common. One Detroiter described to me how 'growing up, people were always saying "Don't cross 8 Mile" or "Be careful when you drive across 8 Mile"; it's always been that divider . . . Most people envision that the dividing line is 8 Mile.' Another urbanite caricatured the suburban view of 8 Mile as 'a portal to a hell dimension . . . where white people venture for sporting events and retreat from as soon as possible', despite it ultimately being 'just a road that divides Detroit from the suburbs'. Even Detroit's mayor from 1974 to 1994, Coleman A. Young, in his inaugural address famously described the road in the manner of an official border, demanding that the city's criminals cross 8 Mile Road and leave for good; as one may expect, the suburbanites to the north were far from impressed with this dictum. Whether it is perceived as dangerous in its own right, as a frontier that should not be traversed, as a barrier that can 'contain' the other side, or as an obstacle across which to expel what one rejects, it is striking how compelling the *concept* of 8 Mile has become. Even though its rangy pylons make 8 Mile a conspicuous physical entity, its real importance lies in the *invisible*, intangible lines it engenders, which divide and help dictate the lives of those on either side. The road may not share the obvious insidiousness of a wall (although one may well argue that by purporting to be innocuous, a mere thoroughfare, it is actually more so), but it has its own power in determining how we imagine and experience city and suburbs.

Representation, then, remains a significant issue: as one Detroiter noted, only 'half a story' tends to be told. If one looks beyond the traditional stereotypes, significant changes can be seen in the city and beyond. For one thing, the Detroit metropolitan area's diversity is frequently overlooked: it boasts the country's largest concentration of people of Arab descent, even if the exact size of this community is concealed by the restrictive categories used in the US census. For another, the old racial and socio-economic boundary of 8 Mile has become blurred over time, as middle-class Black people increasingly live north of the highway, often alongside low-income white communities. Meanwhile, many white suburbanites are opting to move to the south, albeit rarely to the 'border' neighbourhoods around 8 Mile; instead, they tend to choose the rapidly developing Downtown and Midtown areas. Here, significant revitalisation efforts are underway, from the opening and renovation of major sports arenas (which, unlike in many other US cities, can be found downtown) to the establishment of a streetcar system in a city long associated with *private* transport, as well as the granting of state park status to the idyllic Belle Isle in the middle of the Detroit River. With the regeneration of Detroit's core, the traditional city–suburb boundary along 8 Mile Road has thus been somewhat replaced by a series of three concentric belts, comprising an increasingly thriving urban centre, surrounded by a semicircle of long-term disinvestment and poverty, and then another semicircle of suburban prosperity. As central Detroit's appeal to young professionals who would historically have chosen to live in the suburbs continues to grow, the common perception that 'everything in Detroit is cheap, land is cheap, property is cheap', as one person told me, may soon cease to be the case. But until the urban blight around 8 Mile is effectively tackled, the benefits are unlikely to reach this peripheral area, and the long-held notion that there is a strict boundary between the two outer semi-circles is unlikely to be overcome.

One of the few public figures to transcend this boundary is Eminem, especially since the release of the autobiographical film *8 Mile* (2002), in which his white character B-Rabbit attempts to escape this tough area associated with crack houses, strip clubs, liquor stores, pawnbrokers, prostitutes, trailer parks and seedy motels. Through his rap as well as his turbulent childhood, which exposed him to both sides of 8 Mile, Eminem has become something of a mouthpiece for the road and its adjacent neighbourhoods, articulating their angst and anguish. He challenges the rigidity of the United States' entrenched white–Black divide like few others, not least by helping make rap, with its intense depictions of urban life and urban concerns, popular even in white suburban areas that traditionally disparaged it. 8 Mile may seem like the edge of the world, accommodating the 'vices' that other places seek to expel, but it is not without a voice.

Still, 8 Mile's reputation continues to precede it. Conscious of its notoriety, suburbanites who commute into Detroit often prefer to avoid 8 Mile altogether, making sure to select one of the massive freeways that bypass it, as one explained: 'I generally try to avoid that street if I can . . . a lot of strip clubs and liquor stores.' Many of those who do pass through the area in their cars do so hurriedly, speeding past its sizeable unhoused population. Automobiles made Detroit just as Detroit has long made automobiles, but the same vehicles have allowed many in the metropolitan area to become more selective in how they engage with the city. Instead of being a preferred destination, 8 Mile now provides an uncomfortable reminder of the divide between social mobility and despondency, between travelling far away and going nowhere.

Indeed, 8 Mile is a boundary with a conceptual power that transcends merely local relevance. It is a symbol of a country that is polarised in almost every way possible. It exemplifies a divide between those who aspire to realise the 'American Dream', and those for whom this is so fantastical as to be absurd. It forces us to question our presumptions and our privilege, and to recognise the contrasting life chances available in a society that is today *unum** in assertion more than in reality. And it provides expression both in concrete and in mind of how division can be manufactured *anywhere*, through urban policy, design and discourse. It is far more than just a road.

Nor is it the only demarcation between city and suburbs to be associated with severe, seemingly inexorable division, rooted in a history of prejudiced urban planning and policy. But elsewhere in the world, it can be the suburbs – rather than the city – that suffer from stigma and misrepresentation. We can't reach our next destination from Detroit by car, so we'd better fly. At least, because we're heading to the second most visited city in the world, the journey should be straightforward.

---

* Latin for 'one', from the traditional albeit unofficial US national motto *E pluribus unum*, meaning 'Out of many, one'.

Paris's *Banlieues*

---

*Be careful, the stadium is in Saint-Denis . . . not in
Paris . . . It's very near but trust me, you don't want to
be in Saint-Denis. It's not the same as Paris. Trust me.*

Thierry Henry[*]

---

[*] The French former footballer was correcting his CBS Sports colleagues
about the location of the Stade de France, the stadium set to host the
upcoming 2022 UEFA Champions League Final, but unsurprisingly, his
remarks failed to impress Saint-Denis's mayor, who posted the following
on social media: 'Dear Thierry Henry, you are right, Saint-Denis isn't Paris.
Saint-Denis is a city in which the poverty rate is very high. The percentage of
substandard housing is unfortunately one of the highest in France. Insecurity
in public space is a scourge that we have not yet managed to stem. But Saint-
Denis is a city with gigantic potential . . . The contempt with which you have
characterised our city is not acceptable. We are not Paris, but we are not
disreputable because of it.'

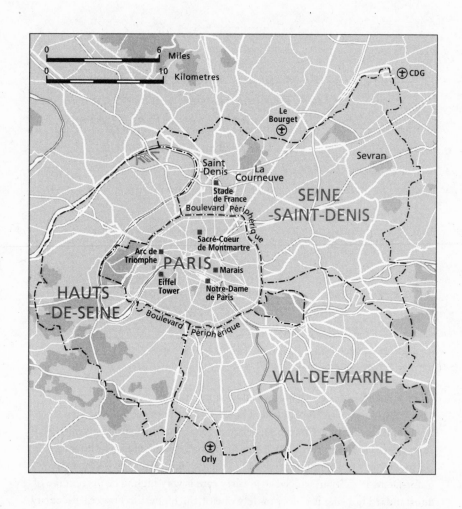

A soft glow emanates from the charming stores and ornate streetlights that line Paris's streets. Along the Seine, the sounds of polyglot commentary can be heard from the *bateaux mouches* (sightseeing boats) chugging past the city's countless attractions. Gustave Eiffel's beloved tower, the world's tallest building when it was completed for the Paris world's fair of 1889,* continues to exert a gravitational pull on the tourists competing to find the perfect angle for their photos. A couple of kilometres away, the Arc de Triomphe is as chaotic as ever, taxis and vans rushing with reckless abandon around the world's most famous roundabout, while on the hill of Montmartre, the evening restaurant crowd is starting to assemble. Although Paris's moniker is owed to its history as a centre of erudition and wisdom during the Age of Enlightenment, the City of Lights was one of the first to adopt street lanterns on a mass scale, and its thriving night-time economy continues to encapsulate the importance of consumption and allure in this teeming icon of modernity, beauty and progress.

Yet while Paris is viewed by millions as the City of Love, its suburbs are generally regarded with far less affection. Whereas suburban areas in countries like the United Kingdom and the

---

* The fair, in French named the *Exposition universelle*, commemorated the centenary of the storming of the Bastille and the start of the French Revolution. Mercifully, the fair's commission rejected a rival proposal for a guillotine measuring a similar height to the Eiffel Tower. Imagine how that would look on a postcard.

United States are often associated – albeit not always accurately – with leafy streets, capacious homes, wealthy residents and cultural homogeneity, those in Paris and many other major French cities are more commonly conceived of as ethnically and racially diverse, impoverished and underfunded districts with high-rise concrete monstrosities and pervasive crime and unemployment. The *banlieue*, a term that roughly translates quite neutrally as the administrative area surrounding a fortified city wall, is consistently portrayed as a place beyond a frontier, where the opulence, extravagance and sense of 'chic' for which French cities are widely known are replaced by deprivation, struggle and suspicion. With around 80 per cent of Paris's metropolitan population living in its *banlieues* and not in the city proper, it can seem surprising that such a broad area retains such a severe stigma.

The origins of this psychological disconnect between city and suburbs, gradually reinforced in brick and concrete, can be found in the nineteenth century. Considering Paris's beauty today, it is easy to overlook how dismal it would have been at that time. Overcrowded, congested, disease-ridden, dark and dangerous, it was regularly described by commentators of the time as the city of *les misérables*, the wretched. In response, Emperor Louis-Napoléon Bonaparte III, nephew of history's most famous Corsican, from 1853 commissioned the civil servant Georges-Eugène Haussmann to modernise the outmoded city. The twisting, dingy medieval streets, so easy for insurgents to barricade – as any Victor Hugo devotee knows, and as the city's officials found to their cost during several armed uprisings – were replaced by long, straight and unprecedentedly wide boulevards, emphasising power, monumentality and efficiency. The insalubrious slums congregated around the central city were razed, while grand homes, stores, arcades, theatres and opera houses, often adopting new building materials such as glass in their designs, took their place. Parks and plazas, sewers and fountains, bridges, aqueducts and railway stations were all constructed. In sum, the city was *beautified* – a novel concept at the time – as aesthetic values, reinforced by strict disciplinary measures, came to supplant the specific needs and interests of long-time residents. Indeed, a major part of the project's appeal among the Parisian bourgeoisie was that it would expel the working classes, whom they often described as *les classes dangereuses* ('the dangerous classes'), from coveted central locations.

Despite its numerous benefits for public health and order, Haussmannisation was thus no altruistic endeavour. Haussmann's project had the overall effect of distinguishing Paris as a wealthy, consumption-oriented city that people on modest incomes would no longer be able to afford. Rather than living in inner-city areas, as remains typical of many working-class residents in the UK and the United States, they were forced beyond the city limits – that is, as long as they had survived the bloodshed of *la semaine sanglante* ('Bloody Week', 21–8 May 1871), during which several thousand socialist 'Communards' were killed in battle or executed by the French army after briefly seizing control of the city.* As far as the Parisian elite was concerned, these despised groups were now out of sight, out of mind.

And this remains the case. The legacy of Haussmannisation is best known in terms of the city's characteristic splendour, while its significant impacts beyond the city limits are generally unknown or ignored. The boundaries of modern Paris had been set before Haussmann arrived on the scene in the form of the Thiers wall, a ring of fortifications constructed to defend the city from invaders,

---

*Rooted in long-standing political and socioeconomic divisions and specifically catalysed by France's humiliating defeat in the Franco-Prussian War of 1870–1, the Commune saw a revolutionary government take command of Paris for a little over two months. During *la semaine sanglante*, which would prove to be the final week of the insurrection, the Communards found that the city's new, wide boulevards were far more difficult to blockade than were the former medieval streets torn up by Haussmann (who had been dismissed in 1870, largely due to concerns about his accounting practices).

after it succumbed in just over a day to Prussian forces in 1814. However, the wall proved inadequate when the Prussian army again besieged the city from 1870 to 1871, and from the 1880s plans commenced to dismantle it, which were later expedited by the challenges it actually posed to the French war effort during the First World War. Nowadays only a few bastions remain. Yet a perceived boundary distinguishing Paris from the wider world never disappeared, and took new physical form in 1973 with the completion of an orbital freeway called the Boulevard Périphérique, which follows the course of the old wall; its junctions are called *portes*, after the gates that once stood there. Today, crossing the 'Périph' is often compared to crossing a national border, as if requiring a passport and visa, when in reality this road simply separates Paris from its suburbs: the *banlieues*.

The *banlieues*' most significant evolution occurred following the Second World War. France was facing a housing crisis due to wartime destruction and a growing population, fuelled by increased immigration from countries such as Algeria as well as a baby boom. Shanty towns called *bidonvilles* were constructed on the urban periphery: the poor living conditions faced by their residents shocked the nation. A solution was needed. The blueprint the authorities used was the blunt modernism of the fascist and antisemitic Swiss-French architect Le Corbusier. In the 1920s, Le Corbusier had proposed levelling the Marais neighbourhood of central Paris so that he could develop his megalomaniac *Plan Voisin*, comprising eighteen identical cross-shaped towers on a rectangular grid. How different Paris would look today had the city not rejected the plan. Nevertheless, instead of being built in the city, his general vision of monolithic tower blocks surrounded by green space, as additionally encapsulated in his *Ville contemporaine* ('Contemporary City') and *Ville radieuse* ('Radiant City') plans, would eventually be regarded as a cheap but superior alternative to the *bidonvilles* in the suburbs.

These public housing estates, called *cités*, were duly constructed with enthusiasm, not least in the industrially oriented *département* of Seine-Saint-Denis to the north-east of Paris, best known by its administrative number as *le quatre-vingt treize* (the 93). But just as has tended to be the case elsewhere, these modernist estates have proved to be almost universally unpopular, generally being poorly built, their austerity standing in stark contrast to the ebullience of central Paris's belle époque and art nouveau architecture. Another cause for concern has been that Le Corbusier's vision called for the separation of functions: residents would need to travel by bus from their apartment to their workplace or the shops, rather than having services in their vicinity. Even more counterintuitively, these neighbourhoods were rarely connected to major roads or railways, trapping their residents and keeping them separated from the employment and leisure opportunities of Paris. Over time, wealthier residents have moved to more desirable private estates where they no longer have to feel constrained by such totalitarian ideas, relinquishing the decaying public estates to those without a choice. Various government interventions especially since the late 1990s have torn down *cités*, replacing them with a wider range of housing types aimed at attracting middle-class people who might support these places' local economies and increase their *mixité sociale* (social diversity). However, meagre (at best) public investment in local infrastructure like transport and education has limited these neighbourhoods' appeal to new residents, while continuing to constrain existing inhabitants' access to employment opportunities. There is also no guarantee that these groups will get along: in reality, many of the former keep largely to themselves, while the latter often resent the fact that the buildings that tend to be demolished are not those in the greatest state of disrepair, but those housing the poorest residents. Adjusting the built environment is mere window dressing if locals' needs and wishes are not considered, and so, far from being regenerated, most neighbourhoods continue gradually to deteriorate.

No surprise, then, that over the past half-century *'banlieue'* has become something of a byword for a low-income housing estate in France, even if it is perceived rather more neutrally in other parts of the francophone world. Crucially, such representations tend to include a clear racial, ethnic or religious component, viewing the *banlieues* as places overwhelmingly populated by poor Muslim immigrants from North and West Africa and the Middle East. In reality there is some uncertainty regarding the accuracy of such a portrayal, for France by law does not collect statistics on race, ethnicity or religious affiliation. Nor does this portrait need to be problematic: there are many popular, high-profile figures in French society who were raised in *banlieues*, from the football star Kylian Mbappé (who is of Cameroonian and Algerian descent) to hit musicians such as Aya Nakamura (who as a child migrated to France from Mali). The issue is that representations of these areas are rarely innocuous. Instead of recognising the contributions to French society that are being made by *banlieusards* on a daily basis, examples like the above are generally treated as exceptions, as people of minority backgrounds who have 'escaped' from these 'foreign' enclaves on French soil and only now can be considered representatives of the country. Moreover, one wrong step and they are chastised as incorrigible children of the *banlieues* once again.*

Certainly, for many people in France, the *banlieues* are the antithesis of French society. Whereas 'authentic' France is generally understood to imply white and rural, and 'republican' France patriotic, law-abiding and secular, the *banlieues* are portrayed as hotbeds of crime and anti-social behaviour, committed by hostile

---

*See for instance how in the immediate aftermath of the French national men's team's disastrous 2010 World Cup campaign, which included a players' strike against their head coach, Raymond Domenech, the French philosopher Alain Finkielkraut denounced 'ethnic and religious divisions' in the team and described the players as 'a gang of thugs who only know one moral, that of the mafia'. Similarly, one sports reporter assigned blame to the team's 'ill-bred suburban brats', while the Minister for Health and Sports Roselyne Bachelot identified the malevolent influence of 'neighbourhood kingpins'.

minority communities (especially young men) who are resistant to assimilation. The sensationalist book *Les Territoires perdus de la République* (*The Lost Territories of the Republic*) – a collection of eyewitness accounts from French school teachers, first published in 2002 by the historian Georges Bensoussan under the pseudonym Emmanuel Brenner – famously contended that *banlieue* youth are being 'Islamised' at school, a threat not only to these communities, but to France in general. Relatedly, the former Minister of the Interior Claude Guéant (a member of the old centre-right Union for a Popular Movement party) in 2011 claimed that French people 'sometimes feel like they are no longer at home' and condemned 'the creation of foreign communities [which] have isolated themselves'. More recently, in the lead-up to the 2022 presidential election, the centre-right Republicans candidate Valérie Pécresse pledged to 'take the Kärcher out of the cellar' in order to 'return order to the streets' and tackle 'the violence of the new barbarians' in the *banlieues*,* areas she had previously described as the 'breeding ground' of Islamism, 'promot[ing] self-segregation, community withdrawal and indoctrination'. Not to be outdone, her National Rally competitor Marine Le Pen told one Muslim woman that 'the headscarf is a uniform imposed over time by people who have a radical vision of Islam', a brusque declaration consistent with her previous declaration that certain *banlieues* are 'areas of lawlessness where there are two drugs: that of drugs and that of radical Islam'. Unfortunately, in the aftermath

---

* Kärcher quickly responded to this pronouncement by demanding 'an immediate halt of all uses of its trademark', fearing that it would become associated with 'violence and insecurity, even though . . . we defend solid civic values'. The German cleaning equipment company has good reason to be frustrated. In 2005, a child was tragically killed by two stray bullets in a stigmatised *cité* in La Courneuve, Seine-Saint-Denis, prompting the Minister of the Interior and future President Nicolas Sarkozy to vow to 'clean' the housing estate with a Kärcher, a metaphor later invoked by the far-right politicians Jean-Marie and Marine Le Pen as well.

of the jihadist attacks that have afflicted the country in recent years, this view that the *banlieues* foment Islamic fundamentalism has become widespread, with the implication that these areas are not only different from 'France', but are intrinsically opposed to the country's core values of *liberté, égalité* and *fraternité*. And while connotations of danger only evolve, implying new content with which to load the disparaged *banlieue* belt, its inner edge continues to act as the perceived boundary, in essentially the same way as 8 Mile Road in Detroit, but with the outside rather than the inside being besmirched.

Such demonisation has invariably involved gross exaggerations and simplifications. For instance, by no means all the perpetrators of the terrorist incidents in France or the nearly 2,000 French citizens who have joined the Islamic State over the past few years have come from deprived *banlieues*, but it has proved much easier to associate these marginalised areas with religious extremism than to pinpoint and analyse broader terrorist networks that additionally implicate comfortable middle-class neighbourhoods. Further, where young Muslims have been involved in skirmishes with the police, for example, they have seldom held a religious agenda and have more typically been seeking to challenge the discrimination they face on a daily basis. In addition, not all *banlieues* are disadvantaged *sensible* ('sensitive') or *prioritaire* ('priority') areas urgently needing a helping hand; some were once small towns in their own right and have remained popular among middle-class buyers and renters for their historic cores and far better value for money than can be found in Paris. As a rule of thumb, the wealthier *banlieues* can be found to the west and thus upwind of France's urban centres, to avoid the pollution carried by prevailing gusts from the west as they pass over the city, a socioeconomic dynamic that also exists in countries like the UK. However, the sizeable French far right especially – although not exclusively – has jumped on the chance to generalise individual incidents in the most troubled neighbourhoods to the *banlieues* as a whole.

'Blame it on the *banlieues*' has thus become a popular political move, providing carte blanche to justify increasingly stringent law enforcement and immigration control,* even where a *banlieue*'s role is not immediately obvious. Regardless of whether the debate pertains to the wearing of the Islamic headscarf,† or the commemoration of the *Charlie Hebdo* attack in 2015 (an act of remembrance declined by a minority of *banlieue* adolescents, outraging much of the country), critical media coverage of *banlieue* residents is rarely far away. For many people, the quintessential image of the *banlieues* involves a gang shooting, a drug bust or a car burning. Such stigmatisation has proved resilient.

Adolescents from racial, ethnic and religious minority backgrounds have borne the brunt of this attention, especially following the violent clashes over citizenship rights and inclusion in French society that have occurred periodically over the past forty years, most infamously in 2005. Many complain that their job applications are rejected as soon as the employer sees their address or name, even if they are qualified for the position.‡ Few major companies are willing to open headquarters or branches in these disparaged districts, further limiting the opportunities available.

---

* An interview with Guéant is, again, informative, as the conversation moves from a drug busting and a shooting in Sevran, a commune in Seine-Saint-Denis where, according to him, 'drug traffickers . . . reign supreme', to the control and integration of immigrants ('It has to be the one who comes to us who obeys our rules, and not the other way round').

† In 2004 these were banned in France's public schools alongside other 'conspicuous' religious symbols. Then, in 2010–11, full-face veils like the niqab and the burqa were prohibited in public areas in general (and while campaigning for the French presidency in 2022, Marine Le Pen vowed to extend this ban to *any* type of Islamic headscarf).

‡ This sense of injustice is backed up by a 2015 report by France's National Observatory of Urban Policy finding that 'all other things being equal, a male graduate with five years of higher education is 22 per cent less likely to be in a higher-level occupation if he comes from a Priority Neighbourhood'.

Several high-profile cases of police brutality and many less publi-cised incidents of racial profiling – paralleling the concerns raised earlier with regard to street gangs in Los Angeles – have under-mined trust in the authorities. The national and international attention gained by the largely white *gilets jaunes* ('yellow vests') protestors from November 2018 has only exacerbated many *ban-lieusards*' frustrations at their comparative lack of political voice. Caught between a country that looks upon them with suspicion and their parents' homelands where they have never lived and to which they feel little connection, many *banlieusards* struggle to see themselves as belonging anywhere. They live near Paris, but crucially not in it. Somehow, they are both French and foreign simultaneously. And without opportunities to change the stigma they experience – especially given that the democratic process excludes adolescents who are too young to vote, and their parents if they are not French citizens – the cycle of poverty and frustra-tion continues.

The word 'apartheid' has often been used by journalists and even the former prime minister Manuel Valls to describe the socioeconomic, racial, ethnic and religious separation that those in the *banlieues* experience from the rest of French society – not without good reason, given the ways in which these areas have been engineered to separate urban and suburban residents. To people beyond the *banlieues*, there tends to be little reason to visit them, entrenching the sense of distance and difference felt by residents on either side of the boundary. And occasion-ally, such sentiments are shared more widely, as was the case of Thierry Henry's warning quoted earlier. Unfortunately, given the chaos that would subsequently mar the Champions League Final between Real Madrid and Liverpool, Henry's caution proved somewhat portentous, but, paradoxically, for a different reason: unduly heavy-handed policing.* Still, try telling that to those who

---

*The principle conclusion of a French Senate inquiry into the trouble around

have already made up their minds about the *banlieues*: the prominent far-right politician Éric Zemmour, for instance, who absolved the police of responsibility by declaring with characteristic crassness that to blame were '*banlieusards*, looters, thieves and the very lot of them . . . the problem is that Seine-Saint-Denis has largely become a foreign enclave' where 'we hardly speak French any more, where people are no longer dressed in the French manner, where mores are hardly French any more'. Many in the *banlieues*, according to Zemmour, are mere *racailles* – a racist word which loosely translates to 'ghetto scum' – who need to be eradicated. It is no shock that he has previous convictions for hate speech.

Unfortunately, Zemmour is far from alone in holding the sentiment that the *banlieues* are dysfunctional places separate from wider French society. After all, along with (often skewed) news reports, one of the few sources of many people's awareness of the *banlieues* is the cinema. Most famously, Mathieu Kassovitz's 1995 film *La Haine* (*Hate*) depicts the shared experiences of unemployment, drugs and a hostile relationship with the police faced by young men of different ethnic origins in the *banlieues*, while Ladj Ly's *Les Misérables* (2019) adopts the title of Victor Hugo's portrayal of the struggles endured by maligned urbanites 200 years ago to highlight both analogous and distinctive themes of crime and conflict with the authorities in these marginalised areas today. Taken together – and despite these films' far more sensitive representations of *banlieue* life – the overall implication seems to be of consistent destitution rather than genuine progress. *Plus ça change, plus c'est la même chose.*

---

the stadium was that the final's organisers were at fault, thereby exonerating Liverpool fans whom had been blamed by the French interior minister, Gérald Darmanin. Although he subsequently provided an apology, albeit a rather weak one, Darmanin also took the liberty of shifting accountability to 'delinquency in Saint-Denis', ensuring that this place and not the authorities would be tarred with the stigma.

Despite this general stasis, in 2016 a new administrative region called Grand Paris ('Greater Paris') was established, one of its aims being to integrate the *banlieues* with the city and in the process reduce the severe inequalities among regions. This may prove to be a positive step, but many in the *banlieues* remain unconvinced, pointing to how even if real change were to be effected, as long as the widely detested Boulevard Périphérique continues to exist, the division between Paris and its immediate surroundings will remain tangible. And yet, although it is true that such physical boundaries can profoundly affect our movement and mobility, the perceptual boundaries they mark are at least as consequential in how we perceive and experience the world. Realistically, if the 'Périph' were to one day be removed, would generations of stigma simply melt away with it? The following example is indicative of the sheer resilience of invisible lines, specifically those that are *reinforced by* but crucially not *reliant on* solid materials.

The Peace Lines

BRING DOWN THE WALLS

End Sectarianism mural, Belfast

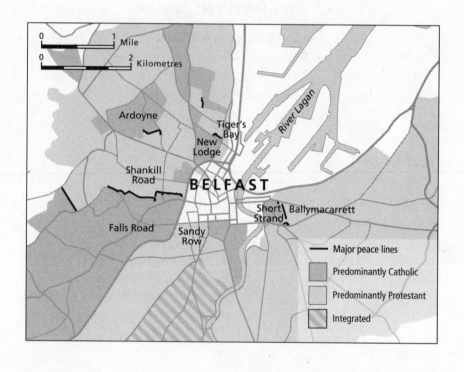

When is a conflict zone no longer a conflict zone? From Angola to Sri Lanka and Guatemala to Kosovo, the post-conflict transition process is almost invariably protracted, arduous and uncertain. The optimism associated with a peace deal can quickly dissipate; an agreement on paper does not imply compliance on the ground. Old wounds, opened and left festering for years, take time to heal. And in spite of popular belief, walls may take far longer to destroy than to build.

For many people in Northern Ireland, walls have become a feature of everyday life. Named the peace lines, in some places these physical barriers – made of corrugated iron, brick or steel and topped with barbed wire – exceed 5 kilometres in length and 6 metres in height. Originally erected during the violence that beset this country, or region, or province (like most matters here, names and definitions remain highly contentious) from the late 1960s, they continued to be built even following the signing of the Good Friday Agreement of 1998, which effectively marked the end of the conflict. Adorned with murals and graffiti, they are not just barriers, but canvases for fiercely opposed political views and identifications. The peace lines provide tangible reminders that despite the successes of the peace process, boundaries and barriers in society do not simply disappear. In fact, they may even advance and evolve.

The territory that would eventually become known as Northern Ireland has a long history of division. In particular, the colonisation of the north Irish province of Ulster by English and Scottish settlers from the early seventeenth century was partly intended to convert a predominantly Irish-speaking and Catholic territory to English-speaking and Protestant. The degree of success achieved by the 'plantation' was limited: although many Catholics were displaced from their lands, as desired by the Crown, they did not disappear. By the early twentieth century, this part of Ireland, by now unified with England, Scotland and Wales as the United Kingdom, was split between two religious groups who enjoyed little mutual *craic:** Catholics, primarily in the west, and Protestants, mainly in the east.

The Home Rule movement had been campaigning for Irish self-government since 1870, but during Easter Week 1916 Irish republicans went a step further, seeking full independence via an armed insurrection against British rule. Although this 'Easter Rising' was quashed by the British army – which had been distracted by the First World War – the violence involved further discredited the UK in many Irish people's eyes and stimulated additional calls for independence. The republican party Sinn Féin achieved a landslide victory in Ireland in the UK's general election of December 1918 and promptly declared full Irish independence. In response, and angered by the killing of two constables by members of the Irish Republican Army (IRA), the British government set about undermining the breakaway government and its advocates. An independence war (which was marked by events as appalling as an indiscriminate shooting by British forces at a Gaelic football match and a mass burning of the city of Cork) ensued until 1921, when a ceasefire was agreed and a treaty eventually signed to grant Ireland its independence. Well, most of Ireland. Whereas twenty-six counties would become a separate

---

* Popular Irish-language term for a fun and entertaining time with good company.

Irish Free State, the precursor to today's Ireland,* a relatively small portion (six counties) in the north would remain part of the UK, albeit with greater autonomy than before. The reasoning was as follows: in 1918, unlike the rest of Ireland, most of the north had voted for the Irish Unionist Party, which sought to remain part of the UK; moreover, its population was predominantly Protestant, the most prominent religion in the UK, whereas the rest of Ireland had a Catholic majority. Partition was thus deemed the best compromise.

The drawing of a new border was a difficult task. Violence continued across much of the island, and the new Irish state was plunged into civil war over the aforementioned treaty. A particular issue of contention was the future of a city that was to become part of the border, albeit narrowly on the Northern Irish side. To Irish nationalists or republicans, who were and still are almost invariably Catholic, this city is known as Derry, and due to its Catholic majority should be part of Ireland; to unionists or loyalists, who tend to be Protestant and generally identify as British rather than Irish, the city is called Londonderry, and owing to its long Protestant history should be part of Northern Ireland and by extension the UK. The usage of either Derry or Londonderry continues to provide a marker of one's politics and religion. The name Ulster in place of Northern Ireland has a similar effect, this being the traditional province of the northern part of Ireland which was split by the partition†; its usage among unionists implies that less

---

* As we shall see in a moment, names remain highly contentious across the island of Ireland. Article 4 of the Irish constitution states: 'The name of the State is Éire, or, in the English language, Ireland.' Either name tends to be used within Ireland, although the Republic of Ireland Act 1948, section 2 uses the longer name Republic of Ireland to describe the state. To this day, the latter also tends to be the choice of, among others, the UK government and the international football association FIFA, although it and the far less common Southern Ireland are much less popular within Ireland.

† Traditionally, Ulster comprises the six counties of modern-day Northern

territory should have become part of 'Catholic' Ireland, to the irritation of many republicans, who may additionally choose to avoid the 'British' name Northern Ireland and instead say 'the North', 'the North of Ireland' or 'the Six Counties'. With continued uncertainty over trade and even the very future of Northern Ireland following the UK's decision to leave the European Union in 2016 – a goal sought by only 44 per cent of Northern Ireland's voters, although fittingly for a divided society, the proportion was far higher among Protestants and unionists than among Catholics and nationalists – the border remains a significant source of controversy.

This context is crucial to understanding the peace lines, which have a more recent history but were relatedly designed to distinguish between two antagonistic sides. Situated within the settlements of Derry/Londonderry, Portadown, Lurgan and especially the capital, Belfast, the peace lines were originally constructed to physically separate predominantly nationalist, republican, Catholic neighbourhoods from predominantly unionist, loyalist Protestant neighbourhoods during 'the Troubles', the conflict that proceeded from the late 1960s to the Good Friday Agreement.* The name 'the Troubles' underplays the violence and hostility that characterised this period; likewise, 'peace lines' is honourably optimistic, as these barriers have achieved not so much peace as an absence of war. The origins of the Troubles are contested: some hold that they started in Derry/Londonderry in October 1968, when a peaceful civil rights march by Catholics upset by their long-standing experiences of discrimination in politics, employment and housing was met with police violence;

Ireland (Antrim, Armagh, Down, Fermamagh, Londonderry/Derry and Tyrone) plus three counties in the contemporary Ireland (Cavan, Donegal and Monaghan).

* Although some peace lines had been built in Belfast during the 1920s and 1930s, they no longer remain.

others date them to August 1969, when an annual parade commemorating a seventeenth-century Protestant victory in war provoked the Catholic residents of the same city's Bogside neighbourhood to protest. This civil unrest was met by resistance from the police and local unionists, a situation quickly replicated across much of Northern Ireland. A couple of nights later, a group of loyalists burnt down the Catholic homes on Belfast's Bombay Street. From this time on, sectarian and paramilitary violence would become the new normal, prompting local communities and the British Army to hastily construct physical barriers to protect the communities on either side of the divide. However, as we have seen throughout this book, drawing lines is not always as easy as it seems. In some cases, one group – even just one house – found itself stranded with its enemy on the wrong side of a barrier. Shootings and bombings, as the Cranberries poignantly describe in their protest song 'Zombie',* were pervasive even in residential areas. In total, more than 3,500 people would lose their lives over the course of nearly three decades. Two-thirds of those deaths occurred less than half a kilometre from a peace line.

The peace process that began with the ceasefire of 1994 did reduce fighting, yet physical and psychological boundaries have continued to grow. This is literally the case with the peace lines, which have become higher as well as more numerous since the Good Friday Agreement. Especially at the edges of the alternating Protestant and Catholic working-class areas of north and west Belfast, they still have a practical purpose: many republican, Catholic residents of Falls Road, for instance, would feel insecure without a barrier dividing them from the loyalist, Protestant Shankill Road. The same is true the other way around.

The peace lines also play an important symbolic role for

---

* The Irish band's singer, Dolores O'Riordan, claimed that the anti-sectarian song was particularly inspired by the tragedy of two fatal IRA bombings in the English town of Warrington in 1993.

residents. Many of the images and messages invoke neighbourhood paragons and martyrs, such as Bobby Sands and Kieran
Nugent for republicans, and Jackie Coulter and Stephen McKeag
for loyalists. Others are international in scope, expressing solidarity with groups deemed to share a wider cause. Palestine is
represented in republican murals due to its common desire for
independence and voice, whereas Israel is cited in some loyalist
murals among broader themes of unity and cooperation. Similarly, some republican murals evince support for Catalonia, the
Basque Country and Cuba, and the civil rights, anti-apartheid and
Black Lives Matter movements, while their loyalist counterparts
often celebrate British monarchs both historical and contemporary. Thus, whereas to those on one side the images and messages
are inspirational, to those on the other, they are potentially incen-
diary. Many even include belligerent imagery, including depictions
of militants and warnings for those deemed not to belong. In
these ways, it is possible to determine a neighbourhood's political
stance and religious identification simply based on their engagement with the local peace line.

Over the past fifteen years, discussions about the peace lines'
removal have continued, and a 2023 target was set for their complete eradication, but progress has been very slow, not least
because many people continue to suggest that these barriers are
necessary for them to feel safe. Remembering how their relatives,
friends and neighbours died, this is understandable. After so long
on either side of a physical boundary, residents are accustomed
to their existence and often favour the maintenance of the status
quo rather than a step into the unknown, even if doing so might
eventually improve relations. Difference has become thoroughly
normalised.

Furthermore, even where there is consent on both sides for a
wall's removal, ambiguities in ownership, legislation and political
responsibility can prove inhibitory. The disappearance of a peace
line could enable the development of a new housing estate, but

politicians have often been sensitive to how their support bases will be affected by changing demographics. The close relationship between local residents' collective identity and their neighbourhood further constrains politicians' willingness to engage in any act that might be regarded as social engineering and as therefore compromising their own electability, even if removing the barriers is likely to have significant long-term economic benefits in what are often deeply impoverished areas. The fact that the peace lines' murals now attract tourists from far afield and thereby generate much-needed revenue, not to mention materialise and reinforce a sense of identity for residents, is also likely to impede efforts to tear them down. To many people, the addition of gates, opened only during the daytime and often staffed by police, is sufficient. The peace lines, which were only ever intended to be temporary, now have an air of permanence.

Northern Ireland's boundaries are not limited to the peace lines, either. Physically, they are just one kind of 'interface', marking where segregated communities abut. Gates or rows of vegetation, for instance, can operate in a similar way, even if they appear less immediately cautionary. Flags, which line many streets in Northern Ireland, provide another important marker of difference, the Union flag and the Ulster banner being favoured among unionists, the Irish tricolour among nationalists. Indeed, even though the tricolour was intentionally designed to include the traditional Protestant colour, orange, in addition to Catholic green, most people associate this flag solely with the latter community. Interestingly, too, what is probably the least contentious flag, the St Patrick's saltire, is not especially beloved among either group. To this day, flags may, like the peace lines, attract rather than deter antagonists by clearly publicising where one's rivals can be found. Even a choice as seemingly innocuous as a favourite football club can stimulate animosity – the two major Glaswegian teams Celtic and Rangers are particularly popular among Catholic and Protestant residents respectively – and as we have already seen in the case of Buenos Aires, sporting the 'wrong' colours in certain neighbourhoods remains risky. Similarly, wearing a Catholic school uniform in some Protestant areas and vice versa still tends to be discouraged.

Education is in itself an important boundary here. Over 90 per cent of children and adolescents still attend schools that are largely or entirely segregated by religion, and although the parent-driven integrated school movement has managed to establish non-denominational alternatives, these remain a tiny minority. With minimal opportunities available to mix with peers of the other faith, people can from childhood easily live parallel lives where they never encounter, at least voluntarily, those on the other side of a peace line. No wonder, then, that many students claim to know little about Catholicism or Protestantism beyond specific stereotypes and possibly prejudices passed down through the generations. Overcoming this knowledge boundary is a difficult task that depends not only on the creditable commitment of many young people to doing so, but also on their elders' amenability to breaking down the walls, both physical and perceived.

Certainly, important social and political boundaries also remain. In many parts of Northern Ireland, especially in working-class communities, marrying outside the faith remains uncommon, and the residents of segregated neighbourhoods may still be targeted with small-scale forms of violence thrown over the peace lines, including threats, verbal abuse and projectiles. These differences at the street level are mirrored at Stormont, the Northern Ireland Assembly, where the two main political parties, Sinn Féin and the Democratic Unionist Party (DUP), represent opposing ideologies, in many ways to an even greater extent than the populace. It transpires that trust can prove more difficult to build than walls.

In this regard, perhaps no issue is as contentious as the summer marching season, when members of the Orange Order, a Protestant, unionist organisation, parade with marching bands in celebration of William of Orange's (or King William III of England's) victory over Catholic forces at the Battle of the Boyne in 1690. For many Catholics, this act is one of triumphalism and, coupled with the enormous 'Eleventh Night' bonfires, at which many Protestant communities additionally burn Irish and Catholic symbols and effigies, there is always the potential for provocation to result in disorder. Republican parades are less common, and instead of commemorating victory, they tend to be used to remember sombre events like the Easter Rising of 1916, 'Bloody Sunday' of 30 January 1972, when British soldiers shot and killed fourteen civilians in Derry/Londonderry protesting the internment without trial of suspected IRA members, and the hunger strikes undertaken by republican prisoners during the 1970s and 1980s, which helped mobilise Irish nationalist politics. Counter-demonstrations are also not uncommon, and accusations of terrorism during the Troubles may be made by either side.

Compared to many other societies that have experienced widespread conflict, attempts to reckon with the past and thereby achieve reconciliation have been fairly limited. Educational organisations, sports clubs and community arts programmes have offered valuable means for individuals to build relations and change mindsets, but they can only do so much. Some of the most confrontational (and conspicuous) murals have been removed or at least altered to depict more 'neutral' images, like Belfast's industrial history or local notables, while new, non-sectarian murals, often created through collaborating artists of different communities, have appeared in recent years. And yet it is still not uncommon to see a mural of children juxtaposed with another of paramilitaries, for instance, or for sectarian murals to take a less militant form, Martin Luther confronting the Catholic Church being just one example. In Northern Ireland, murals do not merely represent a community's outlook: they actively drive it.

After all, as much as the themes depicted on the peace lines change, the canvas ultimately remains the same physical barrier between communities. Many people are reluctant to eliminate the lines, lest doing so implies relinquishing land that they regard as lawfully theirs, and theirs exclusively or at least primarily. They provide feelings of both security and insecurity, belonging and forbiddance, presenting a classic catch-22: as much as there may be a desire to eliminate these barriers, this will only happen when people feel sufficiently free from harm, yet such feelings are in large part contingent on the existence of boundaries. Without concerted efforts to share rather than spar, the potential for conflict remains.

Consequently, these are particularly complicated boundaries, which accordingly say much about the complexity of humans' engagement with space. More than simply being tangible expressions of perceived difference, rooted in a specific period, they help ensure that such sentiments are learnt and thereby maintained in the future. Especially through the use of murals, the peace lines form part of a dialogue: local communities use them to communicate their beliefs and concerns, which are in turn received by others, whether different communities, visitors or future generations. They make invisible attitudes and beliefs visible. A person on either side quickly realises whether or not they belong, and if they do, they may seek to protect the boundary so as to protect their feelings of belonging as well. This requires the continued definition of an 'us' and, at least as importantly, a 'them', understood, however spuriously, as the complete antithesis of oneself. Constantly stereotyping those on either side means that division remains the reality, further compromising any interest in removing boundaries both 'real' and perceived. Indeed, destroying a peace line could be seen as tantamount to erasing a community's understanding of itself and its claims to space.

In a broader sense, then, removing a boundary may be deemed equivalent to dissolving one's identity, or at least endorsing this. Therefore, as much as we may hope to see boundaries that are built on hatred and insecurity disappear – and we should – we must also recognise that the boundaries we *see* are not necessarily the boundaries of most long-term consequence. A wall or fence is rarely built without an intention of keeping someone or something else out, or of explicitly marking out a territory as one's own. Without viewing 'others' as we view 'ourselves', a psychological boundary can always provide the possibility of a physical one. Moreover, once a physical boundary exists – the Boulevard Périphérique around Paris being an analogous example considered earlier – it can be harder for the psychological boundary underpinning it to fade away. Eliminating a tangible boundary like a peace line has proved difficult, but breaking down boundaries in the mind is even harder. Arguably nowhere epitomises the continued relevance of invisible lines following the removal of a physical barrier better than the next example.

The Berlin Wall

Walls in people's heads are sometimes more durable than walls made of concrete blocks.

Willy Brandt

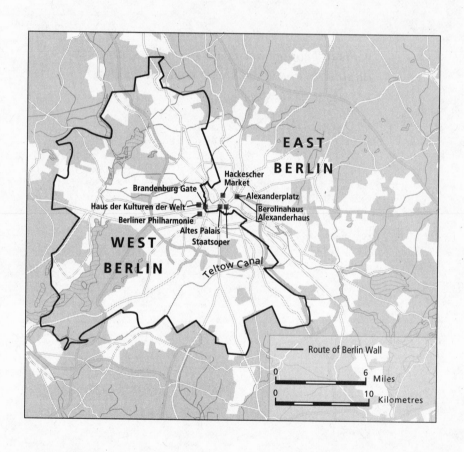

EAST
BERLIN

Hackescher
Market

Brandenburg Gate

Alexanderplatz

Haus der Kulturen der Welt

Berolinahaus
Alexanderhaus

Berliner Philharmonie

Altes Palais

Staatsoper

WEST

BERLIN

Teltow Canal

Route of Berlin Wall

0   6 Miles

0   10 Kilometres

The world is full of examples of boundary lines that became borders. One of the most famous – and notorious – examples is Cyril Radcliffe's boundary demarcation line. It was intended to separate India and Pakistan (the eastern part of which later became Bangladesh) on their independence from the British Empire following the Second World War. Radcliffe, a British lawyer who, despite never having been east of Paris, was commissioned to draw a new border in a distant part of the world,* primarily based his line on religious demographics (with Hindus being placed in India and Muslims in Pakistan; other faiths were more or less ignored), while aiming to minimise disruption to existing infrastructure such as railway lines, canals and irrigation channels. Over seventy years later, the resulting border remains highly contentious and has been the site of several wars and skirmishes. However, there are also cases where formal and often highly policed borders are removed. Do boundaries dissolve when borders disappear? In the case of Berlin, not necessarily.

The story of the Berlin Wall is well known. Constructed by the German Democratic Republic (GDR; East Germany) in 1961, it separated communist East Berlin and the greater GDR from capitalist West Berlin, purportedly to keep out Western 'fascists' who might subvert its far-left ideology. In reality, however, it mainly worked to stem the tide of people – not least professionals

---

* The logic ostensibly being that with ignorance comes impartiality.

and skilled workers – fleeing to the West. Over time, it came to comprise an elaborate system of concrete walls, barbed wire, electrified fences, observation towers, floodlights, anti-vehicle trenches, patrolling soldiers and guard dogs. By the time the wall was opened and promptly chiselled to pieces on 9 November 1989, well over 100 people (exact numbers are uncertain) had died trying to cross it, in many cases after being shot by the GDR's border guards. Crossing it had never been impossible – more than 5,000 people from East Berlin managed to do so via a range of methods, including by tunnelling, swimming along the frigid Teltow Canal and, in the case of the trapeze artist Horst Klein, walking along a disused power cable* – but its demise enabled Berlin once again to become one city, both officially and emotionally.

And yet, even though what was once a formal, tangible border has been reduced to a few exhibits and memorials in the city – individual pieces can also be found in places as eclectic as a men's bathroom in Las Vegas and as apt as the Luxembourgish village of Schengen, where various European countries agreed to gradually abolish their border checks – traces of difference between West and East remain. In some parts of Berlin, it is difficult to imagine there was ever a border here: immediately next to the iconic Brandenburg Gate, for instance, which was rendered inaccessible throughout the Berlin Wall's existence. But look closely, and differences on either side of the wall's former course emerge.

First, the architecture. Following the bombing of Berlin during the Second World War, much of the city needed to be rebuilt. However, whereas West Berlin was able to draw on considerable rebuilding funds through the Marshall Plan and over the subsequent decades saw the construction of numerous new, futuristic structures such as the Kongresshalle (Congress Hall,

---

*Exhausted and cold, Klein ultimately toppled from the cable into West Berlin, breaking both his arms, a landing less graceful than his audiences would typically have witnessed.

now the Haus der Kulturen der Welt or House of the World's Cultures) and the Berliner Philharmonie (Berlin Philharmonic), as well as the restoration of symbolically significant buildings such as the Staatsoper (State Opera) and the Altes Palais (Old Palace), East Berlin opted for a programme of low-cost, high-efficiency modernisation. This was not just an economic choice but an ideological one, as shown by the fact that the GDR's leadership opted to restore the discernibly functional Berolinahaus and Alexanderhaus, but not other buildings that had survived the war. East Berlin's residential *Plattenbauten* ('panel buildings'), consisting of large, prefabricated concrete slabs, were from the 1960s onwards almost invariably constructed following a few standard templates with unceremonious names, such as P2 (*Plattenbau 2*) and WHH Gt 18 (*Wohnhochhaus Großtafelbauweise 18*; 'residential tower, applied large-panel construction with 18 storeys'). Although similar-looking buildings were erected in West Berlin, urban planners on this side also drew on more innovative modernist architectural principles and sought to ensure the availability of open spaces, vegetation and cultural facilities to residents. Such differences are still apparent, albeit quite subtly, today.

Second, when examining Berlin's tram map, it is immediately apparent that the tram network is greatly skewed to the east. Key interchanges that are geographically near the centre of the present-day city, such as Hackescher Markt (which was named 'Marx-Engels-Platz' during the GDR era) and Alexanderplatz/Dircksenstraße, appear towards the western edge, while almost all the lines fan out to the east. Whereas East Berlin retained many of its tram lines, West Berlin opted to extend its underground (U-Bahn) and bus networks, some of which today follow the old tram routes. By the end of 1967, all of West Berlin's trams had disappeared. Since reunification, new tram routes have gradually been opened in what was West Berlin, but they still predominate in the former East. And as one can imagine, Western neighbourhoods of Berlin today tend to be much better served by the U-Bahn than their Eastern counterparts.

The *Ampelmännchen* ('little traffic light men'), which have become perhaps the most enduring symbol of East Berlin, provide further evidence that there was once a formal and enforced divide.* A diminutive male figure with a large head, a distinguishable nose and lips from the side profile and wearing a brimmed hat, the *Ampelmann* design exemplifies several ideological decisions made east of the former border. Designed in 1961 by Karl Peglau, a German traffic psychologist, the *Ampelmännchen* were originally supposed to face the right, for 'go', but given the GDR's political bent, they were soon turned to the left. Their hats, too, became a political subject, being more closely associated with capitalism than communism, but after Peglau saw the key communist politician and future GDR leader Erich Honecker wearing a straw hat on television, they remained in place. With Western values ultimately prevailing in the Cold War, they could have been consigned to history, but following public pressure highlighting their cult appeal (and vividness), their survival has been ensured.

Why are they so popular today? Even as mere silhouettes, the *Ampelmännchen* seem far more expressive than their skinnier and less defined Western counterparts, walking purposefully with a hand outstretched for 'go' and standing steadfast with their arms out and legs in for 'stop'. They command discipline: when an *Ampelmann* tells pedestrians to stop, they do so. During the GDR's existence, they became so beloved and influential that they were used in strip cartoons, games, radio broadcasts

---

*With the benefit of satellite imagery, a different form of illumination provides additional evidence of a formerly divided city: the fluorescent street lamps in the West produce a strident yellow-white, whereas the cheaper sodium-vapour lamps in the East emit a more mellow orange. However, this distinction will eventually disappear as the city gradually replaces the latter in order to minimise its carbon emissions.

and children's television programmes. Such reverence has hardly disappeared since reunification. Indeed, nostalgia has seen them – highly ironically – become deeply commercialised, to the extent that one local told me they actually now 'associate them with being a tourist in Berlin'. Dedicated shops, generally situated in central locations and describing the *Ampelmann* as 'Berlin's iconic brand', sell products ranging from cookie cutters to condoms (marketed in English with the memorable tagline, 'Let's tear down some walls tonight – safely!'), while an *Ampelmann* cafe and an *Ampelmann* coffee bike offer beverages to stay or go. Instead of being replaced by Western traffic lights, they have even started to spread into some Western neighbourhoods and at choice intersections in a few old West German cities, meaning that they do not demonstrate a strict division between East and West, although the vast majority are still to be found in the former. Reflecting Germany's increased commitment to gender equality, a female *Ampelfrau* has also been introduced in places, while same-sex couples called *Ampelpärchen* can be found in parts of neighbouring Austria and in Munich.

The city's streets evince the old divide, too, with names honouring the conflicting ideologies West and East represented. In the East, one finds tributes to communist icons Karl Marx, Friedrich Engels, Rosa Luxemburg and Karl Liebknecht, as well as a park and sculpture commemorating Ernst Thälmann, the leader of the Communist Party of Germany before Adolf Hitler was appointed chancellor in 1933. By contrast, the Western side reveres historic royals such as Queen Sophie Charlotte, the nationalist composer Richard Wagner and Marie Luise Bergmann, a major landowner.

And it is not as if economic and political differences have disappeared, either. In particular, the transition to a capitalist system has not been easy for many in the East, as increased competition has seen thousands lose their jobs and their economic security. Differences in wages and pensions have proved to be controversial matters, and a brain drain from East to West has exacerbated scepticism of the latter in some formerly communist neighbour-hoods. With many on the East side feeling disillusioned about the country's direction over the past thirty years, populists have thus found opportunities to challenge the status quo to a much greater extent than in the West. The far-right Alternative for Germany (AfD) has become one of the largest parties in the German parliament and has made particular inroads in the old East Germany, including in much of East Berlin, whereas its progress in the West has been far more limited. As a local-scale example of this division in action, a visitor is far more likely to come across a memorial to the victims of the Holocaust in western parts of Berlin, given the AfD's denunciation of remembering this event lest it undermine German national pride. The Left Party, the direct descendant of the GDR's single Socialist Unity Party, has also gained support in certain districts of the old East Berlin in recent years, taking advantage of many voters' dissatisfaction with the more main-stream parties associated with western parts of the city and the country in general. Relatedly, and although it is undoubtedly a simplification, many observers and surveys point to contrasting sources of influence on either side of the old divide, with those in the West tending to hold more favourable attitudes towards the European Union and the United States, while those in the East often look the other way: as one Berliner who has lived on both sides of the post-reunification city told me, 'a lot of East Berliners have quite strong pro-Russian sentiment still', alongside 'much stronger anti-American sentiment'. The fact that some Germans continue to distinguish not only politically but also culturally and linguistically between *Wessis* ('Westerners') and *Ossis* ('Eastern-ers') – what is often called *die Mauer im Kopf* ('the wall in the head') – demonstrates how an informal social boundary remains as well.

(Incidentally, an invisible line is still perceived by red deer, which no longer cross where the Iron Curtain between West Germany and Czechoslovakia further south once stood, even though the old electric fences, armed guards and watchdogs are long gone, and the deer living today would not have been alive to remember them. Presumably they have learnt new migration routes from their parents rather than making an ideological decision not to cross the former divide.)

Such resilience to change is part of what makes boundaries so captivating. Although they may originate in a visible phenomenon like a physical border, they can survive, largely or entirely invisibly, even after that phenomenon is long gone. The common assumption that destruction is quicker and easier than construction is thus true only up to a point: despite the fact that more time has now passed since the Berlin Wall fell than this famous divide ever stood, noteworthy manifestations of difference remain. In this respect, division does not rely on conspicuous material phenomena such as walls for survival. It can also endure through more banal means – perceptible, if one looks closely, from the street to the job centre.

But vision, on its own, can also be subject to error. After all, our imaginations play a key role in piecing together our varied observations and experiences, allowing us to identify patterns which may or may not be grounded in reality. Our assumptions, our biases, can shape how we view places we may never have visited. Through constant repetition over time, some myths about 'our' land versus 'their' land even come to be treated as fact. Keeping this thought in mind, who decides what makes one place necessarily different from another, and accordingly, where the boundaries between them are located? Let's zoom out to the continental scale.

The Ural Mountains

There always is this fallacious belief:
'It would not be the same here; here
such things are impossible.'

Aleksandr Solzhenitsyn, *The Gulag Archipelago 1918–1956*

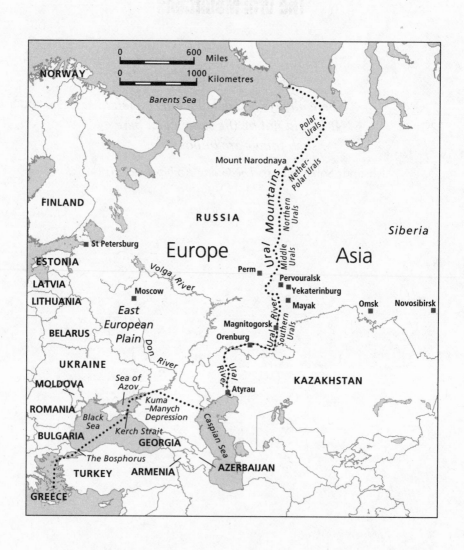

What actually is Europe? The question seems so innocuous, and the answer so obvious: a continent. But like with most things on our planet, there is more than meets the eye. Using a widely accepted definition of a continent – as a large, continuous landmass – it is easy to see that Europe is a very poor example. Unlike Africa, for instance, which merely pecks Asia on the cheek at Sinai and Suez, Europe's land boundary with Asia is thousands of kilometres in length, seemingly making them one continuous landmass rather than two separate ones. Similarly, the Americas are divided by just a narrow strip of land at Panama: no coincidence, then, that both Suez and Panama were identified as convenient geographical shortcuts where seafarers would be able to travel by canal through, rather than around, major landmasses. Geology provides further justification that Africa and North and South America constitute continents, as they sit on discrete tectonic plates.

By contrast, Europe's claim to continental status is far more tenuous. The narrow Bosphorus strait in north-western Turkey provides some support, splitting Europe and Asia along a distinct line that has come to assume considerable cultural as well as geographical relevance, as we shall soon see. There is also a tectonic boundary nearby, between the Eurasian and Anatolian plates, although it runs perpendicular to the Bosphorus rather than through it. And that's about it. The Black Sea to the north and the Aegean Sea to the south of the Bosphorus could *perhaps* be regarded as extensions of a continental boundary. To the north of the Black Sea, however, is a vast stretch of land – the East European Plain – that continues until the Barents Sea, a thousand kilometres north of St Petersburg. As Kievan Rus' found to its cost, this mostly low-lying plain does not provide much of a physical barrier against potential invaders from the east: Mongol forces successfully conquered this once-powerful federation in the thirteenth century. It is difficult to regard Europe as a separate continent when an empire from Asia can so freely spread across the same landmass.

Instead, the 'Eurasian' in the name of the Eurasian tectonic plate provides a clue as to how difficult it is to define Europe. According to the criteria above – a large, continuous landmass, separated by water and most likely plate tectonics as well – Europe is not really a continent at all. It is more like a large peninsula of Asia, one with its own smaller peninsulas, such as Iberia, Italy, Jutland and Scandinavia. In some parts of the world, in fact, this is exactly how Europe is perceived: as merely a portion of a larger Eurasian continent, albeit one that has had an outsized impact on the rest of the planet over the centuries. Nevertheless, it is still conventional in most places to consider 'Europe' as distinct from 'Asia'. And compellingly, a seemingly arbitrary land boundary has long been said to separate the two.

Consulting a map of Europe in an atlas or online, certain consistencies seem to emerge. Iceland, a good thousand or so kilometres from either Scotland or Norway as the crow flies, is positioned in the north-western corner, sometimes alongside a sliver of Greenland. All or most of the Mediterranean is presented to the south, often with the tips of Morocco, Algeria and Tunisia protruding towards Spain and Italy. Turkey is generally represented, either in full or in part; where it is on display in full, so too tend to be Armenia, Azerbaijan and Georgia, sometimes described as the 'balcony of Europe'. Russia, however, presents a dilemma. At over 17 million square kilometres in total, it is nearly three times the size of Europe.* Even its 'European' portion, less than a quarter of its total area, is well over six times larger than Ukraine, the biggest country solely within Europe. Any map that includes the entirety of Russia has the effect of making Europe look – quite accurately – tiny. (This is no inconsequential matter. The Mercator projection, which for many people is *the* standard for world maps, has long enjoyed popularity among Europeans because it inflates the sizes of landmasses towards the poles, making northern Europe especially appear much larger than it actually is. Any European leader seeking to boast about the size of their country is thus advised to use the Mercator rather than its main rival, the Peters projection.) As a result, just the westernmost portion of Russia is typically included in maps of Europe. The cut-off, almost invariably, is the Ural mountain range running north to south, extended by the river of the same name into Kazakhstan.

What is it about the Ural Mountains that means they should be regarded as a boundary between Europe and Asia? After all, they are not particularly remarkable. At approximately 2,500 kilometres in length, the range is the seventh longest in the world, but still shorter than another, far more renowned and formidable mountain chain in Asia, the Himalayas. The Urals are often divided into five sections (Polar, Nether-Polar, Northern, Middle and Southern), with different geologies and climates, but this fact is unsurprising for a range that crosses from Arctic tundra to semi-desert landscapes. There are around 1,300 mountains across the world that exceed 6,000 feet; at 6,217, Mount Narodnaya ('People's Mountain'), the Urals' highest peak, only narrowly qualifies. Are there any points of distinction, either significant or subtle, between the landmasses on either side?

For one thing, geology. It is worth noting that the Urals are

---

*For the purpose of this particular calculation, no part of Russia is included in Europe.

exceptionally old, formed 250–300 million years ago through the colliding of continental plates.* No tectonic plate boundary remains, but a separation of sorts exists between Europe to the west and Asia to the east in the form of the north-to-south Main Uralian Fault. Past tectonic activity here has left traces of difference on either side of the mountain range: the rocks to the west were formed from the sediments of the former Baltica tectonic plate, comprising limestone, sandstone and dolomite, whereas those to the east are primarily basalt, a dense igneous rock strongly associated with the oceanic crust. Limestone is especially prone to weathering and so the western slopes of the Urals are characterised by caves and sinkholes, not dissimilar to parts of Kentucky, Croatia or Slovenia. Given that the prevailing winds here come from the Atlantic Ocean to the west, the climate of the western slopes is milder and wetter and the landscape greener, typified by either broad-leaved trees, conifer forests or mosses going from south to north. By contrast, the eastern slopes are gentler, drier and in winter conspicuously colder, although less snowy. The eastern flora thus includes more pine forests and, to the north, lichen. Also due to various climatic and geological factors, the rivers to the west are generally larger, but the lakes are smaller and less numerous.

As one might suspect given the contrasting geologies on either side, different deposits can be found on the west from those on the east: the former specialises in fossil fuels, whereas the latter has a greater range of metal and mineral resources as well. And crucially, it is the abundance of their natural resources that has since the mid-seventeenth century explained the Urals' importance within Russian society. Bituminous coal, lignite, petroleum and natural gas; economically valuable ores of iron, copper and

---

*In comparison, the Rocky Mountains are only about 70–80 million years old, the Himalayas 40–50 million years and the Andes 25–30 million years in age.

nickel; deposits of precious and semi-precious metals and gemstones, including gold, platinum, diamond, emerald, amethyst and topaz, many of which are showcased in Peter Carl Fabergé's world-famous Easter eggs: all and more are found and extracted here. Cities such as Perm to the west and Yekaterinburg to the east emerged as significant smelting centres during the eighteenth century, and with the construction of the Siberian Route – a trade artery nicknamed the 'Tea Road' – they were eventually connected with Moscow to the west and China to the east. During the 1930s, one of Joseph Stalin's most famous planned settlements, Magnitogorsk, was developed near the southern foothills as the USSR's steel capital in the manner of Pittsburgh or Gary in the United States. Moreover, following Operation Barbarossa in June 1941, when the Nazis mounted a surprise attack against the USSR, Stalin opted to evacuate en masse western Soviet citizens and industries (as well as Vladimir Lenin's embalmed body and the Hermitage Museum's prodigious collection) to this mountain range and beyond, confident that enemy forces would never be able to reach so far east. The subsequent Soviet counter-offensive was fuelled by the productivity of the industries in this region. Later, during the Cold War, the Soviet authorities used the Urals for nuclear weapons testing, offering the ideal combination of an industrial tradition and obscurity to the outside world; even the Kyshtym* disaster of 1957, before Chernobyl the world's most severe nuclear accident in history, received little international attention. The Urals' role in modern Russian history is, in short, considerable.

Today, mining, metallurgy, engineering and chemical processing are central to the economies of Ural cities and, by extension, Russia as a whole. Still, it is highly debatable whether age, geology and natural resources alone are enough to make the Urals a meaningful continental boundary: surely nobody would claim that the Appalachians, which share certain similarities in these respects,

---

* Also known as Mayak.

divide a continent? Population may provide a more effective distinction: despite constituting a far smaller area of Russia, the European part is home to over three-quarters of the country's inhabitants, and almost all its major cities can be found here. Standing in contrast to this more densely populated area is an immense expanse of territory to the east of the Urals that has often been treated as the land equivalent of medieval maps' 'Here be dragons': Siberia. Roughly the size of Canada and India combined, but with a smaller population than Morocco, Siberia is often associated with prisons, Gulags and harsh winters, in contrast to western Russia's elaborate architecture, classical music and literature. Indeed, its reputation as an expansive, remote wilderness rendered Siberia a convenient place for the Soviet authorities to conceal dirty secrets like the forced resettlement of minority-nationality populations, while Western Europeans, so rarely familiar with the Russia beyond the Urals, came to view Siberia as a mysterious and dangerous 'East'. This certainly makes the Urals a boundary of sorts, although not necessarily a continental one. It is also important to avoid overly simplifying this perceived divide: there is plenty of grand architecture to the east of the Urals, such as Novosibirsk's turquoise railway station, or the gold-domed Dormition Cathedral in Omsk. And it's not as if St Petersburg or Moscow are famed for their balmy climes. Nevertheless, and reflecting the power of representation, it has proved easy for a broad distinction between two Russias – one 'known' and 'hospitable', the other 'unknown' and 'hostile' – to emerge, both within Russia itself and beyond.

Indeed, given the general lack of tangible evidence of a continental boundary either side of the Urals – some geological discrepancies, fairly subtle demographic variations, a few differences in climate and landscape – more subjective discrepancies have been sought to justify this boundary. But why the Urals of all places? Ancient Greek scholars such as Anaximander, Hecataeus of Miletus and Herodotus, all of whom made crucial contributions to the foundation of geography as a discipline, distinguished Europe from Asia in their maps further south-west, in the Caucasus Mountains. Importantly, their decisions were based on the belief that these continents are in fact separated by water bodies, an objective criterion, even if it is one that fails to account for size differences between rivers and seas. As their geographical knowledge increased, the Greeks continued to revise and extend the boundary. Gradually the Tanais River (now the Don) became the more conventional divide, a perception reinforced among Europeans with the production in the second century of Ptolemy's map of the world, which positioned this watercourse near the centre of the 'known' world.* Over time, the Eurasian boundary was extended southwards through the Sea of Azov, the Kerch Strait, the Black Sea and the Bosphorus, a tradition that continued until the eighteenth century. That's a very long time for the idea that Europe and Asia are divided along this water-based boundary to take root!

It was not until 1730 that the Swedish army officer and geographer Philip Johan von Strahlenberg, assisted by the Russian statesman and researcher Vasily Tatishchev, provoked a paradigm shift. Drawing on a growing body of research into Russian geography since the sixteenth century, von Strahlenberg contended that the Don is insufficient as a continental divide because it is relatively small and is limited to southern Russia. Instead, he extended the traditional boundary across the Volga River region and northwards along the conveniently spinal Ural Mountains. Von Strahlenberg and Tatishchev identified some of the physical distinctions marked by the Urals mentioned above, such as their contrasting slopes, vegetation and minerals. However, von Strahlenberg also had an important 'cultural' justification in mind.

---

*Incidentally, even though Ptolemy's map did not explicitly identify the river as a dividing line, it did have an appreciable invisible-line legacy of a different kind: it displayed latitude and longitude in an unprecedentedly systematic way.

In recognition of Peter the Great's recent efforts to 'Europeanise' his country, not least by making the old Swedish town of Nyen his new capital, St Petersburg, von Strahlenberg wanted to separate what he deemed the grand, modern, imperial 'Russia' to the west of the Urals from the supposedly wild, ungovernable colony of 'Siberia' to the east. In the process, he hoped to convince European audiences that the tsar was successfully transforming (the western part of) his country into an efficient, meticulously engineered and erudite state that could be welcomed as a European partner. This was of great interest to the new imperial authorities, too, who were still trying to seize control over the south-eastern steppe in particular, whose populations were in large part nomadic, Muslim or Buddhist and difficult to administer from the centre.

Following von Strahlenberg's publication of the dividing line, an accomplished research team was sent to survey the Urals and its inhabitants. They seemed disappointed at the Urals' extent and size, but dutifully agreed to examine and advance our understanding of their physical geography. In their writings, they also reinforced Western assumptions that the 'Asian' people to the east would be resistant to the tsar's authority. This concept of a 'civilisational' divide within Russia has remained a matter of some controversy. For instance, the Slavophile intellectual movement of the nineteenth century, which included the great writer Fyodor Dostoevsky, sought to centre Russian attention on Asia at the expense of Europe.* Disagreements over whether Russia as

---

*Dostoevsky maintained that Russia's 'hopes lie perhaps more in Asia than in Europe: in our future Asia will be our salvation'. He certainly didn't seem to enjoy his time in Geneva, writing to the Russian poet Apollon Maykov: 'If you only knew, what a stupid, dull, insignificant, savage people it is . . . There are parties and continuous squabbles, pauperism, terrible mediocrity in everything. A workman here is not worth the little finger of a workman of ours. The customs are savage . . . Their inferiority of development: the drunkenness, the thieving, the paltry swindling, that have become the rule in their commerce.'

well as Kazakhstan should look to Europe or Asia for a sense of cultural belonging, or whether the countries can uniquely blend the two, remain pertinent to this day.

The notion of there being a boundary – any boundary – between Europe and Asia is thus laden with power, as it is necessarily based on human aspects rather than simply or primarily on the configuration of the Earth's continents. Adolf Hitler's changing mindset during Operation Barbarossa epitomises this point. Whereas the Führer originally took the notion that the Urals constitute a continental divide for granted, pledging to ensure that 'no foreign military forces [exist] west of the Urals', he quickly came to realise that this unassuming mountain range would not suffice, remarking:

It's absurd to try to suppose that the frontier between the two separate worlds of Europe and Asia is marked by a chain of not very high mountains – and the long chain of the Urals is no more than that. One might just as well decree that the frontier is marked by one of the great Russian rivers. No, geographically Asia penetrates into Europe without any sharp break.

And so, in place of this physical but somewhat unassuming mountain range, he decided to invoke the larger Nazi policy of *Lebensraum,** championing a 'living wall' of Aryan German colonisers that could act as a racial dividing line between 'the Germanic world' and 'the Slav world'. Not relying on specific, mappable locations, such a boundary would crucially be malleable and therefore could be moved further and further to the east with incremental German advances. The Ural boundary idea would subsequently be challenged by a Russian leader as well, but for a very different reason. After French President Charles de Gaulle described

---

*Settler colonialism; literally, 'living space'.

Europe as running *'entre l'Atlantique et l'Oural'* ('between the Atlantic and the Urals') in a 1959 speech calling for European integration, the Soviet premier, Nikita Khrushchev, reportedly flew into a rage, displeased that a foreign leader would imply the existence of a partition – any partition – in his country. The French foreign ministry was forced to assure its Soviet counterparts that this mischievous phrase would never be uttered again.

Nonetheless, the belief that there is an invisible continental divide running through Russia has become entrenched over time. To be clear, not every cartographer since von Strahlenberg has precisely followed his line, hardly surprising in a field in which disagreement is commonplace. Some have accused it of being arbitrary, despite proposing similarly tenuous boundaries. The Kuma–Manych Depression to the north of the Caucasus was for a long time a popular rival, connecting the Black Sea to the Caspian Sea, but it gradually declined in usage, especially outside Russia. Factors such as elevation, rivers, watersheds, administrative units and religion have all been used to justify boundary claims in a number of places, but eventually the Ural Mountains – extended by the Ural River, which flows south and west from the southern portion of the range – have come to be the most commonly understood boundary. As symbolic reinforcement, parts of it are today marked by physical structures, including pedestrian bridges over the Ural River in the 'transcontinental' cities of Orenburg and Atyrau and an obelisk in Pervouralsk near Yekaterinburg. Magnitogorsk has even adopted as its official motto, 'The place. where Europe and Asia meet'. Still, while these are all presumably interesting places to visit, or to claim to have visited, the Europe–Asia divide is in many ways a boundary more in name than in substance. There is, simply put, little to distinguish two villages on either side of this line, which is a major reason why its precise location remains so contentious. Further, the Urals have historically been inhabited by various Indigenous groups, many of which are or were formerly nomadic, such as the Bashkirs in the south, the Khanty in the middle portions and the Nenets and Komi in the far north, so any boundary based on demographic lines is subject to flux. More generally, the word 'culture' is often invoked to justify claims of continental difference, even though it can be problematic to define places solely on the basis of such a contested term. For example, Syria and Vietnam are on the same broad landmass and both are considered 'Asian' countries, but their cultural differences are enormous.

So, whereas the Urals provide only a modest physical boundary, as a human one they are truly nebulous. Some broad distinctions between the two sides may be identified – like the greater influence of the Russian Orthodox Church to the west and the higher propensity for people to adhere to minority faiths such as Buddhism, Tengrism and Paganism to the east – but these seem insufficient to justify claiming this mountain range as something as significant as a continental divide. Any cultural boundary between Europe and Asia is gradual rather than sharp, quite counter to efforts to draw a strict demarcation. In Russia and Kazakhstan, instead of a line one might therefore speak of a transboundary *region*, capable of integrating cultures while recognising and respecting the subtle differences that can be discerned if one looks closely enough. After all, at best a cultural-continental boundary between 'West' and 'East' simplifies; at worst, it homogenises. It is better to define continents on the basis of physical than human geography, even if it means fundamentally rethinking how we look at the world. Changing our mind has always been characteristic of humans' engagement with the world, and the Urals have never been unanimously regarded as a continental boundary, despite their recent staying power. The next example has a much longer history of being seen as such, and with its combination of a clearly defined water body and its own claims as a cultural dividing line, represents a crucial boundary to address.

The Bosphorus

On the meeting point of two worlds, the ornament of the Turkish homeland, the treasure of Turkish history, the city cherished by the Turkish nation, Istanbul has its place in the hearts of all citizens.

Mustafa Kemal Atatürk

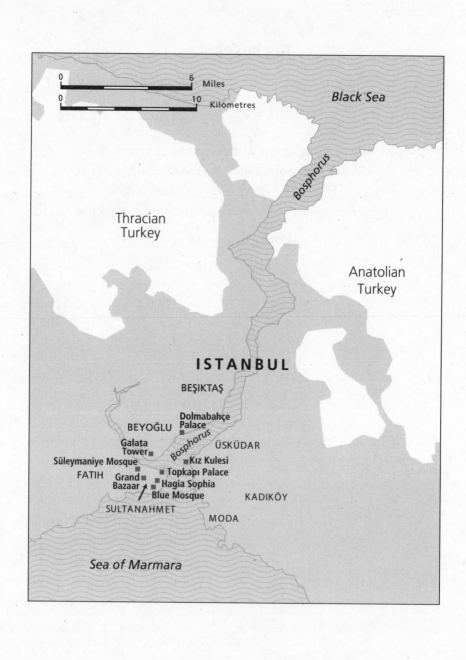

Travelling as a visitor by ferry across the Bosphorus, the narrow strait of water that separates Thracian ('European') and Anatolian ('Asian') Turkey, it is impossible to avoid a burgeoning sense of excitement. While tourists flock the decks to take photographs, munch on *simit* bread rings and search for the intermittent frolicking dolphins, Istanbul's residents read their newspapers or play on their phones, this journey simply forming part of their daily commute. The heat of the sun beating overhead is partially mitigated by the cool breeze blowing from the Black Sea just 30 kilometres to the north. As the conical roof of the hilltop Galata Tower and the apartment blocks on the Thracian side shrink to the boat's stern, the patio restaurants and minarets of Kadıköy and Üsküdar in Anatolian Istanbul come closer into view beyond the bow. Gradually, the diminutive Kız Kulesi (Maiden's Tower) appears. According to legend, it was named for the daughter of a Byzantine emperor who was incarcerated until she reached the age of eighteen because an oracle had prophesied that she would be killed by a venomous snake. In a cruel twist of fate, the emperor's birthday gift to her was a basket of exotic fruits, which unbeknownst to him contained the deadly asp. In expectation of better fortune, the riders disembark and disperse. A new land awaits.

This possibility of visiting two continents in one provides Istanbul with a layer of intrigue that only adds to the city's vast palimpsest of traditions and experiences. After all, even disregarding its ability to straddle such a divide, Istanbul has a certain mystique, enabled by its distinct combination of continuity and change. Having seized the Greek city of Byzantium, the Roman emperor Constantine the Great declared it *Nova Roma* ('New Rome'), a new capital with seven hills and a more strategic location at the geographic heart of the empire than the declining city on the Italian peninsula. In 330 he renamed the city Constantinople after himself and set about erecting numerous churches as part of his mission to convert the region to Christianity. The city's most famous building, the Hagia Sophia, encapsulates Istanbul's many transformations: established as a Christian basilica in 537,* but converted to a mosque when the city fell to Ottoman forces in 1453, in 1935 it was turned into a museum as part of the Republic of Turkey's secularisation, only to be reclassified as a mosque in 2020 by President Recep Tayyip Erdoğan. When the city's comprehensive series of defensive fortifications as well as the many Ottoman mosques that incorporate 'European' Byzantine and Baroque elements are considered, Istanbul can be regarded as a place that has been both bridge and barrier, central to the 'known' world but standing at a frontier.

And yet, like the Ural Mountains, there is no clear physical reason why the Bosphorus should be considered a continental boundary: it is a relatively modest channel† that relies on other humble bodies of water such as the Dardanelles Strait and the Sea of Marmara to form a division between Europe and Asia. Instead, its main relevance is historical and symbolic. During the medieval

---

* What's more, the site previously hosted two churches – *Megale Ekklesia* (the Great Church) and the Theodosian Church – both of which were destroyed during uprisings, in 404 and 532, respectively. It is possible that a pagan temple stood in this location before *Megale Ekklesia* was constructed in the fourth century.

† The Bosphorus measures just 3.7 kilometres (2.3 miles) across at its widest point, and no more than a paltry 750 metres (about 2,450 feet) at its narrowest. No part of the strait is deeper than 124 metres (408 feet).

period it gradually became seen as a dividing line between Christianity in Europe and Islam in Asia; with the Enlightenment in the former, the boundary came to be regarded as one of reason, democracy and 'modernity' versus emotion, despotism and resistance to change. The Ottoman Empire, for centuries a powerful rival to the Christian Habsburg Empire, was viewed in Europe as characteristically 'Asian', reflected in the exoticised artwork created to depict it as inferior and fundamentally *different*.* For their part, the Ottoman leaders did not establish permanent embassies in Europe until the end of the eighteenth century, instead demanding that European diplomats travel to Constantinople. They did not see themselves as a part of Europe even as they conquered most of its south-eastern regions. Nevertheless, with most of Constantinople's Ottoman headquarters being based in the districts of Fatih and Beşiktaş to the *west* of the Bosphorus, this strait was in reality far less important as a boundary than the western frontiers of the Ottoman Empire.

In this regard, the Bosphorus cannot be considered separately from Turkey's broader sense of straddling two different worlds. Although the Ottomans had already passed a number of educational, economic, legal and political *Tanzimat*† reforms during the mid-nineteenth century in an attempt to avoid falling too far behind their rapidly modernising and increasingly powerful European rivals, in the 1920s and 1930s the founder and first president of the new Republic of Turkey, Kemal Atatürk, revamped almost every aspect of his country's society. Last names and the Latin script were adopted, while polygamy and the wearing of the Ottoman hat of choice, the fez, were prohibited. The Ottoman sultanate based in Constantinople, which was renamed Istanbul, was

---

* A particularly good example, famously depicted on the original cover of *Orientalism* by Edward Said, is the French artist Jean-Léon Gérôme's oil painting *The Snake Charmer* (c. 1879).
† Literally, 'Reorganisation'.

replaced with a democratic government in Ankara. The world's last remaining caliphate was supplanted by a secular, French-style model to regulate religion's role in education and politics, and aspects of various European countries' codes of laws took over from Islamic sharia law. However, this process of 'Europeanising' Turkey was traumatic for many, as established traditions were suddenly abandoned for the practices of the old Western adversary. Furthermore, the earlier, controversial population exchange of Greek Orthodox and Turkish Muslim people – mostly refugees – between Greece and Turkey, initiated shortly before Atatürk came to power in 1923, ensured that a sense of difference from 'Christian' Europe would remain.

In Turkey, public attitudes towards 'West' and 'East' are still complex. Culturally, for example, many Turkish people continue to look to the 'East' for religious influence but the 'West' for broader lifestyle preferences, reflected in Turkey's greater average alcohol consumption rates and looser alcohol regulations than in many other Muslim-majority countries. In Istanbul, long-standing religious customs like the Islamic call to prayer and Sufi whirling are juxtaposed with business parks and rooftop bars. Fifteenth-century bazaars compete with gargantuan shopping and entertainment complexes. Diners have the choice of frequenting street vendors offering traditional delicacies such as kebabs, *börek* and flatbread, or high-end restaurants serving up the latest trends in international gastronomy. And despite its official secularism, which in the past included bans on the wearing of headscarves in some public buildings, Turkey is one of only two European member states of the Organisation of the Islamic Conference (Albania is the other), and the majority of its population adheres to Sunni Islam. No wonder then that Turkey's and Istanbul's politics are not always harmonious.

As regards the Europe–Asia boundary, this issue has become especially apparent with respect to Turkey's international relations. In recent years, talks to accede to the European Union (often premised on the idea of Turkey representing a bridge between Europe and Asia) have stalled, while Turkey's relationship with NATO (which it joined in 1952 to help counter Soviet influence in Eastern Europe, the Middle East* and Central Asia) has become strained over questions of democracy, press freedom and human rights, all widely regarded as 'Western' values. Many now claim that Turkey is looking towards the 'East' instead, reflected in the growing role of Islam in some areas of Turkish politics and society and the exchange of rebukes with the EU. At the crossroads between South-Eastern Europe and the Middle East, destabilised by war in neighbouring Syria and associated crises over migration and religious extremism, Turkey is compelled to weigh up competing interests, although the intermediary role it enthusiastically assumed between Russia and Ukraine following the former's 2022 invasion of the latter suggests that it is not frightened to chart its own geopolitical course. Still, this balancing act is fraught with tension, and it is little surprise that the country has become increasingly polarised over the past decade.

Today, Europe and Asia are connected by three bridges and two tunnels (a third has been proposed) across the Bosphorus, all in the effort to decongest a city that with more than 15 million inhabitants is comfortably the largest 'transcontinental' city in the world. The tankers that regularly pass through the Bosphorus, and recent megaprojects like the city's new international airport and a plan to build a new canal to manage ship traffic, further reflect the city's relevance as a key node in a global

---

*In fact, this is another good example of boundaries being drawn to distinguish, somewhat hazily, a geostrategically important region. Indeed, like the 'Fertile Crescent', which is commonly presumed to have partially overlapped its northern edges eleven millennia earlier, the 'Middle East' moniker was popularised remarkably recently – in the early twentieth century – by European and North American intellectuals and politicians, whose perspectives embodied their countries' imperial ambitions.

society. In practice, however, Istanbul manifests few obvious differences on either side of the strait. Most of the city's most
famous attractions as well as hotels, restaurants and embassies
are found on the western, European side of the city, in neighbourhoods including Sultanahmet (the old city), Beyoğlu and
Beşiktaş. The bigger, busier European side thus attracts the vast
majority of visitors and is often regarded as more 'modern'
(read: European), yet Anatolian districts such as Moda are also
cherished for their food scenes, nightlife and other attractions.
The Anatolian side is sometimes seen as more 'traditional' (read:
Islamic), but conservative neighbourhoods such as Fatih are also
common in European Istanbul. Furthermore, both shores are
lined in various places by the grand *yalı* (waterfront houses)
constructed during the Ottoman period. In practice, then, the
boundary is more symbolic than real.

Even so, the Bosphorus continues to encapsulate Istanbul's
ability to balance the old and the new. This can even be seen in
the strait's etymology: the name derives from the ancient Greek
Bósporos, which roughly translates as 'ox passage', and so 'Bosphorus' effectively means 'Oxford'. The story involves the Greek
king of the gods Zeus trying to disguise one of his many lovers
as a cow from his wife and sister, Hera, the perfect combination
of legend and banality. And despite a lack of explicit evidence
of difference on either side, the Bosphorus is still regarded as an
important continental boundary. For instance, Tiger Woods hit
golf balls from Europe to Asia as part of a publicity stunt in 2013,
while on an annual basis the strait is crossed by the participants of
the Bosphorus Cross-Continental Swim and Istanbul's uniquely
'transcontinental' marathon. And returning briefly to football
– for millions around the world a powerful means of distinguishing one's geographically rooted identity from one's rivals – two
of the city's biggest clubs, Galatasaray SK and Fenerbahçe SK,
compete in the 'Intercontinental Derby', a battle thus not just for
themselves, but for Thracian and Anatolian Istanbul, respectively.

Even if the cultural basis of certain boundaries is, as we have seen, rather spurious, there are many that are key to specific groups' senses of uniqueness.

How Invisible Lines Allow Groups to Preserve Their Cultural Distinctiveness

Evidently, invisible lines are frequently laden with power, being used to manufacture and reinforce feelings of difference between groups, which may in reality be poorly defined. Given their subtlety – in large part they exist in the mind, even if their effects may be manifested physically in some way – they are also extremely resistant to attempts at removing them. Unfortunately, prejudices tend to be easier to learn than to unlearn, and although a wall or fence can be demolished without too much effort, a presumption of difference can live on and on. Nevertheless, in certain cases, a group may have good reasons – whether we agree with them or not – for maintaining a degree of separation from the outside world.

Language is commonly implicated in questions of cultural preservation. In Montreal, Anglophones live predominantly in the west, whereas Francophones predominate in the east, helping both tongues to be preserved in a city (and province, Québec) where French is the only official language, but a country, Canada, where English is far more widely spoken. Music provides another basis of geographically rooted cultural distinctiveness. From its origins in the late 1960s, reggae in Jamaica has been intimately associated with the country's 'tenement yards' or shanty towns, which artists consistently acclaim as dignified, genuine places, in opposition to the wealthier but oblivious and arrogant 'hills' that overlook them both geographically and metaphorically. This sense of difference, marked invisibly by a line between those in the shanty town and those who remain in their ivory towers, is conveyed quite frequently in reggae artists' lyrics:

> Living in your concrete castle on the hill
> You don't know what life is like in the ghetto
> Living in a two-by-four with no place to walk around, no-no
> While you're in a castle all alone.

Dennis Brown, Concrete Castle King

Food presents yet another example. Some products enjoy one type of protected status or another, like champagne in the French region of the same name,* or Yorkshire forced rhubarb, which can only be cultivated in the 'Rhubarb Triangle' of this historical English county.† And in fact, Yorkshire more broadly was from 1968 to 1992 known for imposing invisible lines for a very different reason: sport. Specifically, it forbade any player born outside its boundaries from playing for its County Cricket Club, in an effort to maintain the team's 'Yorkshireness'. This rule was modified to allow the future England captain Michael Vaughan, who was born in Greater Manchester, to play for the team; presumably it helped that Vaughan, despite his family's rival Lancashire origins, had lived in Yorkshire since the age of nine. Still, other sports teams have remained more resilient in their commitment to using invisible lines to determine participation. An excellent case is the football team Athletic Bilbao, which champions Basque nationalism and

---

* Wine is in truth distinctly geographical, the concept of *terroir* describing the unique environmental characteristics of an area (including climate and soil) that affect the final product. For this reason, it is possible to map the invisible boundaries of different wine regions in countries like France and Italy, where wines vary significantly by location.

† Remarkably, for a moment in the early twentieth century, this 23-square-kilometre patch of land between Wakefield, Morley and Rothwell is believed to have grown 90 per cent of the entire world's forced rhubarb crop.

has a Basque-only policy,* in accordance with its philosophy of *Con cantera y afición, no hace falta importación*: 'With home-grown talent and local support, there's no need for imports.'

In this final part, we shall see how specific communities have sought to preserve their culture from a wider society that may otherwise eliminate it, whether intentionally or not. The first two cases centre on religious groups: eruvim, effectively invisible boundaries constructed by observant Orthodox Jewish communities to practise their faith on the Sabbath; and Aceh, whose use of Islamic sharia law distinguishes this province from the rest of officially secular Indonesia. We will then consider North Sentinel Island, which, despite being one of India's Andaman and Nicobar Islands, is surrounded by an invisible buffer zone intended to keep the island's 'uncontacted' Indigenous residents uncontactable. The subsequent two chapters focus on unofficial, invisible linguistic boundaries: in Brittany, where the Breton and Gallo languages are seeing something of a resurgence in specific parts of the province, following over two centuries of suppression in favour of French, and in Germany, where geographical differences in dialect remain quite significant, in spite of a degree of standardisation since Martin Luther's influential translation of the Bible in the sixteenth century. The final chapter returns to the theme of religion, but across a far wider and less easily definable area than in the case of eruvim and Aceh: the Bible Belt of the United States, whose high rates of religiosity and religious influence in politics, especially in the case of evangelical Protestant denominations, distinguish it from much of the rest of the country.

---

* The club allows itself to field only players who were born in the Basque Country (in Basque, *Euskal Herria*), or alternatively who came through its own academy or another academy in the territory.

Eruvim

Mark that it is God who, having given you the Sabbath, therefore gives you two days' food on the sixth day. Let everyone remain in place: let no one leave the vicinity on the seventh day.

Exodus 16:29

Route of Eruv

Central
Park

MANHATTAN

Rockefeller
Center

Times
Square

Empire
State
Building

One World
Trade Center

0   1
Mile
0   2
Kilometres

Crossing Broadway, one of the main streets running west to east through Williamsburg in New York's borough of Brooklyn, can be a bewildering experience. The coffee shops, wine bars and Instagram-friendly brunch spots beloved by hipsters quickly give way to discreet synagogues and bustling kosher butchers and bakeries. *Shtreimels* (fur hats) take the place of trilbies and beanies; frock coats replace flannel and denim. But there is a much more subtle boundary here, too, a wire of enormous relevance to one side yet seldom noticed by the other.

This wire makes up part of the Williamsburg eruv (plural eruvim or eruvin), a ritual enclosure that allows thousands of observant Orthodox Jews to practise their faith as desired on Shabbat, the Jewish Sabbath. The Torah prohibits Jews from working from Friday sundown to Saturday sundown, a rule which includes carrying any object between private and public domains. The dilemma is clear: how can one leave the house to walk to synagogue, possibly with a child in arms or pram, a walking stick or a wheelchair? And what to do with the house keys? Many people would be confined to their homes. An eruv (roughly meaning 'mixture') removes this predicament by redefining any space within the enclosure as a single private domain during Shabbat. Not only wires but pre-existing walls, fences, railway lines and even rivers can be used to delineate this space, creating a sort of ersatz building, with vertical posts or poles representing the doorposts. After all, if a building can be deemed to enclose an area even as its doorways open and close, then a system that makes the most of the extant infrastructure, however modest, represents a more practical alternative to erecting a continuous wall around a community. Often just a thin, carefully positioned strip or tube called a *lechi* is affixed to the poles in order to meet the Talmudic (Jewish legal) conditions required of an eruv's 'doorposts'.

As a result, any space that we may conventionally regard as public (streets, parks, pavements) becomes private to strictly observant Jews as long as the eruv's boundaries are unimpaired. Every week in advance of Shabbat, a rabbi or other community authority will inspect the entire length of the eruv to ensure that no part of the wire has fallen or been broken: even one collapsed wire renders it deficient, necessitating a speedy and generally quite rudimentary repair. In an intriguing juxtaposition, many Jewish congregations that eschew electricity on the Sabbath itself have established social media accounts dedicated to monitoring and reporting on their eruv's condition throughout the rest of the week. After all, this can be an exacting task for one person, considering that some eruvim are surprisingly extensive and are often located in busy urban areas: the Manhattan eruv, for instance, stretches across the majority of the borough.

This fact may come as a surprise. And Manhattan is far from the only place to hold this distinction. The Washington, DC eruv, for instance, contains over half of the district, including all its most famous sites. The West Los Angeles eruv covers over 250 square kilometres. Brooklyn is reckoned to comprise at least ten different eruvim, several of which adjoin one another, thereby extending the amount of land that strictly observant Jews can regard as private for the purposes of Shabbat. Eruvim can also be found in dozens of other American cities, most major settlements in Canada, a number of key Jewish population centres in Latin America and Europe (although, quite surprisingly, not Paris, Berlin or Budapest), select districts in Australia and South Africa, and almost every town and city in Israel.

Still, an eruv's virtual invisibility may not conceal it from controversy, including among Jewish people. Even though strictly Orthodox Jews are often portrayed as a somewhat homogeneous group, in reality they comprise numerous denominations with contrasting understandings of the key Jewish texts and rituals. In Israel, many deny the legitimacy of the eruvim constructed by the Israeli government as a matter of policy, and some have taken to erecting their own according to their specific interpretation of Jewish law. And this brings us to another way in which eruvim constitute important boundaries: not just physically between 'public' and 'private', but especially within Judaism, socially, between contrasting perspectives towards the modern world. According to Jews who might broadly be described as more secular-minded, eruvim risk encouraging ghettoisation, attracting antisemitism, or simply bring down property prices given that many are hesitant about living in an area that is deemed to be dominated by religious fundamentalists (although in reality, eruvim tend to be created by communities already living within an area, rather than preceding them). By contrast, some Orthodox Jews claim that eruvim enable their co-religionists to circumvent what they deem the proper observance of the Sabbath and contribute to what they perceive to be a watering down of Jewish practice, while others argue that many of the eruvim in existence fail to meet their own exacting standards. Physical boundaries can be substantial, but social boundaries are often more difficult to transcend.

Certainly, despite their inconspicuousness – most people who live or work within eruvim are not even aware of their existence, and these enclosures do not purport to exclude those with different beliefs or require non-adherents to recognise them – they have stimulated considerable contestation where they have become more widely known, because of what they are presumed to represent. In particular, plans to construct eruvim have been resisted by those who claim that they constitute an attempt to seize territory for the purposes of a religious minority (and one that barely integrates with the wider society), as challenging a long-standing sense of local place identity, and as implicitly suggesting that all 'outsiders' are unwelcome. Depending on the country's planning laws and engagement with questions of religious freedom, advocates of eruvim have often struggled to see their demands realised, although interestingly, in the United States and Canada what may seem to be an unlikely union of utility companies and strictly Orthodox Jews is not uncommon. Nevertheless, protests against the presence of eruvim and even attempts to compromise them through surreptitiously clipping the wires are not unheard of.

Eruvim can be difficult to spot, considering that they are typically made up of utility poles and translucent wires, but it is possible to sense that one has crossed into an eruv on a Saturday morning, when strictly Orthodox Jewish families can be seen walking to or from their congregations. They allow their users to expand their geographical boundaries on Shabbat, and delimit their communal space, the spatial distribution of their key community institutions and the extent to which ancient Jewish rituals can be practised in the present. In this sense, it is somewhat ironic that through the process of enabling their users to access city streets like everyone else, eruvim cause them to stand out through their distinctive dress and Yiddish language. The fact that they additionally assume a temporal dynamic through only existing for a matter of hours each week, the rest of the time being inconsequential to even the strictest believers, makes them all the more interesting.

Eruvim are far from the only religious boundary demarcations across the world,* but they may be the most subtle. Whereas most

---

* Another excellent example is the *miqat*, a boundary connecting five stations and marking where Muslim pilgrims to Mecca must enter a sacred state called *iḥrām*. Before crossing the boundary, they are required to undertake specific cleansing rituals and don particular garments; beyond it, they are prohibited from a number of activities that may be usual elsewhere, including

people can simply dismiss them as wires and posts – where they notice them at all – to strictly observant Jews they define the ease with which they can practise their faith. In so doing, they enable them to balance the challenges posed by both ancient and modern society, between committing to centuries of tradition and living in a world in constant flux. They are thus the lines marking their unique niche in the world, and far less banal than anyone beyond these communities may assume. But don't think that boundaries rooted in strict religious principles are limited to the relatively small scale of urban neighbourhoods. As we shall see next, invisible lines reflecting different religious and/or secular legal systems can even run between entire provinces, in an effort to appease disparate communities and preserve widely contrasting worldviews, philosophies and ways of life.

---

wearing sewn clothing (in the case of men), using perfume or fragrance and engaging in sexual intercourse.

Aceh

---

*Freedom means that we maintain the
distance that separates us from others.*

Hasan di Tiro

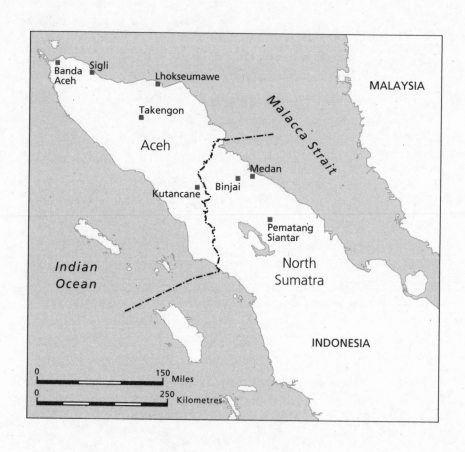

Bhinneka Tunggal Ika. Indonesia's national motto of 'Unity in Diversity' encapsulates the country's efforts to harmonise its almost unfathomably varied society. The country is home to 633 ethnic groups, spread across an area that from west to east exceeds the distance between the United States' Pacific and Atlantic coasts. Although its legal system is primarily based on civil law – in large part influenced by around 350 years of Dutch colonisation – Indonesia also acknowledges traditional, customary *adat* laws that are unique to specific communities throughout the country. In its most recent general election, in 2019, as many as twenty parties competed, representing a wide range of not simply political ideologies and economic stances, but religious or secular philosophies. With six official religions and perhaps 250 others spread across this island nation, faith provides another noteworthy source of difference here.

Sunni Islam is comfortably the most popular religion in Indonesia, and at over 225 million, the country's Muslim population, the biggest in the world, exceeds those of Bangladesh, Afghanistan and Saudi Arabia put together. However, as a country that has officially been secular since its independence in 1945, religion represents a significant area of contention. Indonesia's foundational philosophy, called Pancasila, epitomises the country's challenges in reconciling religious and secular values, its first principle being acceptance of a single God – somewhat problematic for the millions of Hindus who also live here – whereas its third is Indonesian unity.* Even more pertinently, Indonesia's constitution declares that the country is a secular unitary republic, yet one of its provinces is neither secular nor easily compatible with the Indonesian whole. On a map, the boundary between this territory and the rest of the country may thus appear innocuous, but crossing it on the ground is like entering a different world.

Aceh, Indonesia's one province to officially practise sharia, is fittingly nicknamed the 'Veranda of Mecca' on account of its long history of embracing and strictly adhering to Sunni Islam. Its location at the far north-western corner of the island of Sumatra also gives it the appearance of an appendage pointing across the Indian Ocean towards the Arabian peninsula. Although it is uncertain when Aceh first became an Islamic territory, it was probably the first part of modern-day Indonesia to be established as such, presumably by Muslim traders travelling between the Middle East and East and South-East Asia. In the thirteenth century, the Venetian explorer Marco Polo described Muslim settlement here, and in the early sixteenth century Aceh became a sultanate, eventually developing into one of the most politically and economically powerful territories in the region, a formidable local competitor to imperial Portugal in particular. Aceh was invaded by Dutch forces in the 1870s, which under the name Dutch East Indies already controlled most of what is now Indonesia, but despite losing their capital Banda Aceh, the local community violently resisted well into the twentieth century, reflecting and reinforcing the region's long-standing independent streak. The Acehnese, coordinated by

---

* The name Pancasila has its origins in the Sanskrit for 'Five Principles' and echoes the five precepts of Buddhism. In the Indonesian context, the ideology was first outlined by the revolutionary leader Sukarno in 1945, shortly before the country achieved independence. By amalgamating various religious and political philosophies, Sukarno regarded the five principles as non-sectarian and shared by all Indonesians. Even so, finding an appropriate balance between secularism and Islamic particularism (especially) has often proved a challenge.

ulama (religious leaders) such as Teungku Cik di Tiro, tended to adopt guerrilla tactics, including distinctive *parang-sabil* ('holy war') suicide attacks. The 'infidel' Dutch troops, in turn, on occasion opted to slaughter whole communities of Acehnese civilians in the name of 'pacification'. The carnage continued until 1942, when the Imperial Japanese Army successfully invaded the Dutch East Indies during the Second World War.

After Japan surrendered in 1945, the Indonesian revolutionaries Sukarno and Mohammad Hatta – who during the occupation had been permitted to foment nationalist sentiment among the population as long as they supported the Japanese war effort[*] – announced the new country's independence. However, two key groups were displeased. First, the Dutch challenged the legitimacy of this move and Indonesia descended into four more years of conflict, requiring international intervention. Second, in contrast to the general enthusiasm of the archipelago's residents for independence, the Acehnese were divided – to the point of violence – between those who supported the new state and those who had previously collaborated with the Dutch and preferred the old authority. Opposition to the new, highly centralised Indonesian leadership based in Java only increased over the coming decades. Aceh was absorbed into North Sumatra in 1950 despite expecting to enjoy a greater degree of autonomy, and from 1953 to 1959 fought for independence as part of a larger Islamic State of Indonesia. The greater freedoms offered by the Indonesian government during the 1950s appeased the Acehnese insurgents to some extent, but Sukarno's successor Suharto was more uncompromising in his defence of secular principles and as part of his 'New Order' worked to minimise the role of religion, especially political Islam, in Indonesian politics and society. In 1976, angered by the Indonesian government's perceived lack of respect for Islam and

---

[*] Most controversially, this meant turning their backs on the cruelty of the *rōmusha* (forced labour) policy adopted by the Japanese occupiers.

Islamic law, its efforts to profit from the region's oil and natural gas resources seemingly at the local population's expense, and its *transmigrasi* (transmigration) policy by which 'foreign' Indonesians from Java were resettled in less densely populated parts of the country, Aceh once again saw separatist violence, led by di Tiro's great-grandson Hasan di Tiro and the new Free Aceh Movement (GAM).* The following two decades would see both sides accused of various human rights abuses, including torture, executions and the burning down of schools and even entire villages.

Despite this bloodshed and disorder, Aceh is probably best known internationally for being the nearest landmass to the epicentre of the earthquake that triggered the devastating tsunami on Boxing Day 2004, several years after Suharto had fallen from power.† With an astonishing 170,000 estimated casualties, and hundreds of thousands of people made homeless, Aceh bore much of the brunt of the tsunami. If it is possible to find solace in such a catastrophe, it is that GAM and the Indonesian government agreed a ceasefire in order that humanitarian aid could reach desperate populations. In August 2005, the two sides signed a peace treaty in Helsinki, Finland.

Even so, Aceh's historical differences from the rest of Indonesia would not disappear. Today, the main way in which it stands out is its use of sharia. As one Acehnese source told me: 'The very basic difference between the two provinces [Aceh and neighbouring North Sumatra] is the adoption of religious values in the local governance system. In Aceh, the society must follow the governmental system that is associated with Islamic law, whereas in North Sumatra universal or national law is adopted by the local government.' Aceh started to adopt certain sharia-based rules in

---

*In Acehnese, *Geurakan Acèh Meurdèka*.
†Suharto resigned as president of Indonesia on 21 May 1998, in the wake of the 1997 Asian financial crisis (which affected Indonesia particularly severely) and student-led protests demanding political reform.

1999, but these were largely policed by small special interest groups rather than the local government. Greater changes occurred from 2001, when the Indonesian government offered Aceh increased autonomy in order to curb hostilities, enabling it to pass a series of laws with the purpose of criminalising sharia violations, such as alcohol and gambling. The latter is in fact illegal across Indonesia, whereas hypothetically a visitor can purchase and drink alcohol on a journey from east to west across the country, until they reach Aceh, where they are best advised to steer well clear of this substance.

Certainly, the most important contrasts between the two sides of the provincial boundary pertain to the law and law enforcement. For instance, in February 2021 the Indonesian government banned public schools from compelling students to wear religious attire, following the controversial case of a Christian girl who was forced to sport an Islamic *jilbab* (headscarf). Furthermore, from 2005 to 2013, Indonesian policewomen were banned entirely from wearing this garment. The latter prohibition was lifted as part of a change in how secularism can be understood in Indonesia: from being deemed a policy imposed from above as a means of ensuring neutrality over religious matters, to a mechanism capable of respecting individual choice and religious freedom. Safe to say, these laws have never applied to Aceh. Here, policewomen are not only required to wear a *jilbab*, but are also tasked, alongside their male counterparts, with forcing other women to wear one as well. Tight trousers such as jeans are also forbidden to women in Aceh.

Dealing with such offences is not simply a matter of having a quick chat with the 'perpetrator'. In Aceh, public canings are the standard punishment for offences ranging from drinking alcohol to having extramarital 'intimate relations'. Holding hands, hugging or merely being alone together can all result in a flogging from an anonymous hooded figure in front of a baying audience, as the occasional teenaged couple have found to their cost. Homosexuality is considered a taboo subject in Indonesia but it is not illegal – except in Aceh (plus the West Sumatran city of Pariaman), where the punishment has typically involved at least seventy lashes. In recent years Aceh has aimed to move somewhat with the times by opening up traditionally male-dominated professions to women; what this has meant is a new contingent of female floggers available to law enforcement. It should be noted that non-Muslims are only subjected to sharia law if the offence in question is not included in Indonesia's criminal code, although they are often given the option to accept the same punishment as Muslims, for instance a caning instead of a jail term.

The 'morality police' have thus become a particularly distinctive aspect of Aceh, on the constant lookout for behaviour their province deems wicked. Homes, hotel rooms, beaches, beauty salons – a range of places are available for scrutiny. Another credible target would be cinemas – that is, if the province still had any, following the tsunami. Although they are not officially banned, it is easy to understand how rooms where men and women can theoretically sit together, in the dark, watching potentially licentious material, would be opposed. None have been opened ever since. Although dance is a part of Aceh's cultural heritage, in some parts of the province adult women are forbidden from dancing in public lest it inflame men's sexual desire. Moreover, in 2015 Banda Aceh, under the leadership of the city's first female mayor, Illiza Sa'aduddin Djamal, imposed a night-time curfew on women, purportedly to protect them from sexual harassment.*

In fact, there is scope for the society to become even more punitive. A previous attempt to introduce death by stoning as the punishment for adultery was vetoed by the province's governor. Beheading was mooted as recently as 2018 for murder cases, but

---

*Djamal's political career has been groundbreaking: in 2019, she was elected Aceh's first female representative of the People's Representative Council of the Republic of Indonesia (DPR), the lower house of the country's parliament.

the Indonesian government has so far managed to dissuade Aceh's leaders by invoking the restrictions set out in the country's criminal code, whereby the only form of capital punishment permitted is execution by firing squad. So far, human rights activists have managed to make little headway in challenging the legality of Aceh's harshest punishments, given the intricacies of separating Indonesia's and Aceh's laws and authority.

Therefore, whereas Indonesia as a whole is increasingly looking outwards to the international capitalist system and prevailing forms of governance, Aceh has shifted further and further in its own direction. Indeed, there is reasonable evidence to suggest that Aceh is becoming increasingly severe and obdurate as it attempts to set itself apart from the rest of a country that its leaders deem undesirably permissive. An interesting case in this respect is that of Cut Meutia, an Indonesian anti-colonial fighter from Aceh, who since 2016 has appeared on Indonesian 1,000 rupiah banknotes, but without a *jilbab*. Despite some efforts by Aceh's leadership to have her depicted with a headscarf, there is evidence that Meutia and many other Acehnese women of the time opted against this practice, complicating efforts to suggest that the province's strict use of sharia should be treated as some kind of default state. Eventually, however, sharia will become thoroughly normalised, because intentionally or not, Aceh is becoming less susceptible to different ideas and ways of life. For instance, a 2018 law requires that all financial institutions in the province adhere to sharia principles (especially a prohibition of interest on loans), compelling 'conventional' banks to either convert their branches or leave the province for good. How those who do not adhere to Islam will be affected remains to be seen, but it is plausible that the implementation of Islamic practices in such a comprehensive way will enhance the long-standing reluctance of many foreign companies to enter the province, further distinguishing the region on the basis of faith and law.

There are also clear social and economic implications of Aceh's intentional particularity and many businesses' associated hesitation to invest. Admittedly, the 2004 tsunami is an obvious factor behind Aceh's relative underdevelopment, but the ensuing period has inspired little confidence in it keeping up with the adjoining province of North Sumatra. Indeed, even though foreign aid was generally received with gratitude in the immediate aftermath of the tsunami, the disaster response phase also saw tensions emerge in places between international organisations and local institutions sceptical of any perceived external influence. For example, one Islamist organisation was criticised for appearing to exploit people's suffering by propagating fundamentalist ideas – with little success – while international humanitarian groups, which were suspected by some of being fronts for Christian proselytism, were regularly frustrated in their efforts to provide aid by the province's regulations on gender segregation and personal modesty. Aceh has since managed to improve most of its housing and transport infrastructure, and has even attempted to appeal to tourists by opening a tsunami museum and preserving eye-catching memorials to the fateful event (including a floating power plant and a large fishing boat carried inland), though it still attracts fewer international visitors than a region with its coastal landscapes and cultural heritage might expect. It would be fallacious to claim that the tsunami did not significantly set back Aceh's development, but the province's resistance to the pluralism typical of much of the rest of Indonesia must also be acknowledged as an important factor deterring inward investment. As a result, Aceh, as one local affirmed, 'has been left behind North Sumatra so far in terms of economic development. Infrastructure development and economic activities in Medan [North Sumatra's capital] are much more developed and advanced than in Banda Aceh.' And with limited local income sources available, many inhabitants struggle to escape from the considerably above-average levels of poverty that persist here.

The disjuncture between Islam and Islamic law on the one hand and other religions and worldviews on the other is only growing, too. Many survivors maintain that the fact that the elegant Baiturrahman Grand Mosque was one of the few buildings to escape the tsunami practically unscathed provides evidence that Islam is the one 'true faith'; some also inferred from this that any effort to mitigate future disasters is futile if Allah has already decided one's fate. By contrast, even though Christians tend to be exempted from the harsh punishments wielded against their Muslim counterparts, they are frequently regarded as outsiders even though they have lived in Aceh for generations, and attacks on their institutions by vigilantes – often condoned by the local authorities – periodically occur. Christians' general sense of difference in Aceh today is magnified by the fact that nearby North Sumatra has the biggest Protestant population in the country, as well as a large number of Buddhists, offering a far more diverse community and a more pluralistic society.

Over the past two decades, some other local governments, interested in the Aceh model, have sought to impose their own sharia-inspired ordinances, and have been enabled to do so by the political decentralisation that occurred following the fall of Suharto. In several parts of the country, more and more women are now wearing a *jilbab*, and identity politics, including with respect to religious matters, is becoming an increasingly public issue. There are Islamist leaders in Aceh who are duly delighted that they may be pioneering a new model of jurisprudence in the country. Nevertheless, Aceh remains distinctive in its close adherence to sharia at the expense of other legal systems, and accordingly is still perceived quite differently from the rest of Indonesia. Crucially, this sense of dissimilarity is felt and emphasised by Aceh's leaders, too. For instance, as an outcome of the 2005 peace deal, not only is the province legally permitted its own political parties, but in 2013 its leaders audaciously tested the national government's desire to unify the country by adopting GAM's separatist banner as their provincial flag. Even though they quickly backed down, this controversy reflects how Aceh is likely to remain a place that, although officially part of Indonesia, seeks to distinguish itself from the rest of the country, barring an extraordinary U-turn in its relationship to Islam.

In these ways, a boundary does not have to be something fixed: it can be a *process*, changing in magnitude over time. Eventually, through repeatedly invoking the concept of a boundary, and applying stricter and stricter rules, a division can emerge and intensify between two places. What may seem like a mere line on a map – in this case marking the edges of two provinces – can be felt as a meaningful disjuncture in life-worlds on the ground. Via laws, cultural and religious practices, traditions (which, it is often forgotten, are constantly invented as opposed to necessarily being 'old') and the general adherence of much of the population to all of the above, a territory can be distinguished from others. More than just being a political division, the boundary between Aceh and North Sumatra (as well as the rest of Indonesia) both marks and helps make official vastly contrasting ways of life in a country known for its diversity. With the application of new laws – requiring a combination of fear and approval on the part of the population – separation, both real and perceived, can be established. Whether isolation has the effect of restraining one's own economy is unimportant to many political leaders, as long as the society embodies and reproduces dearly held values that for one reason or another are not shared by those on the other side.

Although religion has for centuries proved a significant means by which specific groups can separate themselves from others, it is not the only way. Moreover, it is worth noting that rather than seeking to integrate everyone into the broader society, regardless of minorities' interests in doing so, separation may also be accepted and desired by national governments and other majority powers. As we will see next, boundaries within territories can play a critical role in keeping different people safe as well as in marking out widely contrasting social systems, levels of development and enthusiasm for interaction.

North Sentinel Island

Lord is this island Satan's last stronghold where none have heard or ever had a chance to hear Your Name?

John Allen Chau

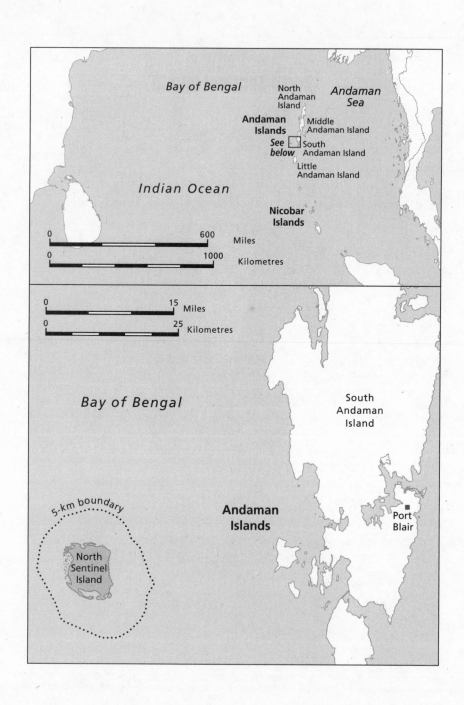

In our globalised society, it can be easy to imagine that there are no untouched places left on Earth, yet there are reckoned to be at least 100 Indigenous groups that remain 'uncontacted'. How can the contemporary world be harmonised – or at least coexist – with those who may well want and moreover need nothing to do with it? And should we even try? North Sentinel Island, officially a part of India's Andaman and Nicobar Islands (A&N) in the Bay of Bengal, provides a particularly compelling example of the challenges of drawing a boundary between groups representing entirely different ages of civilisation. At an administrative level, this is exemplified by the fact that despite falling within the national borders of a modern nation state, the island is protected from interference by this country's government and any other external actor, with non-Sentinelese people prohibited from travelling within 5 kilometres of it. Given that the Sentinelese do not share a language understood by anyone else in the contemporary world and do not seek greater contact either, it is fair to assume that they are neither aware of nor interested in this legal intervention, which reflects some of the ironies involved in drawing a boundary between very different ways of engaging with the world.* But this is not to say that such a boundary is trivial.

---

* The stone tablet claiming the island as a part of India, which was erected during an expedition in 1970, also seems remarkably irrelevant to this population.

A fiercely defended divide is undoubtedly recognised de facto on both sides, as a Christian missionary named John Allen Chau found out the hard way in November 2018.

Chau, a twenty-six-year-old from the United States, a country that for millions stands as an emblem of global connectivity, was by no means the first person to cross the invisible line separating North Sentinel from 'the rest'. Nor was he the first to meet a fatal end for doing so. However, he was quite distinctive in intentionally choosing to traverse the divide and bring something so significant to millions across the globe – his faith – to those on the other side. Those who had reached North Sentinel Island before him had generally done so either accidentally – as was true of the vessels the *Nineveh* in 1867, the MV *Rusley* in 1977 and the MV *Primrose* in 1981, all of which ran aground on the island's reefs – or, more deleteriously, to extract human 'evidence' of difference. The latter was the case of the British naval officer Maurice Vidal Portman's expedition in 1880, which culminated in the kidnapping of an elderly couple and four children, supposedly for anthropological research purposes. Approximately 50 kilometres away in Port Blair, the A&N capital, the adults quickly succumbed to a fatal illness against which they had no immunity. The children were hastily returned to North Sentinel along with some gifts, but it is plausible that they brought with them the disease, potentially leading to the deaths of other Sentinelese. No wonder outside groups have tended to be so vehemently and immediately resisted ever since. Other unwitting encounters include the known or at least strongly suspected killings of an escaped convict from a nearby penal colony in 1896 and two fishermen in 2006.

Through those who have made contact and have lived to tell the tale, the wider world has been able to glean some information about North Sentinel's inhabitants. For instance, we know that rather than being a 'Stone Age' people as they have sometimes been described, on account of appearing to engage in hunter-gathering instead of agriculture, they use the metal from local shipwrecks to make arrows, a productive repurposing of more modern materials. They also build small, narrow canoes which are propelled using a long pole in the manner of a punt, and carry spears and knives as well as bows and arrows. The islanders' clothing comprises, at most, waist belts or strings, necklaces and headbands. Lean-to huts, raw honey, wild fruits, fishing nets, bamboo pots and wooden buckets were all observed by Triloknath Pandit of the Anthropological Survey of India, who through nearly twenty-five years of mostly long-distance engagement with the Sentinelese came far closer than anyone else to befriending this reclusive community. Indeed, although he and his colleagues were sometimes received with hostility, ranging from arrow attacks to obscene gestures (probably not helped by the fact that some of the officers accompanying his team on the first visit seized a range of Sentinelese items, now on display in a museum in Port Blair), on other occasions their encounters were more placid, most notably in 1991, when several islanders peacefully approached the visitors' dinghies. Pandit also noted their varied reactions to his gifts over the years. Coconuts – which do not grow on the island – as well as metal pots and pans were particularly appreciated. By contrast, the pig and the doll he brought on a visit in 1974 were promptly speared and buried in the sand, while the director of a *National Geographic* documentary, whom Pandit was accompanying on this occasion, was hit in the thigh by an arrow.

The rest of our evidently limited knowledge of North Sentinel Island is largely based on conjecture. Through a combination of long-distance photography and anthropologists' calculations of the island's probable food supply, for instance, population estimates range from fifteen to 500 individuals, most likely towards the lower end. Even less is known about everyday matters like household structure, gender relations and island politics. Whether the Sentinelese have been isolated for over 55,000 years, as is sometimes presumed, or only migrated to North Sentinel Island more recently via a land bridge when sea levels were much lower, is another mystery of great intrigue. Satellite imagery can at least indicate that the island is dominated by forest, encircled by a sandy beach and beyond that coral reefs, with a tiny islet at the south-eastern edge. But we know little more than that.

(Looking in the other direction, imagine how mysterious the practices of the visitors must have seemed from the perspective of the Sentinelese. It is difficult to fathom quite what they would have made of the helicopters used to rescue the *Primrose*'s crew in 1981, for instance.)

Furthermore, we are unlikely to find out more any time soon. Despite Pandit's successes, most meetings with the modern world have aroused hostility, as expeditions to check on the condition of the community following the devastating Indian Ocean tsunami in 2004 experienced first hand. Clearly, the island's inhabitants are remarkably resilient and do not need the assistance of outsiders. Indeed, today the consensus – supported by the A&N administration's hands-off policy since 2005 – is that if this community can survive thousands of years of isolation, then the last thing they need is even well-meaning contact with people who may bring diseases that are common to us, such as influenza, but calamitous to them. The fate of various Indigenous groups that have been wiped out by colonisers and others that have come to suffer from alcoholism and diabetes through their contact suggests that this is the most sensible course of (in)action. In the Andaman archipelago, Indigenous populations have shrunk significantly through sustained contact with outsiders over the past two centuries.*

And this remains a major issue. Tourism, a profoundly modern pursuit, represents a particularly significant concern, especially with recent controversies over 'human safari' tourism elsewhere in the region. The Jarawa community of the nearby South and Middle Andaman Islands seems particularly vulnerable, having

---

*For instance, the Onge population of Little Andaman Island is estimated to have fallen from 670 in 1900 to 120 today.

only emerged to a very minor extent from centuries of self-isolation in the 1990s, after one of the community's adolescents was treated in a modern hospital due to breaking his leg in an Indian village. Tour companies now advertise opportunities to drive through Jarawa territory as if searching for rarely seen animals – in the process disturbing the animals on which the group depends for its survival – and poachers often seize local timber and bushmeat while leaving behind alcohol, tobacco and disease. The archipelago's natural beauty lends it enormous tourism potential and there is understandable concern among human rights organisations such as Survival International that some visitors will seek to travel close to North Sentinel, putting both their and the islanders' lives at risk. Although taking photographs or making videos of the Sentinelese is punishable with a prison sentence and the island's vicinity is patrolled by Indian security forces, in 2018 the Indian government relaxed its requirements on visiting twenty-nine islands in the region, potentially making this group more susceptible to exploitation and unwilling engagement. After all, Chau made it past the patrols; it is certainly not beyond the realm of possibility that others will be able to do so, too.

The size of Manhattan but its complete antithesis in terms of development, North Sentinel Island is one of the most captivating places in the world when it comes to the determination of boundaries. Whereas the Indian government assumes certain responsibility for their survival and does not describe the island as an autonomous administrative division in the manner of Assam or West Bengal (among others), the Sentinelese do not regard themselves as part of this country or any other, and hence they effectively constitute an autonomous society. This could be seen in the aftermath of Chau's death, when neither the Indian nor the US government – or Chau's family for that matter – pressed charges against the Sentinelese, whereas the seven fishermen who had assisted Chau in illegally approaching the island were all charged with endangering his life. Furthermore, the fishermen

saw the Sentinelese burying Chau's body, so recovering it was theoretically possible, but the decision was made to relinquish it out
of deference to the community's de facto control of the island and
the fear of spreading diseases against which they are unlikely to be
immune. In this respect, a boundary exists here not just as a line
of protection for the islanders from outsiders and their systems
of governance and law, and not just as a warning to outsiders to
avoid the islanders' own system of justice. It also exists in the very
way in which we in the 'modern world' understand concepts of
society, cooperation and interaction. Given that it is reflective of
entirely different worldviews and communication patterns, this is
a particularly difficult type of boundary to overcome; applying
contemporary perspectives and structures to groups that do not
share the same way of seeing the world is insufficient. Even the
names 'North Sentinel' and 'Sentinelese' are used exclusively by
us as people who have never been able to know the terms used by
the island's inhabitants. Language is a major factor in the creation
and maintenance of boundaries across the world, and as we shall
see next, questions of modernity, culture and heritage are often
not far away.

Brittany's Linguistic Lines

The year is 50 BC. Gaul is entirely occupied by the Romans. Well, not entirely . . . One small village of indomitable Gauls still holds out against the invaders. And life is not easy for the Roman legionaries who garrison the fortified camps of Totorum, Aquarium, Laudanum and Compendium . . .

René Goscinny and Albert Uderzo, *Asterix the Gaul*

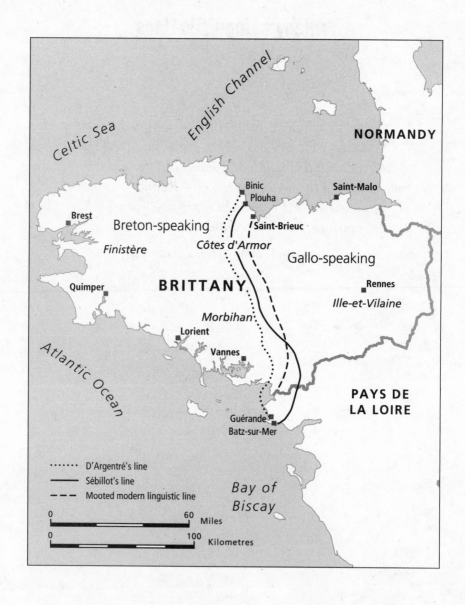

Looking out across the Atlantic from France's north-westernmost province, it is easy to see why Brittany was long regarded as a far-flung boundary of Europe. Fierce waves batter the craggy coast, with just the occasional ship in the distance suggesting a degree of human assurance in the face of a dangerous natural environment beyond. The stories of Asterix, the region's internationally beloved fictional son, concern the courage of a diminutive warrior from a tiny Gaulish village, which, despite being cornered by the mighty Roman Empire, repeatedly fends off its advances. Even the name of Brittany's most remote department – Finistère – attests to its being somehow at the end of the world, being derived from the Latin *Finis Terrae* (*Penn-ar-Bed* in the local Breton tongue). But Brittany does not only represent a boundary between the familiar mainland Europe and thousands of mysterious square kilometres of ocean; it is faintly scored by invisible linguistic lines that themselves represent partitions between different regional identities, generations, social classes and aspirations for the future.

Although some will know that Brittany is home to mainland Europe's only surviving Celtic language, Breton, which is related to the Cornish and Welsh still used by minority speakers across the English Channel to the north, far fewer realise that Brittany also has a second regional language, Gallo. Reflecting the divide between the two languages, the word *Gallo* is actually derived from the Breton word for 'foreign', *gall*, and observers have long sought to draw a geographical line separating the settlements where they are spoken. As early as 1588, a local historian named Bertrand d'Argentré described a line running from Binic on the northern coast to Guérande in the south, with Breton speakers in the west and Gallo speakers in the east. A local folklorist and painter called Paul Sébillot in 1886 adjusted the boundary to run from the town of Plouha (Breton) or Plóha (Gallo) in the northern Côtes-d'Armor department to Batz-sur-Mer on the Bay of Biscay. Taking a slightly different approach, three years earlier the historian Joseph Loth drew two lines delimiting the maximum extension of the Breton language as well as a 'mixed zone' of Romance and Breton influences. Today any line or lines are less clearly defined, largely owing to the various challenges wrought by the modern period, but the notion of an invisible boundary distinguishing Breton from Gallo communities is still accepted among many residents and observers, some of whom place it several kilometres to the east of these older delimitations, running from Saint-Brieuc to the mouth of the River Vilaine. Further, even though these names are not administratively recognised, it is still common to speak of a 'Lower Brittany' (*Breizh-Izel* in Breton; *Basse-Bretagne* in French) to the west, and an 'Upper Brittany' (*Breizh-Uhel* in Breton; *Haùtt-Bertaèyn* in Gallo; *Haute-Bretagne* in French) to the east. Upper Brittany may also be deemed a sort of boundary in its own right, a buffer zone for Breton speakers, as the Gallo language borrows quite significantly from both Breton and French, whereas Breton has traditionally remained fairly separate from French influence.

These linguistic distinctions have long helped Brittany to maintain an independent streak. Historically the western part of the province was Celtic, especially thanks to the in-migration of Celtic Britons from Cornwall and Wales in response to the Anglo-Saxon settlement of Britain during the fourth to sixth centuries. Meanwhile, the eastern half of what was then called Armorica was subjected to greater Roman influence, probably stimulating the emergence of Gallo here via Vulgar Latin. Eventually the name Brittany (*Bretagne* in French; *Breizh* in Breton; *Bertaèyn* in Gallo) became more common, and the region – albeit with some changes to its external and internal borders alike – functioned autonomously until it was annexed by France in 1532. Brittany has clung onto this rich and distinctive history and culture ever since, as seen in cultural activities like its *festoù-noz*,* as well as in the region's gastronomy and distinctive *Gwenn-ha-Du* (white-and-black) flag. The fact that Brittany was one of the only French regions whose name and borders were not amended in a major administrative overhaul by the French government in 2016 evidences its strong sense of uniqueness.

Nevertheless, particularly since the French Revolution towards the end of the eighteenth century, Brittany's languages have come under threat. They are not unique in this respect. Various policies have been enacted since this time to intentionally marginalise France's many regional languages, including Occitan, Alsatian, Corsican, Flemish and Basque. Breton was portrayed as contrary to the national unity that only the French language was said to guarantee (at this time, speaking or understanding French was far from universal), and children were shamed and physically punished for speaking it in school. Then, as Brittany's isolation began to diminish, especially with the expansion of the railroads in the late nineteenth century and the resultant increase in the movement of people between Brittany and the rest of France, it came to be regarded not only as less conducive than French to achieving economic success, but also as indicative of one's 'backwardness'. It was seen as the language of farmers, who rarely travelled beyond their local villages. By contrast, French had long been associated with the more powerful classes, and speaking it came to be regarded as a sign of one's loyalty to the new regime. Meanwhile,

---

* 'Night festivals', which provide a modernised version of traditional music and dance, and whose proceeds help support Breton organisations.

Gallo, which is much more similar to Standard French, was disparaged as an incomprehensible *patois*, a word commonly used to label regional tongues as languages of the uneducated rural classes. Indeed, the traditional expression *se remettre à parler gallo* ('resume speaking Gallo') has long been used to imply that the language is merely flawed French, an attitude that many speakers internalised over time, limiting it to private conversations such as within the family. As a result of this harassment, Brittany's urban residents became increasingly determined to speak French, often at the expense of their ancestors' tongue, effectively drawing sociolinguistic and socioeconomic lines between 'modern' towns and 'primitive' villages.

France's popular media reinforced negative representations of Brittany as a centre of folklore and absurd traditionalism until the Second World War, when real or potential secessionist movements such as Bretons were instead portrayed, in most cases speciously, as Nazi collaborators. Set against the common portrayal of French as the patriotic language of the Resistance leaders, the outcome was the further delegitimisation of Brittany's regional languages. More and more, parents spoke French with their children, creating ever stronger sociolinguistic boundaries between grandchildren and grandparents, while the traditional geographic boundaries separating Breton from Gallo and Gallo from French were gradually eroded. Whereas around 2 million people could speak Breton in the 1880s, only 500,000 to 600,000 were believed to have this capacity a century later. The number of Gallo speakers has always been harder to determine given this language's greater ties to French, but today there are estimated to be just around 200,000 of each and, being concentrated among the older age brackets, both tongues are regarded by UNESCO as 'severely endangered'.

French politicians slowly started to warm to the idea of preserving regional languages after the Second World War as long as it did not undermine the predominance of the French language.

To this end, a small number of laws have been passed following popular pressure, most recently the 2021 Molac Law conceived to protect and promote regional languages.* It is important to mention here that the Council of Europe and the European Union, of both of which France is a key member, have enabled minority-language advocates to expect more inclusive national language policies. Especially via its *Ya d'ar brezhoneg* ('Yes to Breton') programme, emboldened by the Basque *Bai Euskarari* ('Yes to Basque') scheme, the *Ofis Publik ar Brezhoneg* (Public Office for the Breton Language) has played a key role in promoting businesses and organisations' use of Breton, from street signage to promotional material. Since the 1960s, French citizens have gradually been given greater freedoms to name their children what they want (within reason), following a long-standing clampdown on names that were not those of Catholic saints or celebrated French historical figures, which had the effect of banning Breton and other regional names. Breton-language education is also becoming increasingly commonplace, most notably through the province's *Diwan* (Germination) schools, which, inspired by Basque *ikastolas* and Welsh *ysgolion*, have been established since 1977. Despite encountering some significant financial challenges, these institutions have made great strides in redressing the gaps left by a general

---

*This law allows schools to teach fully in regional languages (previously the maximum was 50 per cent), permits community-run schools to access funding from the municipalities where their students live, and authorises the use of regional diacritical marks in civil status acts like the registration of a baby's name. Spearheaded by Paul Molac, a member of parliament from Brittany, the bill received substantial support in the French National Assembly, with 247 votes for, 76 against (including that of President Emmanuel Macron) and 19 abstentions. Molac celebrated by singing Brittany's anthem *Bro Gozh ma Zadoù* ('Old Land of My Fathers', which incidentally has the same meaning plus melody as the Welsh and Cornish anthems *Hen Wlad Fy Nhadau* and *Bro Goth agan Tasow*, respectively) with colleagues from his region.

lack of family-based intergenerational transmission in recent decades, and students can now take the language at university, too. Gallo activists likewise made inroads from the 1970s, promoting their language through the organisations Bertaèyn Galeizz (Gallo Brittany), Maézoe (Henceforth) and the Gallo Teachers' Association. Although its progress has been slower than Breton's, Gallo is gradually enjoying a greater presence in local radio, television and print media, through cultural activities such as *fêtes gallèses* ('Gallo festivals') and via various creative endeavours, as well as in the education system.

At the same time, the linguistic boundaries between Brittany and the rest of the country as well as within the province have continued to blur. Immigration to Brittany and other French provinces, especially from North Africa in the past forty years, has rendered languages such as Arabic as well as the place of Islam within French national identity much more pertinent topics to many political leaders, not least with regard to education. Of particular relevance to Brittany, though, there is little agreement on what Breton and Gallo even look or sound like today. Breton is widely reckoned to comprise four major dialects (Kerne, Leon, Treger and Gwened), each with its own internal variations, such that the language differs quite substantially from village to village. Standardising Breton spelling has proved an unenviable task, as at least three versions exist. All this has rendered it impossible to identify a single Breton language to teach a younger generation of people who are increasingly interested in reconnecting with their roots, but who never learnt the tongue because their parents or grandparents felt too ashamed to transmit it. The result has been the emergence of a Neo-Breton language, primarily in Brittany's main population centres, where the majority of schools and universities are located. This language is quite similar to the Leon dialect, but whereas 'native' Breton uses numerous French loanwords, Neo-Breton introduces various neologisms formed from Celtic roots and pronounced like one would expect in French.

However, the growth of Neo-Breton has not been uncontested. The generally older group of native speakers almost invariably learnt Breton orally and can only read and write in French, whereas the *néo-bretonnants* develop a broader range of language skills, but their tongue is commonly accused of being unintelligible, concocted by regional elites for young urban speakers, rather than representing the language of local farmers and fishers. Through additionally standardising the traditional language via print, radio, television and the internet, Neo-Breton has hence created fault lines between 'traditional' and 'new' speakers, based on people's level of education, place of residence (especially the regional capital of Rennes versus the rest) and age.

Similarly, little consensus has been found with respect to Gallo. For decades Gallo was understood even by its speakers as a mere dialect of French, and in some places it can be difficult to clearly distinguish from Standard French, as like Breton, it varies across villages (where it remains much more common than in urban areas). Further, some of the descendants of Gallo speakers have only recently found that their ancestors spoke this language and not Breton as they had suspected, having never learnt either. Progress is being made: in 1978 Gallo was described in the *Charte culturelle de la Bretagne* (Cultural Charter of Brittany) as a *parler* (local dialect) rather than a *patois*, and from 2004 by the *Conseil régional* (Regional Council) as a *langue* (language), reflecting its growing status. New learners appear to be more confident in speaking the language and regard it more positively than their older counterparts who have internalised considerable scepticism as to its worth. Consequently, Gallo is still working out how best to survive in a country that is more willing to embrace linguistic difference than before, but where the increased movement of people has made it more difficult to define.

In this respect, a new division has emerged: between the respective statuses of Breton and Gallo in twenty-first-century France. Breton is increasingly regarded as the more 'authentic' of the two, aided by its greater geographical distance from the rest of France (as is true also of Corsican) and linguistic similarities to other Celtic languages. Tourists – an important contributor to Lower Brittany's economy – often value the conspicuousness of the region's contemporary bilingualism and Celtic or quasi-Celtic traditions, sensing that it 'feels' different from the rest of the country. Meanwhile, being far more similar to French, Gallo has struggled to attain the same widespread legitimacy in popular consciousness as a symbol of Brittany and as a language in its own right, to the exasperation of many of its speakers. It is also much less common in different types of media, and whereas Breton is today demanded by many schools, libraries and nursing homes, among other institutions, knowledge of Gallo tends still to be considered a 'bonus' at most. Noteworthy too is that rather than uniting against the long-time linguistic centralism of the French state, Breton speakers have often distanced themselves from their Gallo counterparts, seeing their language as 'too Romance' to merit collaboration. It is thus Breton that has become the more powerful symbol of Breton distinctiveness: the language reinforces regional identity while providing a degree of protection against French assimilation.

Of course, there are numerous examples of language borders across the world*; Brittany is not alone in this regard. However, the region offers a rare glimpse into the struggles faced by two neighbouring languages in a country that still does not officially recognise them, as well as the associated boundaries that have emerged on the basis of worldview, social class, generation and more. The case demonstrates that language can provide a powerful source of identity, marking one's distinctiveness and defining

---

* Although perhaps none have as evocative names as Switzerland's gastronomical *Röstigraben/rideau de rösti* and *Polentagraben/rideau de polenta* – effectively the 'Rösti Curtain' and the 'Polenta Curtain' – separating French from German and Italian speakers, respectively.

one's sense of belonging. By identifying where minority languages are spoken, and hence where the invisible boundaries separating them from 'the outside' are to be found, it becomes possible to discern the current condition of unique communities whose future survival are in question. As we will consider next, in some places it is also helpful to map dialects, whether one's intention is to identify, understand and perhaps maintain differences across space, or, alternatively, to melt these differences to achieve a degree of standardisation.

Germany's Dialect Lines

Ich verstehe nur Bahnhof
'I only understand train station'

German idiom

Catching the train in Germany is often a pleasant experience. Not only famously punctual, German trains are invariably also clean, comfortable and fast, and stations are clearly labelled. However, misunderstandings are still possible. A train scheduled at 8.15 a.m. on Saturday will be *viertel neun* ('quarter nine') on *Sonnabend* to one speaker from Rostock in the north-east, but *viertel nach acht* ('quarter past eight') on *Samstag* to a second speaker from Rosenheim in the south. Even that final sound, the *Tag* in *Samstag*, is far more prevalent in southern Germany than in the north, where *Dag*, the same word as in Dutch and more similar to the English 'day', prevails. In fact, Germany is home to numerous variations in its choice of consonants and even words, resulting in a range of dialects – potentially up to 250, depending on how strictly a distinct dialect is defined – across the country.

Admittedly, the German language is not alone in having a distinct geography to its dialects. In England, a person from Newcastle upon Tyne will typically sound very different from a person from Bristol, and in the United States the same can be said of Boston versus New Orleans. Lines can be drawn demarcating different pronunciations: note for instance the north–south divide in England concerning 'bath' or 'scone', or in the United States between 'you all' and 'y'all'.* Even the words or phrases we use

---

* The Pittsburgh area, intriguingly, has a term of its own, 'yinz', derived from the Scots-Irish 'you ones'.

vary significantly: if a British person says 'bun', 'bap', 'barm', 'batch', 'cob' 'teacake', 'muffin' or another of the seemingly countless names for what many call a bread roll, it is possible to gain a sense of where they grew up. The same is true of a long American sandwich: is it a sub, a hoagie, a hero, a grinder, a zeppelin . . . ? In fact, there is something both wonderfully unifying and maddeningly divisive about bread goods. But hungrily, I digress. As a country that was only unified late in the nineteenth century and then forcibly divided into two for much of the twentieth century, Germany provides a particularly compelling case of a place where regional dialects have been able to enjoy a relatively high level of staying power. Of particular interest for this book, in Germany several invisible linguistic lines called isoglosses have been drawn over time to demarcate three broad dialect areas in particular, thereby distinctly mapping variations in the German language. The fact that German has words to describe not only a strong desire to travel (*Wanderlust*), but also a more specific longing for distant places (*Fernweh*) and a perhaps related obsessive yearning for the unattainable (*Sehnsucht*) only increases its *Anziehungskraft* (appeal, or 'attraction force') as we depart from an age of pandemic-related travel restrictions. So before I *verschlimmbesser* this paragraph (make something worse in attempting to improve it) with my favourite German words, I shall proceed.

The German language is roughly grouped into three dialect areas: Upper German (*Oberdeutsch*), Central German (*Mitteldeutsch*) and Low German (*Niederdeutsch* or *Plattdeutsch*). Confusingly for anyone consulting a map of Germany, Upper German refers to the southernmost portion, for its name is related to the upland landscapes that characterise much of this area. Low German by contrast means northern German, for the low plains found in this part of the country. The variations are the result of a slow historical process called the High German consonant shift, whereby the southern dialects gradually underwent a phonological (sound) evolution, especially implicating the consonants 'p', 'd', 'k' and 't', which in many words became respectively 'f', 't', 'ch' and either 'ß'/'ss' or 'z'. Some remote southern Alpine regions underwent further modifications that never took hold elsewhere, as is still evident in parts of Switzerland, where the German word for 'child', *Kind*, is replaced by *Kchind*. By contrast, most northern dialects were unaffected by this process. The central German dialects, conveniently, represent a middle ground, with local dialects here adhering to the consonant shift to differing extents. The timing of the process remains uncertain, although many linguists believe that it occurred between approximately the third or fourth and ninth centuries in a series of waves that had greater reach in some communities than others. Events such as the Hunnish invasions and associated population movements from the fourth century, notably the Lombards and the Franks, appear to have been particularly influential in shaping not only the geography of the Germanic peoples, but their languages and dialects as well.

The overall result of the consonant shift is a patchwork of dialects. To make better sense of this *Mischmasch*, the three groups Low, Central and Upper German are used to categorise dialects by the extent to which they changed due to the consonant shift. Although they are not perfect groupings, and many linguists are refining them to reflect more specific regional variations, including west from east as well as solely north from south, their existence is still commonly described by German speakers. Further, being easily mappable under three overarching headings, divided by isoglosses, they offer a concise way of making sense of a complex language. And with its many compound nouns, such as *Ohrwurm* (literally 'ear worm', referring to a catchy tune that is stuck in one's head), *Treppenwitz* ('staircase joke', a rejoinder concocted too late) and *Naschkatze* ('nibble cat', someone with an insatiable sweet tooth), the German language certainly endorses succinctness.

One isogloss, the Benrath Line, separates the dialects to the north, which use the 'k' sound in words like *maken* ('to make'), from those to the south, which during the consonant shift adopted the 'ch' sound instead, resulting in *machen*. The isogloss runs across northern Germany, fittingly starting near most atlases' first entry, Aachen, to Benrath just south of Düsseldorf, looping around Berlin before passing Frankfurt an der Oder and finally crossing the Polish border. A second isogloss is the Uerdingen Line, which is named after a district of Krefeld a few kilometres up the River Rhine from Düsseldorf, where the word for 'I' is *ik*, in contrast to the southern *ich*. Again, this isogloss crosses national borders, passing through both the Netherlands and Belgium. The Uerdingen Line, unsurprisingly given its shared tendency to separate 'k' and 'ch', follows a similar course to the Benrath Line, although it does deviate in places, including in Berlin's state of Brandenburg, where it travels south of the capital and not north like its counterpart. Furthermore, near the Dutch and Belgian borders the two isoglosses part and effectively bound the Limburgish dialect, which is centred on Maastricht but is also spoken in the Düsseldorf area. Considered together, however, the two lines roughly divide Low German from Central and Upper German.

Within the Central German region, there are several shorter isoglosses, especially near Germany's western borders with the Netherlands, Belgium, Luxembourg and France, a complex triangular-shaped region called the Rhenish Fan, after the Rhine. Here, not only can the Limburgish dialect be discerned from Standard Dutch, but various Franconian tongues can also be identified, covering an area from roughly Nijmegen in the Netherlands to the north-eastern corner of France and encompassing major German cities like Köln (Cologne) and Bonn. The local Central German dialects here can be distinguished north from south on the basis of consonants such as 't' versus 's' (the Sankt Goar Line), 'v' versus 'b' (the Boppard Line) and 'p' from 'f' (the Bad Honnef Line) in certain words. In short, this is the region with the most intricate set of isoglosses, where speakers can still use their local dialect to communicate with others across national borders, despite clear differences in the *standard* versions of their national languages.

Finally, to distinguish Central and Upper German, the Speyer Line runs north-east as an inverted V from approximately Strasbourg in present-day France, to an apex near Erfurt in Thuringia, central Germany, and then south-east into the western, Bohemia portion of the Czech Republic near Plzeň. From the European Parliament to the world's centre of pilsner beer, the Speyer Line specifically separates the plosive 'pp' from the affricate 'pf', as in *Appel* versus *Apfel* ('apple') or *Peper* versus *Pfeffer* ('pepper'). Examining a map, it is also possible to see that place names with 'pf' are far more common in southern Germany, for example Pforzheim, Pfaffenhofen an der Ilm and Pfeffenhausen. Settlements with 'pp' tend to be further north, like Wuppertal and Meppen. And of course, English, as a Germanic language not to undergo the consonant shift, has like Low German retained 'pp' rather than adopting 'pf'. More whimsically, some Germans refer to a north–south culinary divide roughly following the Speyer Line, called the *Weißwurstäquator*, south of which the traditional Bavarian white sausage is far more common. The Main River, which following the Austro-Prussian War in 1866 briefly became the basis of the border between Otto von Bismarck's Prussia-led North German Confederation and the generally Austria-leaning southern states, is regarded by others as the divide between Central and Upper German.

These lines are of course imperfect: a person speaking one dialect can easily move to another part of the country but retain their form of speech, even if their dialect is likely to assimilate somewhat after a more extended period. Although they look strict, the isoglosses actually mark transition zones where people's pronunciations gradually shift. After all, any language comprises a continuum of dialects, such that the further one travels to the 'purest' form, the more unintelligible the language becomes to other speakers. This means that crossing an isogloss does not

351

suddenly result in an entirely different dialect; instead, one can expect to hear subtle variations in people's speech and choice of words. Nevertheless, at a larger scale, a person from a northern city such as Hamburg or Bremen may struggle to understand their compatriots' speech (albeit not written language) in southern states like Bavaria, especially in more rural, mountainous areas, and to a greater extent than is the case in England, say, even though my wife likes to remind me of my occasional struggles with the rural Yorkshire dialect with which she grew up. Incidentally, the dialect that stimulates the strongest loathing among German speakers is often said to be Upper Saxon, a Central German dialect from the east of the country, which is characterised by its unusual vowel sounds and 'mushy' consonants.

Long before Germany was unified in 1871, efforts were underway to standardise this hodgepodge of regional dialects. The theologian Martin Luther, aided by a printing boom in the early sixteenth century, was pivotal in this process. Whereas the once-powerful Hanseatic League in the north used Middle Low German, people in the south used a range of Upper dialects and the leaders of the Catholic Church whom Luther denounced tended to prefer the Medieval Latin unknown by the larger society. Translating first the New Testament (1522) and then the whole Bible (1534), Luther chose to adapt the language of the court of his native Saxony in east-central Germany so that it would incorporate elements of Upper German vernacular, rendering it more widely understood. In this way, he opened up the Good Book to an unprecedented readership across the multilingual Holy Roman Empire, managing not only to reform a religion, but also to set in motion the reformation of the German language. This linguistic baton was later taken up by the notoriously pedantic philosopher Johann Christoph Gottsched, whose *Grundlegung einer deutschen Sprachkunst (Foundation of a German Art of Language)*, published in 1748, helped establish a consistent written system. From then on it was largely a matter of letting schools normalise this new version of German, a fusion of Central and Upper dialects called 'High German'. Today it is typically used in the national media as well as in government and the education system, in much the same way as England's Received Pronunciation.* Fittingly, the German words used to describe this standard remain varied, including *Standarddeutsch*, *Hochdeutsch* and *Schriftdeutsch*, the latter being typical in Switzerland.

Other German-speaking countries and communities unsurprisingly have their own dialects as well. Some Swiss German dialects, following centuries of geographical isolation in the Alps, can be barely intelligible to other German speakers, especially those from northern Germany. By contrast, most versions of German spoken in Austria are similar, to differing degrees, to the Upper German dialects typical of Bavaria, the exceptions being in the westernmost part of the country, where the language is generally more like the various Alemannic (*Alemannisch*) dialects used in Liechtenstein, the eastern portion of Switzerland and south-western Germany. In the Americas, the language used by minority German-speaking communities is drawn from the dialects of their founders, so Pennsylvania 'Dutch' originated in the Palatinate region of south-western Germany and remains somewhat like this area's *Pfälzisch* dialect (there's that 'pf' sound again), while the Hunsrik language spoken in parts of southern Brazil, north-eastern Argentina and southern Paraguay is related to the *Hunsrückisch* dialect to the Pfalz's immediate north.

These emigrant dialects' survival has strongly depended on their speakers' willingness to communicate in the language among themselves, without allowing the features of other dialects to permeate. In this regard, isoglosses are contingent on at least one side's determination to impede 'external' traits, and so such

---

* In comparison, American English does not have a clear standard, although some argue that accents from Nebraska and Iowa tend to be the least inflected.

boundaries rely on the lack of mixing their existence may imply. However, in the modern world, complete isolation is difficult to achieve. In fact, perhaps no place better exemplifies the opposing dynamics of boundary maintenance and boundary blurring with respect to dialects than Germany during the second half of the twentieth century. The mass migration that occurred from East to West Germany following the Second World War undermined various regional dialects while strengthening Standard German even in rural areas traditionally unaccustomed to significant influxes of people, as speakers were suddenly spread across the country rather than being limited to a specific geographical area. As existing communities were generally unwilling to change their traditional dialects for the benefit of newcomers, while the latter did not yet feel sufficiently at home to adopt an unfamiliar regional dialect, the standard form came to be seen as both convenient and relatively prestigious, especially among younger generations, who felt torn between the dialect of their parents and that of their peers. During the era of the Iron Curtain, certain linguistic differences did emerge between West and East, the former adopting new words from English, the latter from Russian (for instance, *astronaut* versus *Kosmonaut*). Still, the majority of variations between West and East to have survived to the present day have an origin far pre-dating this relatively short-lived boundary and hence are more entrenched in local speech.

With the rise of mass media and the increasing tendency for people to move around the country, dialect distinctions have continued to fade, although local media often work hard to preserve regional dialects. A generation gap has expanded as younger people are often more mobile and digitally connected, exposing themselves to new voices (particularly in urban areas, which as one Berliner told me can 'have a certain levelling effect' on dialects), whereas their elders, especially those in rural areas, may continue to interact primarily or solely with people with the same dialect and thereby maintain their traditional tongue. Indeed, over time it is plausible that new isoglosses of sorts will emerge between those rural areas where in- and out-migration remain uncommon, and the rest of the country. Mapping these boundaries may provide insights into the degree of cultural exchange at play throughout this and other nations.

Just as Luther's standardisation of the German language never resulted in the complete disappearance of local dialects, his Protestant Reformation's reach across the states that would eventually become united as Germany was inconsistent, leaving a broad division between a Protestant North and a Catholic South that exists to this day. Germany is not the only country to manifest a geographical split on the basis of religion, however. One particularly compelling example, an entire region named for the religious fervour that distinguishes it from its surroundings, is where we shall turn to next.

The Bible Belt

If there's a church for every four people, and two in every strip mall . . . you might live in the Bible Belt.

Neil Carter

A giant cross overlooks the freeway. A billboard commands drivers to praise Jesus. Christian radio plays from a nearby car. The vehicle has an *ichthys* (Jesus fish) sticker on its rear window and its registration plate invokes God's name. Descending into a valley, a small town can be seen ahead, the steeples and spires of its churches emerging above the low roofs of its houses. The United States may officially be a secular nation, but across much of the South, Christian influence is palpable.

I teach a university course called Religious Geography, and in the first class I tend to ask students to think of instances where they have noticed evidence of a local religious community, without naming a religious institution such as a church. They always have lots of ideas: streets named after saints, cemeteries, halal or kosher restaurants – the list goes on. But invariably, something from 'the South' will be mentioned by a student either from or familiar with that region. Often the student will recount a memorable message they have seen on a billboard, warning of eternal damnation or encouraging viewers to visit a specific church. They will speak of the cultural differences they have come across between Chicago, where the university is located, at the north-eastern point of Illinois, and somewhere just a few hours south, at the intersection of Illinois, Kentucky, Missouri and southern Indiana. As our discussion proceeds, I consistently find that the student who first shared an anecdote from the South is not alone in seeing this as the most obvious example of a religiously infused place.

The term 'Bible Belt' was coined nearly a century ago by the American journalist and satirist Henry Louis Mencken to refer, derisively, to the pervasiveness of evangelicalism in the South and rural Midwest. However, just as 'Yankee Doodle' came to be reappropriated by American soldiers in defiance of the British troops who had sung it to mock their supposedly simple ways, so too did Southerners come to adopt the phrase as a descriptor of their piousness. Over time, broad divides have been identified between the Bible Belt and the rest of the country. Most significantly, rates of religiosity (which is measured in various ways, such as by asking respondents to rate their strength of personal belief in God, the degree to which religion is important to them, their attendance at weekly worship services and their participation in daily prayer) are consistently found to be much higher here than elsewhere, with the possible exception of Utah, a Western state where more than half of the population identifies as a member of the socially conservative Church of Jesus Christ of Latter-Day Saints. Yet the Bible Belt also stands out in other ways. Whereas Catholicism and mainline Protestant denominations such as Methodism, Lutheranism, Presbyterianism and Episcopalianism have traditionally predominated in most other states and have also tended to see the most significant declines in religious identification over the past fifty years or so, Southern states are characterised by thriving evangelical Protestant churches, particularly Baptist and Pentecostal as well as non-denominational. Of course, the latter are also represented elsewhere in the country, but here another divide emerges: between the churches within the Belt, which broadly stand firm against abortion and homosexuality, and those beyond, where a far greater proportion are gradually softening their stances on these subjects.

Indeed, religion may now constitute the most conspicuous difference between the South and the rest of the country. Although there has never been a religious dividing line as formal as the Mason–Dixon line, which was originally drawn to settle a border dispute between two powerful families in colonial America, but gained notoriety as the boundary between the states of the South (where enslavement was legal) and the North (where it was not), religion has long played a key role in shaping the South's politics. Southern states such as Mississippi, Alabama, South Carolina and Tennessee have proved to be among the most resolutely Republican in recent elections. Reflecting the close relationship between religion and politics in the South, even today some communities frame the American Civil War as a 'theological' conflict over the future of Christianity, with the 'pious' soldiers of the South defending their faith from the 'heretical' North.

The Southern-oriented Moral Majority was key to mobilising conservative Christians in US politics for the long term, revitalising the Christian nationalism* championed by previous generations of white evangelicals, most notably the televangelist Billy Graham in the 1940s and 1950s. Officially established in 1979, this movement under the leadership of Jerry Falwell rallied against a number of liberalising trends in American society since the 1960s (including the sexual revolution, the gay rights movement, the women's liberation movement, various Supreme Court rulings that limited the place of religion in public schools, and the nationwide legalisation of abortion by another Supreme Court ruling, *Roe v. Wade* in 1973), all of which it claimed amounted to a decline in traditional Christian morality in politics and everyday society. By purporting to save and promote American 'family values', and by publicising their values both through the media

---

*The belief that the United States is a Christian nation and that this Christian heritage therefore needs to be defended. Note also that the Moral Majority was far from the only Christian Right group to come into the wider American public's consciousness at this time, although it was by far the most prominent; other groups with differing levels of influence included Christian Voice, the Religious Roundtable, the National Christian Action Coalition and Intercessors for America.

and at the grassroots, the Moral Majority succeeded in mobilising a broad association of religious conservatives under a patriotic banner. The election of the Republican Ronald Reagan, the group's preferred candidate, as president in 1980 increased the Moral Majority's confidence as a political force for much of the decade, before it was ultimately disbanded in 1989 for a range of reasons, including the emergence of new conservative rivals with different 'enemies' against which to rail, disagreement among its leadership as to who should succeed Reagan, and a drastic decline in funds.

Yet in spite of its own demise, the Moral Majority has had a powerful legacy with respect to the sheer influence and leverage enjoyed by Christian Right voices today, helping shape socially conservative positions on issues including homosexuality, sex education, euthanasia and abortion. In many ways, Republican Donald Trump's election as president in 2016 was the culmination of the Christian Right's efforts over multiple decades. Twice divorced and having long cultivated a 'playboy' reputation, Trump is hardly the archetype of a traditional religious conservative, but he was nevertheless endorsed for the presidency by Falwell's son, also named Jerry. Appealing directly to the Christian nationalist narrative that the country's Christian heritage is under threat* – and lauding Falwell Jr as 'one of the most respected religious leaders in our nation' – Trump would go on to win 77 per cent of the white evangelical Christian vote, a similar percentage to previous, more avowedly religious Republican candidates such as George W. Bush and Mitt Romney. Conservative Christianity has also assumed a central role in the highest court in the

---

*There are certain signs that the US public today is less religious than in the past, and yet even now, nearly 90 per cent of members of the US Congress identify as Christian, while only a single representative – the former Democrat, now independent senator Kyrsten Sinema of Arizona – identifies as religiously unaffiliated.

land, determining laws that affect *everyone*, regardless of faith, and regardless of public opinion. In no case has this been more apparent than in the controversial overturning of *Roe v. Wade* via *Dobbs v. Jackson Women's Health Organization* in 2022, which restored individual states' former autonomy to define their own abortion laws. After all, polls suggest that the general public is far less averse to abortion than the six conservative Supreme Court justices (three of whom were appointed by Trump), who now appear willing to revisit previous rulings pertaining to matters historically opposed by many staunch Christians, including contraception and same-sex relationships. Furthermore, and reflecting the significance of geography, in the immediate aftermath of the 2022 ruling a pattern quickly emerged with regard to abortion laws, states in the presumptive Bible Belt generally being the most decisive in banning or seriously restricting abortion,* whereas state protections for this right exist in most of the North-East, along the West Coast and in Illinois and Hawaii.

The Bible Belt's general sense of differentiation from the wider United States is experienced culturally as well. Transplants from other parts of the country, especially those who do not identify as Christian, regularly describe being struck by the extent to which evangelical forms of Protestantism are so pervasive as to constitute the default in the South. It is not uncommon to be asked which church one attends, for blessings to be said before meals and for meetings to open with a prayer. 'God bless you' is often used in place of 'thank you' and, in some regions, 'have a blessed

---

*Thirteen states, eight of which one might consider 'Southern', had already established 'trigger laws' to make abortion illegal within the first two trimesters, in anticipation of the eventual repeal of *Roe v. Wade*. At the time of writing, not all these states have yet enacted their trigger laws, although two – Texas and Oklahoma – managed to ban almost all abortions *prior* to the 2022 ruling, by enabling the law to be enforced via civil lawsuits as opposed to state prosecution. A further six states still have abortion bans predating *Roe v. Wade* in their laws.

day' substitutes for 'goodbye' (even though this also has Christian origins, being a contraction of 'God be with you'). Thanksgiving in many counties is treated as a Christian holiday, on which the sale of alcohol is banned; some other counties refuse to sell and serve alcohol throughout the year or have time restrictions on Sundays. Pastors such as Joel Osteen, Paula White and Creflo Dollar have become celebrities, using radio, television, print media and the internet to share their sermons with a much wider audience than is possible in a single geographical location.* Many students in the South report having teachers lead their class in prayer despite this being illegal in the country's public schools. Intriguingly, from 1993 to 2021 the state of Alabama banned yoga in public schools due to it supposedly endorsing a 'non-Christian belief system'; meditation and the greeting 'namaste' are still forbidden. And according to some of the region's residents, the very existence of the United States is the result of divine inspiration.

Admittedly, given variations in the public presence of Christianity across the South, including between urban and rural areas, it can be difficult to determine exactly where the Bible Belt's invisible boundaries are to be found, but this has not stopped people from trying. Part of the issue pertains to what exactly constitutes the Bible Belt. Most agree that it concerns areas with a significant evangelical Protestant (especially Baptist) presence and socially conservative views. This means that areas that are far from unanimously considered 'Southern', such as Texas and Oklahoma, as well as certain parts of Kansas, Missouri, Illinois and Indiana, can be said to fall within the Bible Belt as long as they display similar religious and political characteristics. But there is little agreement

---

*For example, soon after the COVID-19 pandemic started afflicting the United States, Osteen's sermons would draw well over 4 million viewers online. At present, he has more than 10 million Twitter followers and is the author of seven number one *New York Times* bestsellers. That's quite the flock.

as to whether certain denominations should be discounted when determining the boundaries, or how they should be defined. Any spatial boundaries are thus always going to be contested.

There is also only minor consensus as to what represents the 'buckle' or unofficial capital of the Belt, with Jackson, Memphis, Nashville, Dallas, Charlotte, Oklahoma City and Tulsa (the latter two of which are both in Oklahoma rather than the 'geographical' South) just some of the cities postulated. By contrast, some parts of the 'geographical' South, like southern Florida and Louisiana, are not always described as part of the Bible Belt owing to their significant Catholic populations. Within the Belt there is an additional racial divide, as many cities remain highly segregated, the overwhelming majority of churches are made up of exclusively white or Black parishioners, and Black voting patterns do not tend to accord as well with religion as their white counterparts. Relatedly, some have claimed that the Bible Belt can be divided into a broadly western region and a broadly eastern region, based in large part on demographic variations. Unsurprisingly given the premise of a Bible Belt, the United States has also been described as having the inverse elsewhere, an 'Unchurched Belt' in the North-West, where church membership is lower than in the majority of the rest of the country. Nevertheless, the 'Bible Belt' as a concept has achieved much greater prominence in popular discourse, and analogous but far smaller examples have been identified in other parts of the world, too, including in Scandinavia, Central Europe and certain Australian suburbs.

Given the continued and in some places growing popularity of evangelical Protestantism, it is also reasonable to expect the Bible Belt to expand in the future, its invisible boundaries moving further north and west across states such as Kansas, Missouri and Illinois, exemplifying the continued significance of faith across much of the South. Through repeatedly invoking the main tenets of a religion and viewing these as central to a place's identity, that faith can become normalised, a default standard to which residents are expected to adhere. Those who approve are likely to remain (or move here, if they come from elsewhere), whereas those who do not may well choose to move away, in the process strengthening the territory's association with that specific religion. And owing to the frequently close entwinement between religion and politics – as this region demonstrates so openly – the stretching of boundaries marking out a religiously distinctive place can additionally imply shifts in voting patterns. Seemingly small changes in the religious demographics of a particular county, for instance, may have profound ramifications during election season, and thus be of interest locally *and* nationally.

In these ways, and somewhat akin to the case of Northern Ireland, the boundaries of the Bible Belt are not merely relevant to those who live within them, through hinting at the likely extent to which an individual will feel comfortable and compatible with their surroundings. They also provide insights into large proportions of citizens' worldviews, helpful in political advocacy and forecasting by those on the 'outside' as well. In an increasingly fractured society, they can quite reasonably be deemed the fault lines of public opinion, on matters that affect us all. And so, if we are to truly understand the divisions we feel, we must seek out the lines we cannot see. Lines like these may be invisible, but their existence is palpable. They can be rigid, or they can be dynamic, but one thing is consistent: they are not going away any time soon.

Epilogue

The Imaginary Lines of Ukraine, Russia and 'Europe'

---

*From the very first steps they [Ukrainians]
began to build their statehood on the denial of
everything that unites us. They tried to distort the
consciousness, the historical memory of millions
of people, entire generations living in Ukraine.*

Vladimir Putin

*Neighbours always enrich one another culturally,
but that does not make them one, does not dissolve
us in you. We are different. But it is not a reason
to be enemies. We want to determine our history
by ourselves. In peace, calm and honesty.*

Volodymyr Zelenskyy

In this book, we have considered many types of invisible lines, perceived and drawn to distinguish between sides, and to assume control over our world. Sometimes these lines emerge intentionally, through laws, policies and human decisions. Other times we scarcely notice we are distinguishing between two sides, but through experience develop a sense that 'this' place is different from 'that' place, that 'here' we feel safe and comfortable, whereas 'there' we consider ourselves somehow 'out of place', possibly compelling us to withdraw or to alter our behaviour. The lines we draw in our mental maps of the world reveal different aspects of our engagement with the planet – cultural, social, political, environmental, meteorological, really any way in which one *can* feasibly divide the world. Given the intricacies of our globe and the diversity of its people, is it any wonder that we are tempted to seek the simplest answers?

Lines constitute the most accessible and efficient mechanism by which to both understand the world and shape it as we see fit. Regardless of whether we are speaking of scientists seeking patterns with the potential to explain our planet's workings, governments deciding where to prioritise investment and resources, or religious groups aiming to ensure their adherents can practise their faith as they desire, lines provide a means of distinguishing between one side and another. Even where lines emerge organically, they reflect our biases, our assumptions about 'us' and 'them', about what being on either side represents or demands. And by being continuously perceived, felt, discerned, they can have far-reaching impacts on people's relationship with the world.

Russia's horrific invasion of Ukraine exemplifies the significance of boundaries, and the diverse ways in which these are constructed, articulated, reiterated and challenged by various individuals and groups. While it is easy to focus on questions of borders – most notably, Russia's failure to respect Ukraine's sovereignty through its military advances – the war is rooted in various, competing identity narratives, with boundaries drawn to distinguish between sides. However, these boundaries are not only highly subjective, but in many cases phenomenally spurious, more reflective of presumptions and biases than having empirical support.

Consider the common claim, including in 'the West' (itself a loaded construct), that there are 'two Ukraines'. Ever since Ukraine's independence from the USSR in August 1991, various observers have spoken of a fault line dividing a broadly western or north-western part from a broadly eastern or south-eastern part, on the basis of ethnicity and language (Ukrainian versus Russian), religion (Ukrainian Orthodox and Catholic versus Russian Orthodox)* and outlook (Europe and the 'West' versus Russia and the 'East'). Some even invoke the existence of a line between the cities of Uman' and Kharkiv as a means of reinforcing this view, while additionally taking into account differences in physical geography (forests versus steppe) and human settlement (a largely rural north-west versus a more urbanised and industrial south-east). Foreign speculation about the possible break-up of Ukraine along such a divide, and its potential security implications for the rest of Europe, has dominated much of the discourse and reporting of Ukraine for three decades.

Such representations are highly problematic. For example,

---

*Further reflecting the politicisation of division, it is worth noting that the Ukrainian Orthodox Church only officially gained its independence from its larger Russian counterpart in January 2019.

many people who regard their ethnicity as Ukrainian consider Russian their mother tongue. National-scale maps suggesting a general north-west–south-east linguistic divide also tend to mask dynamics at the local scale, with the Ukrainian language generally more common in rural areas, whereas Russian speakers are often concentrated in urban districts. Moreover, it is necessary to recognise that Ukraine contains a large bilingual population, who may choose to speak one language or another in different social contexts, especially since Ukrainian was made the only official state language in 2019.* Similarly, numerous citizens consider their ethnicity a combination of Ukrainian and Russian. The common narrative that Ukrainian national identity has been developed in contradistinction to Russian national identity ignores not only that a significant percentage of the population identifies as dual-national, but also that Poland to the west has long provided a rival 'Other' in Ukrainian nation building. Even the idea that western Ukraine represents some kind of 'heartland' of Ukrainian national identity is limited. According to some accounts, the articulation of a separate Ukraine actually originated in the eastern part of the modern-day country, but the threat of Russification eventually pushed this ideology westwards, where it flourished as it competed with Polish nationalism.

---

*Relatedly, and like we have seen with Northern Ireland, one's choice of names here reflects one's identity or political worldview, as can be observed in the growing tendency of Western media outlets to refer to the country's capital as Kyiv (Київ in Cyrillic) according to the Ukrainian language, as opposed to the Russian-language Kiev (Киев), especially since the launch of the Ukrainian Ministry of Foreign Affairs' 'KyivNotKiev' online campaign in October 2018. Other major cities of interest include Odesa/Одеса (as opposed to Odessa/Одесса), Lviv/Львів (as opposed to L'vov/Львов) and the aforementioned Kharkiv/Харків (as opposed to Kharkov/Харьков). Similarly, English-language publications are increasingly dropping the article 'the' before the country's name, to avoid implying that the country is a mere region of a larger entity (historically implying Russia).

How can one therefore speak of a dividing line within Ukraine? Not easily. As with other subjective boundaries, the Uman'–Kharkiv line is an imaginary construct, but through being repeatedly invoked, it risks being made real. In March 2022, the Ukrainian military intelligence chief Kyrylo Budanov brought this point home by emphasising how Russian military action constitutes 'an attempt to create North and South Korea in Ukraine'. In this war, division benefits Russia, but with the Ukrainian population so far demonstrating considerable solidarity and unity in opposition to the invasion, any such line appears more as a Muscovite myth than a solid basis for partition. One would hope that lessons have been learnt from the horrors of the Partition of India and the break-up of the former Yugoslavia, which in certain ways are analogous examples of ethnically diverse places that had been occupied by external powers,* and where boundaries were perceived and drawn to imply and foster cultural homogeneity. Only time will tell, but at the time of writing, beyond the contested peninsula of Crimea and the two rebel-held territories of Donetsk and Luhansk in the Donbas region (the latter two of which have, like Russia, banned Facebook and Instagram as well as Google, forming invisible lines determining one's access to news media), there appears to be little appetite for Russian control.

Ukraine as a whole is far less divided today than many external observers and actors believe, or *choose* to believe. Rather than being split Cold War-style somewhere through the middle, the war so far has revealed the determination of the majority of the country's population to be embraced by 'Western' institutions. To be clear, it is true that since independence, the country has been pulled in different geopolitical directions, and voting patterns have

---

*In the case of Ukraine, different parts have been occupied in the past millennium by the Mongol Empire, the Polish–Lithuanian Commonwealth, the Russian Empire, the Austrian (and later Austro-Hungarian) Empire, Czechoslovakia, Romania, the USSR and, today, the Russian Federation.

on occasion suggested a geographical division between north-west and south-east, not least in the fraught presidential elections involving the more western-looking Viktor Yushchenko in 2004 and Yulia Tymoshenko in 2010 versus the Kremlin-allied Viktor Yanukovych. Nevertheless, in the main, membership of the European Union (EU) and the North Atlantic Treaty Organization (NATO) has been coveted far more than the Eurasian Economic Community and its successor the Eurasian Economic Union (EEU), as well as the Commonwealth of Independent States (CIS), which Ukraine never fully joined.* Accordingly, perhaps the two most significant events to put Ukraine 'on the map' (the 'Orange Revolution' of November 2004 to January 2005, which saw mass protests against electoral fraud and corruption, and 'Euromaidan' from November 2013 to February 2014, comprising mass demonstrations following Yanukovych's decision to move the country politically closer to Russia and the EEU rather than the EU)[†] both reflected a popular if not unanimous desire for the country to operate in line with and, no less importantly, to *be seen* like any other European country. Here were powerful moments of national awakening, which enabled Ukrainians from all walks of life to come together as one, call for functioning democratic institutions and, in the process, detach their country from the vote-rigging and intimidation frequently characteristic of their larger neighbour to

---

* Ukraine agreed to the formation of the CIS as a natural successor to the USSR, making it a founding state, but remained reluctant to hand over too much of its newfound autonomy to a supranational organisation that was likely to be dominated by Russia. Given this concern, it refused to ratify the CIS Charter which would have made it a full rather than associate member, and ultimately ceased participating in CIS statutory bodies in 2018 as its relationship with Russia proceeded to deteriorate.

† Yanukovych made this move in large part as a means of prolonging his presidency, rendering it a decision that was at least as much individual and pragmatic as it was ideological or reflective of a broadly held desire to ally with Russia.

the east. Ukraine's future, these events suggested, would be 'European' and, by extension, *not* 'Russian'.

In this respect, Europe exists, as we have seen in the case of the Urals, first and foremost as a concept, an ideological construct whose values include liberty, democracy, the rule of law and public order. A major challenge that Ukraine still faces is to legitimise its positioning on this 'western' side of the political divide, and simultaneously to distance itself from the collectivism, repression and corruption so frequently associated with the 'eastern' 'Other'. Ukraine's second president Leonid Kuchma once sought to emphasise Ukraine's cultural differences from Russia, but was undone when his second term (1999–2005) adopted an authoritarian bent. Invoking 'Europeanness' – or at least 'not-Russianness' – is not enough on its own.

Achieving this objective is complicated – and perhaps rendered impossible – by the need to balance ideological commitment to the European project with appeasement of the Kremlin. After all, Russian President Putin has viewed the above, alongside the gradual eastern enlargement of NATO, as a threat to his country. See for instance his address to the Russian people on 24 February, the first day of the 2022 invasion, in which he described a figurative and thus in practice *invisible* 'red line' between his country and 'the West':

> For our country, this ['policy of containment of Russia'] is ultimately a matter of life and death, a matter of our historical future as a people ... This is the very red line that has been talked about many times. They ['the United States and its allies'] crossed it.

The speech marked the culmination of years of denouncing 'Western' policies and initiatives – not least the European Neighbourhood Policy (ENP, launched in 2003) and the Eastern Partnership (EaP, initiated in 2009) – for bringing Ukraine closer to EU institutions, and by extension implying increased cultural and political distance from Russia. Accordingly, and especially since Euromaidan and the ousting of the autocratic Yanukovych in February 2014, Putin has aggressively sought to bring Ukraine 'back' within Russia's sphere of influence, again a line both invisible and imaginary.*

Where can this line be found? Putin's rambling essay of July 2021, which accompanied new movements of Russian troops on the Ukrainian border, is particularly informative. In this treatise, he contends that Russians and Ukrainians are 'one people', whose 'close cultural, spiritual and economic ties' have been repeatedly undermined by 'external patrons and masters' responsible for 'sow[ing] discord' and 'pit[ting] the parts of a single people against one another'. In this vein, Ukraine's leaders have, in Putin's mind, begun 'to mythologise and rewrite history, edit out everything that united us, and refer to the period when Ukraine was part of the Russian Empire and the Soviet Union as an occupation'. Additionally, they have 'robbed the people of Ukraine and kept their stolen money in Western banks', just as Russia, too, has long been 'robbed' through 'foreign intervention':

Well before 2014, the US and EU countries systematically and consistently pushed Ukraine to curtail and limit economic cooperation with Russia . . . Step by step, Ukraine was dragged into a dangerous geopolitical game aimed at turning Ukraine into a barrier between Europe and Russia, a springboard against Russia.

To Putin, then, any notion of Ukraine acting as a boundary

---

*Paradoxically, many pro-Western Ukrainians are also dissatisfied with the ENP, because it implies that Ukraine is outside the boundaries of Europe and has no greater claim to 'Europeanness' than the countries of North Africa, the Levant and the Caucasus.

between 'West' and 'East' is a Western myth, a manipulation designed to tame the Russian bear. The invisible line is not Ukraine per se; in actuality, it exists at Ukraine's western border, making this country merely a part of Russia. This distinctive understanding of 'Russia's' land and its boundaries helps explain what has transpired since. It is an invasion rooted in narcissism, couched in the language of self-determination ('What Ukraine will be – it is up to its citizens to decide'), and vain disregard and audacity ('I am becoming more and more convinced of this: Kiev simply does not need Donbas'). As has become increasingly clear, Putin has no interest at all in respecting what Ukraine's citizens want, regardless of what his supporters may suggest of his bogus annexation referendums in regions under military occupation, including several years earlier in 2014, in Crimea. All that matters to him is that Ukraine be subsumed within Russia's boundaries: to hell with what 'the West' thinks. And all the while, he has worked hard to increase the strength of Russia-centric Eurasian alliances like the EEU and the Collective Security Treaty Organization (CSTO), in hopes that they can contend with the EU and NATO to the west. This international geopolitical divide is far more significant than any geographical divide *within* Ukraine. This is the invisible line that needs to be discerned.

Fatefully, and to the particular and obvious vexation of many of its residents, Ukraine has long seemed more meaningful to Russia than to 'Western' institutions. Indeed, Putin has for years expressed greater determination to embrace Ukraine – in his own megalomaniacal way – than have institutions like the EU, which have tended to view the country through an economic lens as a free trade partner, rather than as a geopolitical asset.* It is thus more than a little ironic that Ukraine, for so long overlooked in

---

*As the Eastern European politics expert Kataryna Wolczuk wrote in 2016: 'The conundrum for Ukraine is that the EU does not care enough about Ukraine's European choice while Russia cares too much.'

'the West', has now become its primary foreign policy concern, portrayed as a symbolic borderland between core 'European' values of democracy and sovereignty on one side, and tyranny and violation on the other. The country whose name is widely believed to derive from a Slavic word for 'frontier region' or 'borderland',* out of sight and out of mind, has suddenly been thrust front and centre of the world's attention. The war so far appears to have shifted it, belatedly, to the western side of Europeans' invisible, cognitive boundary, a mindset which Ukrainian President Zelenskyy has been working hard to cultivate when addressing the EU, for example:

> We are fighting to be equal members of Europe . . . Do prove that you are with us. Do prove that you will not let us go. Do prove that you are indeed Europeans, and then life will win over death and light will win over darkness.

Whether this translates into Ukraine receiving the EU and NATO membership much of its population has long craved, however, remains to be seen.†

Whatever transpires, it seems unlikely that more than a minority of Ukraine's population, seeing the obliteration of their cities and the mass graves of fellow civilians, will be cajoled to look 'East'. The EU is now Ukraine's main trading partner, and the latter's gradual adoption of EU trade rules has pushed Ukraine and Russia further and further apart. In the minds of those in

---

*This is not unanimous, however: a competing theory, especially popular among scholars committed to foregrounding rather than marginalising this part of the world, states that its meaning is closer to 'in the country'.
† Arguably reflecting the legacy of the Cold War and assumptions about different countries' 'Europeanness', it is interesting to note that only three former Soviet republics have managed to join the EU and NATO: Estonia, Latvia and Lithuania, all in 2004.

the unquestioned 'West', too, viewing the brutality with which Russian forces attack their neighbour, Ukraine appears increasingly as a separate and necessarily independent entity. Today, instead of running along Ukraine's western borders with Poland, Slovakia and Hungary as a boundary between the 'Western' and 'Orthodox' civilisations, as Samuel Huntington famously posited following the fall of the Iron Curtain, any geopolitical boundary would seem to exist much further east, cleaving at least the vast majority of Ukraine from the Russian state's actions and assumptions. Indeed, the conflict may well ensure that in the long term, Ukraine can distance itself from Russia in the collective imagination, as Zbigniew Brzezinski, former United States national security advisor, argued in 2016: 'The key point to bear in mind is that Russia cannot be in Europe without Ukraine also being in Europe, whereas Ukraine can be in Europe without Russia being in Europe.'

The borders on a map can depict where two countries abut, but they struggle to represent where people actually believe one place ends and another begins. Such boundaries – imagined, shifting, contested, infused with assumptions and stereotypes, appearing so simple and yet constituted from complexity – always need to be considered. These are the lines that we more frequently encounter, and which, through being continuously reproduced in words and in minds, shape and frame our thinking and behaviour in return. Looks can be deceiving, but the lines we do *not* see may be just as persuasive, and far more effectual. Only by addressing the invisible, the perceptual, the emotive, the discursive, can we truly understand our place in the world.

Notes

In conducting the research for *Invisible Lines*, I enjoyed reading thousands of books, journal and news articles and websites, and speaking with people in various countries. Although I realise that some readers will be curious about the origins of a specific fact or story, a bibliography comprising every single source that inspired my thinking would likely almost double the size of this book. Therefore, listed below are a variety of sources that proved particularly informative in my research and that readers may accordingly want to explore for themselves. The notes are structured by chapter. Sources containing quoted text (where applicable) are listed first, in the order that they appear. Additional sources are then listed alphabetically by author. I translated some of the sources myself (primarily those in French) or with the help of a native speaker (mainly those in German) and take full responsibility for any errors.

Introduction

Sources

Antony Galton, 'On the ontological status of geographical boundaries', in Matt Duckham, Michael F. Goodchild and Michael Worboys (eds), *Foundations of Geographic Information Science* (New York, Taylor & Francis, 2003), pp. 151–71.

Doreen Massey, *For Space* (London, SAGE Publications, 2005).

Yi-Fu Tuan, *Space and Place: The Perspective of Experience* (Minneapolis, University of Minnesota Press, 1977).

The Wallace Line

Quoted sources

'In this archipelago': Alfred Russel Wallace, letter to Henry Walter Bates,

4 January 1858, in John van Wyhe and Kees Rookmaaker (eds), *Alfred Russel Wallace: Letters from the Malay Archipelago* (Oxford, Oxford University Press, 2013), p. 147.

'a dead leaf'; 'perhaps the most perfect case'; 'the variability of the toes'; 'not only as a token': Alfred Russel Wallace, *The Malay Archipelago* (Singapore, Periplus Editions, 2008), pp. 99, 101, 32, vi.

'solved the problem of existence' and 'I took thought': Thomas Henry Huxley, *Science and Christian Tradition: Essays* (New York, D. Appleton, 1894), pp. 238, 239.

'My work is now nearly finished': Charles Darwin, *On the Origin of Species: By Means of Natural Selection, or the Preservation of Favoured Races in the Struggle for Life* (London, John Murray, 1859), pp. 1–2.

Additional sources

Jason R. Ali and Lawrence R. Heaney, 'Wallace's line, Wallacea, and associated divides and areas: History of a tortuous tangle of ideas and labels', *Biological Reviews*, vol. 96, no. 3 (2021), pp. 922–42.

Edward J. Larson, *Evolution: The Remarkable History of a Scientific Theory* (New York, Modern Library, 2006).

Peter Raby, *Alfred Russel Wallace: A Life* (London, Chatto & Windus, 2001).

Ross A. Slotten, *The Heretic in Darwin's Court: The Life of Alfred Russel Wallace* (New York, Columbia University Press, 2004).

Alfred Russel Wallace, 'On the physical geography of the Malay Archipelago', *Journal of the Royal Geographical Society of London*, vol. 33 (1863), pp. 217–34.

Tornado Alley

Quoted source

'I had never been': Chris Paul, in Joe Gerrity, 'New Orleans Hornets buzz: The quotable Chris Paul', *Bleacher Report* (26 December 2009).

Additional sources

Walker S. Ashley, 'Spatial and temporal analysis of tornado fatalities in the United States: 1880–2005', *American Meteorological Society*, vol. 22, no. 6 (2007), pp. 1214–28.

Matthew Cappucci, 'Tornado Alley in the Plains is an outdated concept. The

South is even more vulnerable, research shows', *Washington Post* (16 May 2020).

P. Grady Dixon et al., 'Tornado risk analysis: Is Dixie Alley an extension of Tornado Alley?' *Bulletin of the American Meteorological Society*, vol. 92, no. 4 (2011), pp. 433–41.

John P. Gagan, Alan Gerard and John Gordon, 'A historical and statistical comparison of "Tornado Alley" to "Dixie Alley"', *National Weather Association Digest*, vol. 2 (2010), pp. 145–55.

World Population Review, 'What countries have tornadoes?' and 'Tornado Alley states' (2023).

The Doldrums and the Sargasso Sea

Quoted sources

'This second arm': Jules Verne, *Twenty Thousand Leagues under the Sea* (New York, Butler Brothers, 1887), p. 250.

'He was continually laughing': William Smith, *A Natural History of Nevis, and the Rest of the English Leeward Charibee Islands in America. With Many Other Observations on Nature and Art* (Cambridge, J. Bentham, 1745), Letter VIII, p. 188.

'So, by a calenture misled. . .': Jonathan Swift, 'Upon the South-Sea Project', *The Works of Jonathan Swift*, vol. 2 (Dublin, George Faulkner, 1744), p. 137.

'Most of the day': Christopher Columbus, journal entry (Friday 21 September 1492), in *The Journal of Christopher Columbus (During His First Voyage, 1492–93), and Documents Relating to the Voyages of John Cabot and Gaspar Corte Real*, ed. and trans. Clements R. Markham (London, Hakluyt Society, 1893), p. 27.

Additional sources

Leslie Acton et al., 'What is the Sargasso Sea? The problem of fixing space in a fluid ocean', *Political Geography*, vol. 68 (2019), pp. 86–100.

Jeff Ardron et al., 'Where is the Sargasso Sea? A report submitted to the Sargasso Sea Alliance', *Duke University Marine Geospatial Ecology Lab & Marine Conservation Institute* (2011).

Mélanie Béguer-Pon et al., 'Direct observations of American eels migrating across the continental shelf to the Sargasso Sea', *Nature Communications*, vol. 6 (2015), 8705.

Eric Betz, 'Mystery of the vanishing eels', *Discover Magazine* (7 September 2017).

Daniel Klocke et al., 'Rediscovery of the doldrums in storm-resolving simulations over the tropical Atlantic', *Nature Geoscience*, vol. 10 (2017), pp. 891–6.

National Oceanic and Atmospheric Administration (NOAA), 'What is the Sargasso Sea?' (4 January 2021) and 'What are the doldrums?' (16 December 2021), oceanservice.noaa.gov/facts/sargassosea.html and oceanservice.noaa.gov/facts/doldrums.html#:~:text=Known%20 to%20sailors%20around%20the%20world%20as%20the%20 doldrums%2C%20the,and%20south%20of%20the%20equator.

Sargasso Sea Commission, 'The protection and management of the Sargasso Sea: The golden floating rainforest of the Atlantic Ocean', *Sargasso Sea Alliance* (2011).

The Antarctic Circumpolar Current and the Antarctic Convergence

Quoted source

'Great God!': Robert Falcon Scott, diary entry (17 January 1912). Scott Polar Research Institute, Cambridge, www.spri.cam.ac.uk/museum/diaries/ scottslastexpedition/page/7/.

Additional sources

Antarctic and Southern Ocean Coalition (ASOC), 'Protecting Antarctica' (2023), www.asoc.org.

Ceridwen Fraser, 'Antarctica may not be as isolated as we thought, and that's a worry', *The Conversation* (26 May 2016).

Zambra López-Farrán et al., 'Is the southern crab *Halicarcinus planatus* (Fabricius, 1775) the next invader of Antarctica?', *Global Change Biology*, vol. 27, no. 15, pp. 3487–504.

P. Mark O'Loughlin et al., 'The Antarctic region as a marine biodiversity hotspot for echinoderms: Diversity and diversification of sea cucumbers', *Deep-Sea Research II*, vol. 58, nos 1–2 (2011), pp. 264–75.

Ryan Smith et al., 'The Antarctic CP Current' (2013), oceancurrents.rsmas. miami.edu/southern/antarctic-cp.html.

Elizabeth Truswell, *A Memory of Ice* (Canberra, ACT, ANU Press, 2019).

The Arctic Tree Line

Quoted source

'Yesterday was wood': Yoji K. Gondor, *Fine Aphorisms, Proverbs and Philosophical Quotes From Around the World* (Sacramento, CA, Sintesi Point Publishing, 2014), p. 11.

Additional sources

ACIA, *Arctic Climate Impact Assessment* (Cambridge, Cambridge University Press, 2005).

Kevin Krajick, 'Where trees meet tundra, decoding signals of climate change', *Columbia Climate School* (16 November 2016).

G. M. MacDonald, K. V. Kremenetski and D. W. Beilman, 'Climate change and the northern Russian treeline zone', *Philosophical Transactions of the Royal Society of London B: Biological Sciences*, vol. 363, no. 1501 (2008), pp. 2285–99.

Ben Rawlence, '"The treeline is out of control": How the climate crisis is turning the Arctic green', *Guardian* (20 January 2022).

Ben Rawlence, *The Treeline: The Last Forest and the Future of Life on Earth* (New York, St Martin's Press, 2022).

Andrew D. Richardson and Andrew J. Friedland, 'A review of the theories to explain Arctic and Alpine treelines around the world', *Journal of Sustainable Forestry*, vol. 28, nos 1–2 (2009), pp. 218–42.

The Malaria Belt

Quoted sources

'Defeating malaria is absolutely critical': Tedros Adhanom Ghebreyesus, 'Ending malaria for good', *HuffPost* (25 April 2016).

'This disease is habitual': *The Genuine Works of Hippocrates*, trans. Francis Adams, vol. 1 (London, Sydenham Society, 1849), pp. 196–7.

Additional sources

Rachel Carson, *Silent Spring* (Boston, Houghton Mifflin, 1962).

Centers for Disease Control and Prevention (CDC), 'Malaria' (19 August 2022), www.cdc.gov/parasites/malaria/index.html.

Ismaël Chakir et al., 'Control of malaria in the Comoro Islands over the past century', *Malaria Journal*, vol. 16, no. 387 (2017).

Richard G. A. Feachem et al., 'Malaria eradication within a generation:

Ambitious, achievable, and necessary', *The Lancet*, vol. 394, no. 10203 (2019), pp. 1056–112.

Timothy C. Winegard, *The Mosquito: A Human History of Our Deadliest Predator* (New York, Dutton, 2019).

World Health Organization (WHO), 'Malaria' (6 December 2021), www.who.int/news-room/fact-sheets/detail/malaria; and 'Global Malaria Programme' (2023), www.who.int/teams/global-malaria-programme/reports.

The Kokaral Dam

Quoted source

'We cannot expect charity': Joseph Stalin, quoted in Lydia Mihelič Pulsipher and Alex A. Pulsipher, *World Regional Geography: Global Patterns, Local Lives*, 3rd edition (New York, W. H. Freeman, 2006), p. 179.

Additional sources

Nikolay Vasilevich Aladin et al., 'The zoocenosis of the Aral Sea: Six decades of fast-paced change', *Environmental Science and Pollution Research*, vol. 26 (2019), pp. 2228–37.

Dene-Hern Chen, 'The country that brought a sea back to life', BBC Future (23 July 2018).

Igor S. Plotnikov et al., 'Modern state of the Small (Northern) Aral Sea fauna', *Lakes and Reservoirs: Research and Management*, vol. 21, no. 4 (2016), pp. 315–28.

Aliya Uteuova, 'Northern Aral's promise stunted by dam height, international disputes', Eurasianet (28 October 2020).

Kristopher D. White, 'Nature–society linkages in the Aral Sea region', *Journal of Eurasian Studies*, vol. 4 (2013), pp. 18–33.

The Qinling–Huaihe Line

Quoted source

'We will declare war': Li Keqiang, quoted in Lucy Hornby, 'China declares war on pollution', *Financial Times* (5 March 2014).

Additional sources

Douglas Almond et al., 'Winter heating or clean air? Unintended impacts of

China's Huai River policy', *American Economic Review*, vol. 99, no. 2 (2009), pp. 184–90.

Avraham Ebenstein et al., 'New evidence on the impact of sustained exposure to air pollution on life expectancy from China's Huai River Policy', *Proceedings of the National Academy of Sciences of the United States of America*, vol. 114, no. 39 (2017), pp. 10384–9.

Hannah Gardner, 'China's unlikely divide over home heat', *National* (25 January 2013).

Xiaopeng Ren, Xiaohui Cang and Andrew G. Ryder, 'An integrated ecological approach to mapping variations in collectivism within China: Introducing the triple-line framework', *Journal of Pacific Rim Psychology*, vol. 15, no. 1 (2021), pp. 1–12.

Ai Yan, 'As winter arrives, will the debate over heating systems in China continue?', CGTN (19 November 2020).

Green Belts

Quoted source

'Human society and the beauty of nature': Ebenezer Howard, *Garden Cities of To-morrow* (London, Swan Sonnenschein, 1902), p. 17.

Additional sources

Marco Amati and Makoto Yokohari, 'Temporal changes and local variations in the functions of London's green belt', *Landscape and Urban Planning*, vol. 75 (2006), pp. 125–42.

Robert Beevers, *The Garden City Utopia: A Critical Biography of Ebenezer Howard* (New York, St Martin's Press, 1988).

Robert Fishman, *Urban Utopias in the Twentieth Century: Ebenezer Howard, Frank Lloyd Wright, and Le Corbusier* (New York, Basic Books, 1977).

Peter Hall, *Cities of Tomorrow: An Intellectual History of Urban Planning and Design Since 1880*, 4th edition (Chichester, Wiley-Blackwell, 2014).

Alan Mace et al., 'A 21st century Metropolitan Green Belt', London School of Economics report (2016).

Lewis Mumford, *The City in History: Its Origins, Its Transformations, and Its Prospects* (New York, Harcourt, Brace & World, 1961).

The Chernobyl Exclusion Zone

Sources

Victoria Gill, 'Chernobyl: The end of a three-decade experiment', BBC News (14 February 2019).

R. F. Mould, *Chernobyl Record: The Definitive History of the Chernobyl Catastrophe* (Bristol, Institute of Physics, 2000).

William C. Roberts, 'Facts and ideas from anywhere', *Baylor University Medical Center Proceedings*, vol. 33, no. 2 (2020), pp. 310–16.

Jim T. Smith and Nicholas A. Beresford (eds), *Chernobyl: Catastrophe and Consequences* (Berlin, Springer, 2005).

World Nuclear Association, 'Chernobyl accident 1986' (2021), www.world-nuclear.org/information-library/safety-and-security/safety-of-plants/chernobyl-accident.aspx.

Eyam

Quoted sources

'To some the sermon': Albert Camus, *The Plague*, trans. Stuart Gilbert (New York, Vintage International, 1991 [1947]), p. 100.

'a watch is constantly kept': Samuel Pepys, *Diary* (4 September 1665).

Additional sources

Colin Hall, 'The Boundary Stone', Stoney Middleton Heritage Centre Community Group website (3 November 2014).

Victoria Masson, 'Why is Eyam significant?', Historic UK website.

Philip Race, 'Some further consideration of the plague in Eyam, 1665/6', *Local Population Studies*, vol. 54 (1995), pp. 56–65.

Eleanor Ross, 'Did this sleepy village stop the Great Plague?', BBC Travel (29 October 2015).

Giovanni Spitale, 'COVID-19 and the ethics of quarantine: A lesson from the Eyam plague', *Medicine, Health Care, and Philosophy*, vol. 23, no. 4 (2020), pp. 603–9.

The International Date Line

Quoted source

'Only the Krauses let him down': Arthur C. Clarke, *Childhood's End* (1953; repr. New York, Del Rey Books, 1966), p. 76.

Additional sources

Clarke Blaise, *Time Lord: Sir Sandford Fleming and the Creation of Standard Time* (London, Weidenfeld & Nicolson, 2000).

Tom Garlinghouse, 'The international date line, explained', *Live Science* (23 June 2021).

Seth Mydans, 'Samoa sacrifices a day for its future', *New York Times* (29 December 2011).

Allen W. Palmer, 'Negotiation and resistance in global networks: The 1884 International Meridian Conference', *Mass Communication and Society*, vol. 5, no. 1 (2009), pp. 7–24.

Eviatar Zerubavel, 'The standardization of time: A sociohistorical perspective', *American Journal of Sociology*, vol. 88, no. 1 (1982), pp. 1–23.

How Invisible Lines Allow People to Claim Territory as Their Own

Quoted source

'Long live free Flanders': Vlaams Belang politician, quoted in 'Parliament dissolves itself, paving the way for June vote', France 24 (6 May 2010).

Additional source

'Yellow car owners join rally in support of "ugly" car', BBC News (1 April 2017).

The Treaty of Tordesillas

Quoted source

'No one can give away' and 'Rulers and to the Free': Hugo Grotius, *The Freedom of the Seas: Or the Right which Belongs to the Dutch to Take Part in the East Indian Trade*, 1633, trans. Ralph Van Deman Magoffin (Kitchener, ON, Batoche Books, 2000), pp. 47, 7.

Additional sources

Eneko Arrondo et al., 'Invisible barriers: Differential sanitary regulations constrain vulture movements across country borders', *Biological Conservation*, vol. 219 (2018), pp. 46–52.

Stephen R. Brown, 'Treaty of Tordesillas: The 1494 decision still influencing today's world', *History Reader* (12 April 2012).

Lawrence A. Coben, 'The events that led to the Treaty of Tordesillas', *Terrae Incognitae*, vol. 47, no. 2 (2015), pp. 142–62.

William Eleroy Curtis, *The Authentic Letters of Columbus*, vol. 1, no. 2 (Chicago, Field Columbian Museum, 1895).

Charles Garcia, 'Was Columbus secretly a Jew?', CNN (24 May 2012).

Papal Enyclicals Online, '*Inter Caetera*: Division of the undiscovered world between Spain and Portugal', (4 May 1492); '*Dudum siquidem*' (26 September 1493); '*Ea quae*' (24 January 1506); '*Aeterni regis*' (21 June 1481).

Tatiana Waisberg, 'The Treaty of Tordesillas and the (re)invention of international law in the Age of Discovery', *Meridiano*, vol. 47, no. 18 (2017), e18003.

Simon Wiesenthal, *Sails of Hope: The Secret Mission of Christopher Columbus* (New York, Macmillan, 1973).

Bir Tawil

Quoted source

'This is your chance': Jeremiah Heaton, 'The world's first crowdfunded nation' (2015), www.indiegogo.com/projects/the-world-s-first-crowdfunded-nation#.

Additional sources

Alastair Bonnett, *Unruly Places: Lost Spaces, Secret Cities, and Other Inscrutable Geographies* (Boston: Houghton Mifflin Harcourt, 2014).

Gareth Johnson, '5 micronations that have claimed Bir Tawil', Young Pioneer Tours, www.youngpioneertours.com/micronations-claimed-bir-tawil.

Dean Karalekas, *The Men in No Man's Land: A Journey Into Bir Tawil* (Global Adventures Press, 2020).

Rudraneil Sengupta, 'Meet Suyash Dixit, the man who would be king', *Mint* (5 January 2018).

Jack Shenker, 'Welcome to the land that no country wants', *Guardian* (3 March 2016).

Notes

The Outback

Quoted source
'Australia lives with a strange contradiction': Kate Grenville, interview, Penguin Random House, www.penguinrandomhouse.com/books/286492/the-idea-of-perfection-by-kate-grenville/9781101175033/readers-guide.

Additional sources
Director of National Parks, Australian Government, 'Uluru-Kata Tjuta National Park: Values statement' (14 May 2015).

Phoebe Everingham, Andrew Peters and Freya Higgins-Desbiollesc, 'The (im)possibilities of doing tourism otherwise: The case of settler colonial Australia and the closure of the climb at Uluru', *Annals of Tourism Research*, vol. 88 (2021), 103178.

Pew Trusts, 'A modern Outback: Nature, people and the future of remote Australia' (2014), www.pewtrusts.org/en/about/news-room/opinion/2014/10/a-modern-outback-nature-people-and-the-future-of-remote-australia.

Allan James Thomas, 'Camping outback: Landscape, masculinity, and performance in *The Adventures of Priscilla, Queen of the Desert*', *Continuum*, vol. 10, no. 2 (1996), pp. 97–110.

Jillian Walliss, 'The right to land versus the right to landscape: Lessons from Uluru-Kata Tjuta National Park, Australia', in Shelley Egoz, Jala Makhzoumi and Gloria Pungetti (eds), *The Right to Landscape: Contesting Landscape and Human Rights* (Farnham, Ashgate, 2011), pp. 153–64.

Landmines and the Inter-Entity Boundary Line

Quoted source
'The political union': Gavrilo Princip, quoted in Vladimir Dedijer, *The Road to Sarajevo* (New York, Simon and Schuster, 1966), p. 341.

Additional sources
ITF Enhancing Human Security, 'Annual report 2021', www.itf.si/publications/annual-reports.

Ajdin Kamber, 'Bosnian countryside scarred with landmines', Institute for War & Peace Reporting (1 November 2013).

Mine Action Review, 'Bosnia and Herzegovina: Clearing the mines 2022',

389

www.mineactionreview.org/assets/downloads/BiH_Clearing_the_Mines_2022.pdf.

Snjezana Musa, Željka Šiljković and Dario Šakić, 'Geographical reflections of mine pollution in Bosnia and Herzegovina and Croatia', *Revija za geografijo*, vol. 12, no. 2 (2017), pp. 53–70.

Frank D. W. Witmer and John O'Loughlin, 'Satellite data methods and application in the evaluation of war outcomes: Abandoned agricultural land in Bosnia-Herzegovina after the 1992–1995 conflict', *Annals of the American Association of Geographers*, vol. 99, no. 5 (2009), pp. 1033–44.

Football in Buenos Aires

Quoted source

'I'm from the craziest gang of all': River Plate supporters, quoted in William Huddleston, 'Kicking off: Violence, honour, identity and masculinity in Argentinian football chants', *International Review for the Sociology of Sport*, vol. 57, no. 1 (2022), p. 46.

Additional sources

Pablo Alabarces et al., 'Argentina', in Jean-Michel De Waele et al. (eds) *The Palgrave International Handbook of Football and Politics* (London, Palgrave Macmillan, 2018), pp. 469–84.

Eduardo P. Archetti, 'Argentinian football: A ritual of violence?' *International Journal of the History of Sport*, vol. 9, no. 2 (1992), pp. 209–35.

Teun Heuvelink, '"Mobsters and hooligans": The identity construction of the *barra brava* of Boca Juniors in the Buenos Aires neighbourhood La Boca' (unpublished master's thesis, Universiteit Utrecht, 2010).

Joel Horowitz, 'Football clubs and neighbourhoods in Buenos Aires before 1943: The role of political linkages and personal influence', *Journal of Latin American Studies*, vol. 46 (2014), pp. 557–85.

Salvemos al Fútbol, 'Muertes en la historia por la violencia en el fútbol argentino' (2022), salvemosalfutbol.org/lista-de-victimas-de-incidentes-de-violencia-en-el-futbol.

Fernando Segura M. Trejo, Diego Murzi and Belen Nassar, 'Violence and death in Argentinean soccer in the new millennium: Who is involved and what is at stake?', *International Review for the Sociology of Sport*, vol. 54, no. 7 (2019), pp. 837–54.

Street Gangs in Los Angeles

Quoted sources

'When you in the hood': Snoop Dogg, quoted in Elizabeth Day, 'Snoop Dogg: "Women are getting empowered. Now I have a daughter, I understand"', *Guardian* (19 June 2011).

'race, color, religion': United States Civil Rights Act (1964).

Additional sources

Anti-Defamation League (ADL), 'With hate in their hearts: The state of white supremacy in the United States' (3 March 2017), www.adl.org/resources/reports/hate-their-hearts-state-white-supremacy-united-states.

Avishay Artsy, 'Gang borders create invisible walls in Los Angeles', KCRW (13 March 2018).

Gregory Christopher Brown, James Diego Vigil and Eric Robert Taylor, 'The ghettoization of Blacks in Los Angeles: The emergence of street gangs', *Journal of African American Studies*, vol. 15, no. 2 (2012), pp. 209–25.

Mike Davis, *City of Quartz: Excavating the Future in Los Angeles*, 2nd edition (London, Verso, 2006).

John Gramlich, 'Black imprisonment rate in the US has fallen by a third since 2006', Pew Research Center (6 May 2020).

James Queally, 'Los Angeles must change use of gang injunctions under court settlement', *Los Angeles Times* (26 December 2020).

Southern Poverty Law Center (SPLC), 'Intelligence report special edition: Aryan prison gangs' (7 January 2014), www.splcenter.org/20140106/intelligence-report-special-edition-aryan-prison-gangs.

Al Valdez, 'The origins of Southern California Latino gangs', in Thomas Bruneau, Lucía Dammert and Elizabeth Skinner (eds), *Maras: Gang Violence and Security in Central America* (Austin, University of Texas Press, 2011), pp. 23–42.

Vera Institute of Justice, 'Incarceration trends in California' (2019), www.vera.org/downloads/pdfdownloads/state-incarceration-trends-california.pdf.

How Invisible Lines Allow People to Divide 'Us' From 'Them'

Sources

Nicholas Lees, 'The Brandt Line after forty years: The more North–South relations change, the more they stay the same?', *Review of International Studies*, vol. 47, no. 1 (2021), pp. 85–106.

Marcin Wojciech Solarz, '"Third World": The 60th anniversary of a concept that changed history', *Third World Quarterly*, vol. 33, no. 9 (2012), pp. 1561–73.

8 Mile

Quoted source

'I issue a warning': Coleman A. Young, quoted in *Deadline Detroit*, 'Gallery: 8 Mile Road, name-checked by Coleman Young, immortalized by Eminem' (25 June 2020).

Additional sources

Douglas S. Massey and Nancy A. Denton, *American Apartheid: Segregation and the Making of the Underclass* (Cambridge, MA, Harvard University Press, 1993).

Johnny Miller, 'Roads to nowhere: How infrastructure built on American inequality', *Guardian* (21 February 2018).

Scott A. Mitchell, 'Spaces of emergent memory: Detroit's 8 Mile wall and public memories of civil rights injustice', *Communication and Critical/Cultural Studies*, vol. 15, no. 3 (2018), pp. 197–212.

Jeff Rice, *Digital Detroit: Rhetoric and Space in the Age of the Network* (Carbondale, Southern Illinois University Press, 2012).

Richard Rothstein, *The Color of Law: A Forgotten History of How Our Government Segregated America* (New York, Liveright, 2017).

Paris's *Banlieues*

Quoted sources

'Be careful, the stadium': 'Thierry Henry, "Le stade est à Saint-Denis, pas à Paris, croyez moi vous ne voulez pas être à S-D"', YouTube (5 May 2022).

'Dear Thierry Henry': Mathieu Hanotin, quoted in 'Thierry Henry: Ses propos sur la ville de Saint-Denis, en direct à la télévision américaine, engendrent la polémique!', *Public* (8 May 2022).

'ethnic and religious divisions . . . a gang of thugs': Alain Finkielkraut, quoted in 'Finkielkraut: Une équipe de "voyous"', *Europe 1* (20 June 2010).

'ill-bred suburban brats': 'Insupportables', *So Foot* (19 June 2010), www.sofoot.com/insupportables-128020.html.

'neighbourhood kingpins': Roselyne Bachelot, quoted in Stéphane Beaud (with Philippe Guimard), *Traîtres à la nation? Un autre regard sur la grève des Bleus en Afrique du Sud* (Paris, Éditions La Découverte, 2011), p. 18.

'sometimes feel like': Claude Guéant, quoted in 'Guéant: les Français "ont parfois le sentiment de ne plus être chez eux"', *Le Point* (17 March 2011).

'the creation of foreign communities': Claude Guéant, quoted in 'Guéant en banlieue de Paris pour plaider contre le communautarisme', *Le Point* (17 November 2011).

'take the Kärcher out . . . return order . . . the violence': Valérie Pécresse, quoted in 'Election présidentielle 2022: Valérie Pécresse veut "ressortir le Kärcher de la cave" en matière de sécurité', *Le Monde* (6 January 2022).

'an immediate halt . . . violence . . . we defend': Kärcher, quoted in 'German pressure-hose maker asks French politicians to stop using its name', *The Local* (11 January 2022).

'clean [the housing estate]': Nicolas Sarkozy, quoted in '19–29 juin 2005: France. Annonce par Nicolas Sarkozy du "nettoyage" de la cité des 4 000 à La Courneuve', *Universalis* (20 June 2005).

'breeding ground . . . promot[ing] self-segregation': Valérie Pécresse, quoted in Christine Ollivier, 'Valérie Pécresse: "On n'éradiquera pas l'islamisme si on ne casse pas les ghettos urbains"', *Le Journal du dimanche* (5 December 2020).

'The headscarf is a uniform': Marine Le Pen, quoted in William Dupuy, 'Le Pen confronté à des femmes musulmanes portant le hijab lors d'un procès de campagne, leur disant que le voile est "radical"', *Dernières Nouvelles* (15 April 2022).

'areas of lawlessness': Marine Le Pen, quoted in Abel Mestre, 'Marine Le Pen entend "mettre l'islam radical à genoux"', *Le Monde* (25 March 2012).

'drug traffickers . . . reign supreme . . . It has to be the one': Claude Guéant, quoted in 'Interview de M. Claude Guéant, ministre de l'intérieur, de l'outre-mer, des collectivités territoriales et de l'immigration', *Vie Publique* (28 June 2011).

'All other things being equal': Observatoire national de la politique de la ville (National Observatory of Urban Policy), annual report 2015, www.onpv.fr/uploads/media_items/ra-2015-synthese-uk.original.pdf, p. 28.

'delinquency in Saint Denis': Gérald Darmanin, quoted in 'Champions

League final: French interior minister apologises to Liverpool fans for ticketing chaos', Sky Sports (28 June 2022).

'*banlieusards*, looters . . . the problem is . . . we hardly speak French': Éric Zemmour, quoted in 'Incidents au Stade de France: Pour Eric Zemmour, "les racailles font la loi" en Seine-Saint-Denis', *La Dépêche* (30 May 2022).

Additional sources

Emmanuel Brenner, *Les Territoires perdus de la République* (Paris, Éditions Mille et une nuits, 2002).

Juliet Carpenter, 'The French banlieue: Renovating the suburbs', in Bernadette Hanlon and Thomas J. Vicino (eds), *The Routledge Companion to the Suburbs* (Abingdon, Routledge, 2019), pp. 254–65.

David Garbin and Gareth Millington, 'Territorial stigma and the politics of resistance in a Parisian *banlieue*: La Courneuve and beyond', *Urban Studies*, vol. 49, no. 10 (2012), pp. 2067–83.

Tanvi Misra, 'The othered Paris', Bloomberg CityLab (16 November 2017).

Matthew Moran, 'Terrorism and the *banlieues*: The *Charlie Hebdo* attacks in context', *Modern & Contemporary France*, vol. 25, no. 3 (2017), pp. 315–32.

George Packer, 'The other France', *New Yorker* (24 August 2015).

Justinien Tribillon, 'Dirty boulevard: Why Paris's ring road is a major block on the city's grand plans', *Guardian* (26 June 2015).

The Peace Lines

Sources

Stanley D. Brunn, Sarah Byrne, Louise McNamara and Annette Egan, 'Belfast landscapes: From religious schism to conflict tourism', *Focus on Geography*, vol. 53, no. 3 (2010), pp. 81–91.

Cain Burdeau, 'Will Northern Ireland's "peace walls" ever come down?', Courthouse News Service (28 June 2019).

Peter Geoghegan, 'Will Belfast ever have a Berlin Wall moment and tear down its "peace walls"?', *Guardian* (29 September 2015).

Andrew Hill and Andrew White, 'Painting peace? Murals and the Northern Ireland peace process', *Irish Political Studies*, vol. 27, no. 1 (2012), pp. 71–88.

Siobhán McAlister, Deena Haydon and Phil Scraton, 'Violence in the lives of children and youth in "post-conflict" Northern Ireland', *Children, Youth and Environments*, vol. 23, no. 1 (2013), pp. 1–22.

Laura McAtackney, 'Peace maintenance and political messages: The significance of walls during and after the Northern Irish "Troubles"', *Journal of Social Archaeology*, vol. 11, no. 1 (2011), pp. 77–98.

David McKittrick and David McVea, *Making Sense of the Troubles: The Story of the Conflict in Northern Ireland* (Chicago, New Amsterdam Books, 2002).

The Berlin Wall

Quoted source
Willy Brandt, quoted in Marc Fisher, 'Leader of a shattered nation', *Washington Post* (15 November 1992).

Additional sources
'In Berlin, quirky reminders linger from East–West divide', Al Jazeera (4 November 2019).

Rachel Boate, 'East–West relations at a crossroads: German reunification and the GDR: *Ampelmännchen*', *Shift*, vol. 10 (2017).

Rick Noack, 'The Berlin Wall fell 25 years ago, but Germany is still divided', *Washington Post* (31 October 2014).

'For red deer, Iron Curtain habits die hard', NPR (1 May 2014).

Emily Pugh, *Architecture, Politics, and Identity in Divided Berlin* (Pittsburgh, PA, University of Pittsburgh Press, 2014).

Dana Regev, 'Deutsche Wiedervereinigung: Was Ost und West noch trennt', DW (3 October 2020).

Michael John Williams, 'Die Mauer im Kopf: The legacy of division in German politics', Atlantic Council (7 November 2019).

The Ural Mountains

Quoted sources
'There always is': Aleksandr Solzhenitsyn, *The Gulag Archipelago 1918–1956*, trans. Thomas P. Whitney and Harry Willetts (London, Vintage, 2018 [1973]), p. xxiv.

'hopes lie perhaps'; 'If you only knew': Fyodor Dostoevsky, quoted in Hans Kohn, 'Dostoevsky's nationalism', *Journal of the History of Ideas*, vol. 6, no. 4 (1945), pp. 408, 393.

'no foreign military forces': Adolf Hitler, in 'Martin Bormann's minutes of
 a meeting at Hitler's headquarters (July 16, 1941)', *German History
 in Documents and Images*, germanhistorydocs.ghi-dc.org/docpage.
 cfm?docpage_id=2289.
'It's absurd to try'; 'living wall': Adolf Hitler, in H. R. Trevor-Roper, *Hitler's
 Table Talk, 1941–1944: His Private Conversations*, trans. Norman
 Cameron and R. H. Stevens (London, Enigma Books, 2008), 23–5
 September 1941.
'between the Atlantic and the Urals', Charles De Gaulle, speech, 25 March
 1959, quoted in Anton W. DePorte, 'De Gaulle's Europe: Playing the
 Russian card', *French Politics and Society*, vol. 8, no. 4 (1990), p. 30.

Additional sources

Pekka Korhonen, 'Changing definitions of Asia', *Asia Europe Journal*, vol. 10
 (2012), pp. 99–112.
Joshua Kucera, 'The friendliest border', *Roads & Kingdoms* (13 February
 2017).
Colum Leckey, 'Imagining the Urals: Academic travelers and Russia's
 Europe–Asia divide', *Eighteenth-Century Studies*, vol. 53, no. 4 (2020),
 pp. 647–65.
Lila Leontidou, 'The boundaries of Europe: Deconstructing three regional
 narratives', *Identities*, vol. 11, no. 4 (2004), pp. 593–617.
W. H. Parker, 'Europe: How far?', *Geographical Journal*, vol. 126, no. 3
 (1960), pp. 278–97.
Yevgeny V. Yastrebov and Thomas M. Poulsen, 'Ural Mountains',
 Encyclopædia Britannica.

The Bosphorus

Quoted source

'On the meeting point': Mustafa Kemal Atatürk, quoted in Bettany Hughes,
 Istanbul: A Tale of Three Cities (London, Weidenfeld & Nicolson,
 2017), p. 585.

Additional sources

Joshua Kucera, 'Continental rift: Searching for the real border between East
 and West in Istanbul', Pulitzer Center (24 January 2017).
Alexander Lyon Macfie, *Ataturk* (London, Routledge, 1994).

Sigrid Rettenbacher, 'Hagia Sophia and the third space: An enquiry into the discursive construction of religious sites', in Ulrich Winkler, Lidia Rodríguez Fernández and Oddbjørn Leivik (eds), *Contested Spaces, Common Ground: Space and Power Structures in Contemporary Multireligious Societies* (Leiden, Brill Rodopi, 2017), pp. 95–112.

Edward Said, *Orientalism* (New York, Pantheon Books, 1978).

Thomas Scheffler, '"Fertile Crescent", "Orient", "Middle East": The changing mental maps of Southwest Asia', *European Review of History: Revue européenne d'histoire*, vol. 10, no. 2 (2003), pp. 253–72.

How Invisible Lines Allow Groups to Preserve Their Cultural Distinctiveness

Quoted sources

'Living in your concrete castle': Dennis Brown, 'Concrete Castle King', lyrics written by Lloyd 'Gitsy' Willis, *Visions of Dennis Brown* (Lightning Records, 1978).

'With home-grown talent and local support': Athletic Bilbao, quoted in Matthew Chandler, 'Athletic Bilbao transfer policy: Basque rule explained', *Sports Quotes and Facts* (2021).

Additional sources

Ed Cumming, 'Mysteries of the Rhubarb Triangle, revealed by Martin Parr', *Guardian* (30 January 2016).

Sarah Daynes, 'A lesson of geography, on the riddim: The symbolic topography of reggae music', in Ola Johansson and Thomas L. Bell (eds), *Sound, Society and the Geography of Popular Music* (London, Routledge, 2009), pp. 91–105.

Eruvim

Sources

Michael Inscoe, 'The wire that transforms much of Manhattan into one big, symbolic home', *Atlas Obscura* (16 October 2017).

Michele Rapoport, 'Creating place, creating community: The intangible boundaries of the Jewish "Eruv"', *Environment and Planning D: Society and Space*, vol. 29, no. 5 (2011), pp. 891–904.

Nechama Rosenberg, 'Eruv. NYC', *Manhattan Eruv* (25 January 2023), eruv.nyc/#map.

Oliver Valins, 'Stubborn identities and the construction of socio-spatial boundaries: Ultra-Orthodox Jews living in contemporary Britain', *Transactions of the Institute of British Geographers*, vol. 28, no. 2 (2003), pp. 158–75.

Peter Vincent and Barney Warf, 'Eruvim: Talmudic places in a postmodern world', *Transactions of the Institute of British Geographers*, vol. 27, no. 1 (2002), pp. 30–51.

Sophie Watson, 'Symbolic spaces of difference: Contesting the eruv in Barnet, London and Tenafly, New Jersey', *Environment and Planning D: Society and Space*, vol. 23, no. 4 (2005), pp. 597–613.

Aceh

Quoted source

'Freedom means that': Hasan di Tiro, *The Price of Freedoms*, diary entry (4 December 1981), published by National Liberation Front of Acheh Sumatra (1984).

Additional sources

Jon Emont, 'As shariah experiment becomes a model, Indonesia's secular face slips', *New York Times* (12 January 2017).

Arndt Graf, Susanne Schröter and Edwin Wieringa (eds), *Aceh: History, Politics and Culture* (Singapore, ISEAS-Yusof Ishak Institute, 2010).

Ben Hillman, 'Ethnic politics and local political parties in Indonesia', *Asian Ethnicity*, vol. 13, no. 4 (2012), pp. 419–40.

'Q&A: What you need to know about sharia in Aceh', *Jakarta Post* (4 March 2018).

Muhammad Riza Nurdin, 'Disaster "caliphatization": Hizbut Tahrir Indonesia, Islamic Aceh, and the Indian Ocean tsunami', *International Journal of Mass Emergencies and Disasters*, vol. 33, no. 1 (2015), pp. 75–95.

North Sentinel Island

Quoted source

'Lord is this island': John Allen Chau, journal entry (15 November 2018), transcribed by Craig Dunning, p. 10.

Additional sources

Alastair Jamieson, Elisha Fieldstadt and Associated Press, 'American killed by isolated tribe on India's North Sentinel Island, police say', NBC News (21 November 2018).

M. Sasikumar, 'The Sentinelese of the North Sentinel Island: Concerns and perceptions', *Journal of the Anthropological Survey of India*, vol. 67, no. 1 (2018), pp. 37–44.

M. Sasikumar, 'The Sentinelese of North Sentinel Island: A reappraisal of tribal scenario in an Andaman Island in the context of killing of an American preacher', *Journal of the Anthropological Survey of India*, vol. 68, no. 1 (2019), pp. 56–69.

Kiona N. Smith, 'Everything we know about the isolated Sentinelese people of North Sentinel Island', *Forbes* (30 November 2018).

Survival International, 'Outrage as tour operators sell "human safaris" to Andaman Islands' (17 October 2017); 'The Jarawa' (5 March 2019); 'The Sentinelese' (18 December 2020); 'The Onge' (12 April 2021).

Brittany's Linguistic Lines

Quoted source

'The year is 50 BC': René Goscinny and Albert Uderzo, *Asterix the Gaul*, trans. Anthea Bell and Derek Hockridge (Leicester, Brockhampton Press, 1969 [1961]).

Additional sources

Madeleine Adkins, 'Will the real Breton please stand up? Language revitalization and the problem of authentic language', *International Journal of the Sociology of Language*, vol. 223 (2013), pp. 55–70.

A. S. Bukhonkina V. P. Sviridonova and U. S. Dzubenko, 'Minority languages of Brittany in regional economy and regional enterprises', *IOP Conference Series: Materials Science and Engineering*, vol. 483 (2019).

Michael Hornsby, 'From the periphery to the centre: Recent debates on the place of Breton (and other regional languages) in the French Republic', in Robert McColl Millar (ed.), *Marginal Dialects: Scotland, Ireland and Beyond* (Aberdeen, Forum for Research on the Languages of Scotland and Ireland, 2010), pp. 171–97.

Ronan Le Coadic, 'Brittany's borders', presentation at the International Symposium *Crossing Borders: History, Theories and Identities*, University of Glamorgan (2–4 December 2004).

Kerstin Mendel, 'Regional languages in France: The case of Breton', *LSO Working Papers in Linguistics*, vol. 4 (2004), pp. 65–75.

John Shaun Nolan, 'The role of Gallo in the identity of Upper-Breton school pupils of the language variety and their parents', *Sociolinguistic Studies*, vol. 2, no. 1 (2008), pp. 131–53.

Germany's Dialect Lines

Sources

Hyde Flippo, 'German dialects: Dialekte' (27 July 2018), *ThoughtCo.*

Werner F. Leopold, 'The decline of German dialects', *WORD*, vol. 15, no. 1 (1959), pp. 130–53.

Anja Lobenstein-Reichmann, 'Martin Luther, Bible Translation, and the German language', *Oxford Research Encyclopedia of Religion* (Oxford, Oxford University Press, 2017).

Peter Schrijver, 'The High German consonant shift and language contact', *Studies in Slavic and General Linguistics*, vol. 38 (2011), pp. 217–49.

Philipp Stoeckle, 'Country report Germany' (2016), www.researchgate.net/publication/304247217_Country_Report_Germany.

The Bible Belt

Quoted sources

'If there's a church': Neil Carter, 'You might live in the Bible belt if . . .', YouTube (27 May 2014).

'one of the most respected': Donald Trump, quoted in Eugene Scott and Tom LoBianco, 'Trump picks up endorsement of evangelical leader Jerry Falwell Jr', CNN (26 January 2016).

Additional sources

Stanley D. Brunn, Gerald R. Webster and J. Clark Archer, 'The Bible Belt in a changing South: Shrinking, relocating, and multiple buckles', *Southeastern Geographer*, vol. 51, no. 4 (2011), pp. 513–49.

Center for Reproductive Rights, 'After Roe fell: Abortion laws by state' (2023), reproductiverights.org/maps/abortion-laws-by-state.

Kristin Kobes Du Mez, *Jesus and John Wayne: How White Evangelicals Corrupted a Faith and Fractured a Nation* (New York, Liveright, 2020).

Robert C. Liebman and Robert Wuthnow (eds), *The New Christian Right: Mobilization and Legitimation* (New York, Aldine, 1983).

Joseph L. Locke, *Making the Bible Belt: Texas Prohibitionists and the Politicization of Southern Religion* (Oxford, Oxford University Press, 2020).

Pew Research Center, 'Religious landscape study' (2014), www.pewforum. org/religious-landscape-study.

Epilogue

Quoted sources

'From the very first steps': Vladimir Putin, quoted in 'Extracts from Putin's speech on Ukraine', Reuters (21 February 2022).

'Neighbours always enrich': Volodymyr Zelenskyy, quoted in Tim Lister and Katherina Krebs, 'Ukraine's president: "Trigger can appear any minute" for a Russian invasion', CNN (23 February 2022).

'an attempt to create': Kyrylo Budanov, quoted in Daniel Boffey, 'Putin wants "Korean scenario" for Ukraine, says intelligence chief', *Guardian* (27 March 2022).

'For our country . . . This is the very red line': Vladimir Putin, quoted in '"No other option": Excerpts of Putin's speech declaring war', Al Jazeera (24 February 2022).

'one people'; 'close cultural'; 'external patrons'; 'sow[ing] discord . . . pit[ting] the parts'; 'to mythologise'; 'robbed'; 'foreign intervention'; 'Well before 2014 . . . Step by step'; 'What Ukraine will be'; 'I am becoming more and more convinced': Vladimir Putin, 'On the historical unity of Russians and Ukrainians' (12 July 2021), en.kremlin. ru/events/president/news/66181.

'The conundrum for Ukraine': Kataryna Wolczuk, 'Ukraine and Europe: Reshuffling the boundaries of order', *Thesis Eleven*, vol. 136, no. 1 (2016), p. 69.

'We are fighting to be': Volodymyr Zelenskyy, quoted in Philip Blenkinsop and Ingrid Melander, 'Ukraine's Zelenskiy tells EU: "Prove that you are with us"', Reuters (1 March 2022).

'The key point to bear in mind': Zbigniew Brzezinski, *The Grand Chessboard: American Primacy and Its Geostrategic Imperatives* (New York, Basic Books, 2016), p. 122.

Additional sources

Kristin M. Bakke, 'Survey: Ukrainians do overwhelmingly not want to be part of Russia', *Science Norway* (3 March 2022).

Peter Dickinson, 'How Ukraine's Orange Revolution shaped twenty-first century geopolitics', Atlantic Council (22 November 2020).

Samuel P. Huntington, *The Clash of Civilizations and the Remaking of World Order* (New York, Simon & Schuster, 1996).

Dávid Karácsonyi et al., 'East–West dichotomy and political conflict in Ukraine: Was Huntington right?', *Hungarian Geographical Bulletin*, vol. 63, no. 2 (2014), pp. 99–134.

John O'Loughlin, Gerard Toal and Gwendolyn Sasse, 'Do people in Donbas want to be "liberated" by Russia?', *Washington Post* (15 April 2022).

Gwendolyn Sasse, 'The "new" Ukraine: A state of regions', *Regional and Federal Studies*, vol. 11, no. 3 (2001), pp. 69–100.

Stephen White, Ian McAllister and Valentina Feklyunina, 'Belarus, Ukraine and Russia: East or West?', *British Journal of Politics and International Relations*, vol. 12 (2010), pp. 344–67.

Tatiana Zhurzhenko, 'The myth of two Ukraines', *Eurozine* (17 September 2002).

Acknowledgements

In contrast to the boundaries and belts presented above, the support I have received ever since I first considered writing *Invisible Lines* has been conspicuous and unequivocal. Thank you to Andrew Nurnberg and your wonderful team at Andrew Nurnberg Associates for seeing potential in this book, with special thanks due to my marvellous agent Michael Dean for your perceptive, erudite comments on an early version of the manuscript, for your constant advice as I navigate the world of trade publishing for the first time, and for your genuine enthusiasm for the project as a whole. I am grateful also to Profile Books for providing a perfect home for *Invisible Lines*: to Andrew Franklin for your palpable faith in my debut book; to Georgina Difford for your astute oversight of the managing editorial process; to Robert Greer for your savvy handling of the publicity campaign; and most of all to Calah Singleton for your deft editing of the manuscript as well as the guidance and encouragement you have provided me ever since our initial meeting. The book would look far inferior without your diligence, zeal and expertise. Additionally, I am greatly appreciative of House of Anansi Press for bringing *Invisible Lines* to North America: thank you in particular to Shivaun Hearne for your clear passion for the book, Michelle MacAleese for overseeing its seamless crossing of the Atlantic, Emma Rhodes for promoting it in Canada and the United States, and Greg Tabor for designing the clever and striking cover. Further, I would like to recognise the efforts of the marketing/rights teams at Andrew Nurnberg, Profile and House of Anansi for building interest in this work internationally. Thank you, too, to Robert Davies for your conscientious and judicious copyediting, and Dominic Beddow for so successfully conveying the book's invisible lines as eye-catching maps.

Invisible Lines could easily have remained a personal pandemic project, but various people spurred me – consciously or not – to try and turn it into something tangible. Thanks are due in the first instance to Ted Naron, who helped me realise how enjoyable it is to write simply for the sake of writing. I am grateful also to those who, upon learning of my idea, generously suggested an assortment of invisible lines to explore, or introduced me to people and resources with additional insights to offer: Pascale-Anne Brault, Euan Hague, Pratheek Nagaraj, Gabriel Pankhurst, Sundeep Patel, Lulu Raczka, Michael Rebak, Robert Vanderbeck, Arizka Wargenagara and Bo Zhang, your contributions in this respect cannot be overlooked. While I have agreed to keep the names of the individuals I interviewed anonymous, please know that I owe you, too, a debt of gratitude for the time you kindly made available from your busy schedules.

Last but certainly not least, a huge thank you to my immediate family, who, in different ways, have made indispensable contributions to this work. To my father, Alan, for your support in conceptualising *Invisible Lines*, for familiarising me with the publication process, and for our shared passion for the eclectic. To my brother, Nathaniel, for sending me illuminating news stories, informative charts and humorous maps, all of which have helped inspire this book. To my mother, Leone, for initiating our weekly online quizzes during lockdown, which spurred me to extend the boundaries of my knowledge and interests, as well as for your unwavering confidence in Invisible Lines. And to my wife, Eleanor, for your love and companionship, as well as your patience while I replicated our university days, buried in piles of books and journals, trying to research the minutest details. The connections I cherish with all of you have rendered this book real.

© Alex Papadopoulos

MAXIM SAMSON is is a geographer with specific interests in religion, education, and cities. Originally from England, Maxim is currently based in Chicago, where he teaches at DePaul University and chairs an international research group specializing in the geographies of religions and belief systems. In his spare time, he enjoys long-distance running, maintaining his Duolingo streak, and gradually adding to his kaleidoscopic flag collection. *Invisible Lines* is his first book.